THE WANDERERS

THE WANDERERS

A Story of Exile, Survival, and Unexpected Love in the Shadow of World War II

DANIELA GERSON

GRAND CENTRAL

New York Boston

Copyright © 2026 by Daniela Gerson

Cover design and illustration © Kelly Winton
Cover copyright © 2026 by Hachette Book Group, Inc.

Hachette Book Group supports the right to free expression and the value of copyright. The purpose of copyright is to encourage writers and artists to produce the creative works that enrich our culture.

The scanning, uploading, and distribution of this book without permission is a theft of the author's intellectual property. If you would like permission to use material from the book (other than for review purposes), please contact permissions@hbgusa.com. Thank you for your support of the author's rights.

Grand Central Publishing
Hachette Book Group
1290 Avenue of the Americas, New York, NY 10104
grandcentralpublishing.com
@grandcentralpub

First edition: March 2026

Grand Central Publishing is a division of Hachette Book Group, Inc. The Grand Central Publishing name and logo is a registered trademark of Hachette Book Group, Inc.

The publisher is not responsible for websites (or their content) that are not owned by the publisher.

Grand Central Publishing books may be purchased in bulk for business, educational, or promotional use. For information, please contact your local bookseller or the Hachette Book Group Special Markets Department at special.markets@hbgusa.com.

Library of Congress Cataloging-in-Publication Data has been applied for.

ISBNs: 9780306834301 (hardcover), 9780306834325 (ebook)

Printed in Canada

MRQ-T

10 9 8 7 6 5 4 3 2 1

To Talia
To our fathers, Allan and Nachum
And to our children, Alma Pearl and Aviv Nachum

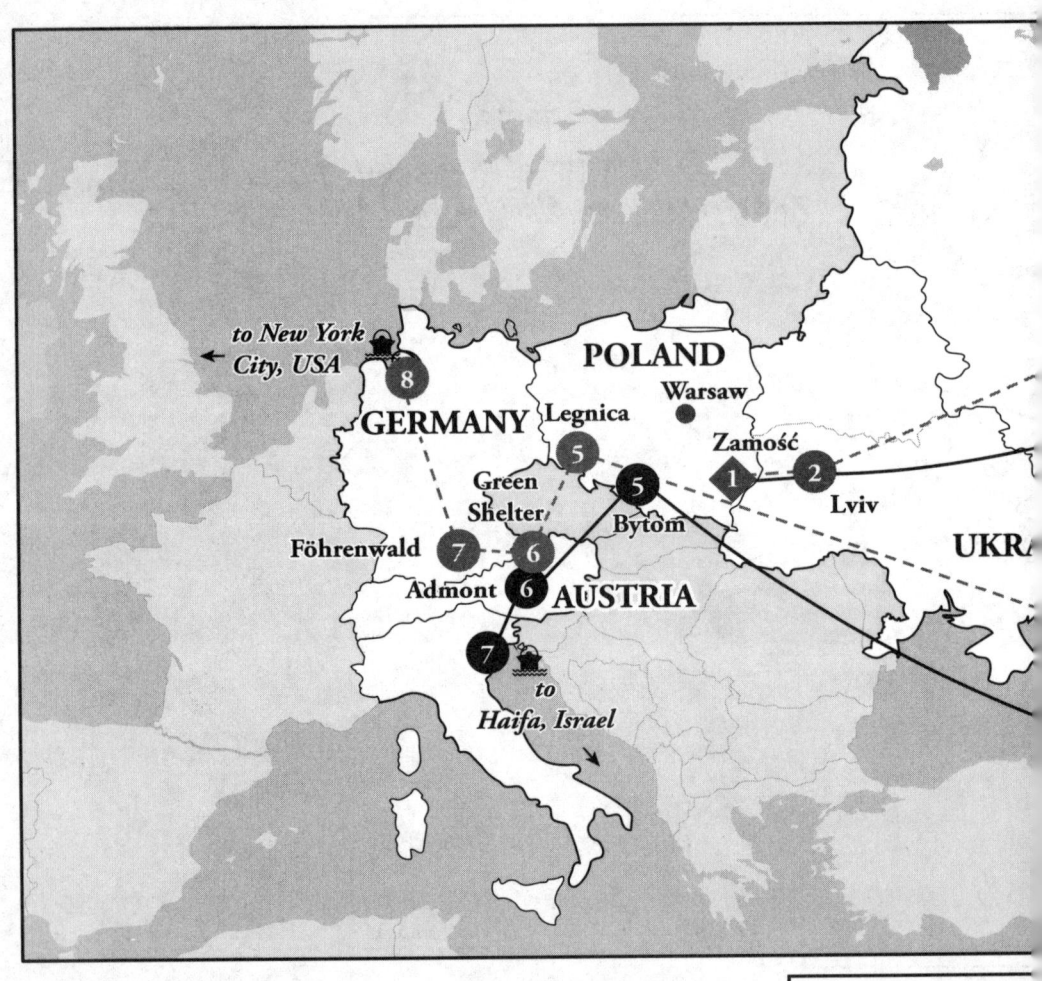

Contents

Preface — xi
Introduction — xiii

Chapter 1: Peshke and Mottel — 1
Chapter 2: Never Forget, Never Forgive — 4
Chapter 3: Seekers — 9
Chapter 4: Leon's Secrets — 18
Chapter 5: Finding Adi — 25
Chapter 6: Motherland — 33
Chapter 7: The Book of Memory — 39
Chapter 8: Origin Stories — 44
Chapter 9: Radical Moderns — 53
Chapter 10: The Pendulum — 64
Chapter 11: Rainbow Square — 70
Chapter 12: Stay or Go — 77
Chapter 13: Other Side — 86
Chapter 14: The Ones Who Run — 96

Chapter 15: City of Lions	99
Chapter 16: Return	107
Chapter 17: Territory of Terror	114
Chapter 18: Sybiraks	124
Chapter 19: Index of the Repressed	131
Chapter 20: An Outstretched Arm	142
Chapter 21: Tashkent Station	148
Chapter 22: Samarkand Blessings	157
Chapter 23: Kaganovich Street	164
Chapter 24: Repatriates	178
Chapter 25: Alive and Free	184
Chapter 26: Flight	199
Chapter 27: Displaced Persons	207
Chapter 28: Lies	220
Chapter 29: Promised Lands	230
Chapter 30: Home	245
Afterword	*253*
Acknowledgments	*257*
Note on Language and Reporting	*267*
Notes	*269*
Index	*301*

Preface

As you know very well, during the Holocaust Jewish life in Zamosc—the town of our parents and their parents before them—was totally obliterated. Zamosc had been the jewel of the crown of Polish Jewry. The whole range of Jewish life vibrantly thrived there... Today we have only the memory...

Dear children, if not now, when? If not you, who? We are tired and old. Our ranks are getting smaller. We look to you.

Long after my grandfather died in 1991, I uncovered this letter in a stack of correspondence lodged in my parents' basement. His writing revealed a single-minded focus to "never forget, never forgive" the Nazi destruction of Jewish Zamość. He proposed nailing steel plates with the names of slaughtered family members to trees in an Israeli forest, rallied support for a monument to the martyrs in a New Jersey cemetery. And, again and again, he penned solicitations like this one from 1986 urging the children of Zamość survivors to take up the burden of preservation efforts.

As I reached the end of the letters, I realized that for all his advocacy, my grandfather failed to commemorate his own confounding story—how a cataclysmic deportation to the Soviet hinterlands led to his salvation.

I knew well the outlines of my grandparents' saga—brutal forced labor in the Gulag, perilous black-market activity in Uzbekistan. But I assumed it was relatively rare. I didn't yet know how the hundreds of thousands of Polish Jews who fled *east*, to the Soviet Union, became pawns in a battle across borders and politics, where the line between lies and truth, good and evil, was often hard to decipher. And how their journey and its legacy, which ripples into our violent present, was largely overlooked. Only after an unexpected meeting transformed my life would I begin to grasp the magnitude of my grandparents' journey to survival.

Introduction

Our story could easily never have happened. Neither of us was particularly eager to attend the birthday picnic for a man we had both flirted with and who was now seriously involved with a close friend of mine. We were approaching our mid-thirties, when dating often slips toward more high-pressure stakes for women. Our online profiles closely resembled each other's. We shared a love of foreign languages, stories from far-flung travels, and a mutual surprise at having landed in Los Angeles. "I never thought I'd live in this city." "I still wake up some mornings wondering how I ended up back here." And then we described our ideal matches—smart, kind, and preferably Jewish men.

I'd brought a date like that to the party. A lanky guy, wavy hair just beginning to thin, from New York. The type of person I imagined I would one day marry. On that Saturday afternoon in June, I strolled with him across a grassy field toward Griffith Park's abandoned zoo. Under a small grove of eucalyptus and pine trees, a group had gathered around picnic tables. Standing in their midst was a small woman, her brown hair pulled back neatly.

Talia had an infectious laugh that belied her size, and I was immediately drawn to her. I don't remember our first words, if I said them or she did, nor what happened to my date at that moment. We relaxed into a perch on top of a concrete picnic table, sunglasses pulled back over our brown hair, heads tilting toward each other. Talia told me she was a lawyer working in a local immigrant detention center. I shared that I had reported on immigration in New York and produced a series where I followed deportees to the Dominican Republic. I was relatively new to Los Angeles and moving into a more academic space. I missed reporting stories and interviewing lawyers and advocates. Maybe she could be a source?

The cake was served; I barely noticed.

Leaving the party, I climbed up into my date's truck, and he began to opine about music. A thought whispered: *I wish I could date Talia instead.*

But a relationship with another woman was not an option I had seriously considered. When I emailed Talia the next day about a radio story I had recently reported, I still assumed it was about connecting with her as a source, perhaps a new friend, who shared my passion for immigration.

At almost 11:00 p.m., an email from Talia lit up my inbox. "Thanks for sending... it was great to meet you yesterday."

Over the next hour, we exchanged messages about everything from which public pool was best in LA to the intricacies of immigration policies. Finally, at 11:47 Talia messaged: "Okay, conversation to be continued," and sent me a link to a Hebrew song we had discussed about my name. I grew up adjacent to Israeli culture but not part of it. Hebrew was my parents' language from when they lived in Jerusalem before I was born, spoken in our home only when they didn't want us kids to understand. Until high school, I attended Hebrew instruction at our synagogue a few times a week, and after graduating college, I studied the language in Israel but still had only a proficient command. Talia's Hebrew was fluent. Her father was Israeli, and she had spent summers north of Tel Aviv with her grandparents as a kid.

That link to the Hebrew song elicited not just a rush of connection. With it also came an entrance to realms that had long felt inaccessible.

INTRODUCTION

The way Talia moved through the world intrigued me. She spoke Nepali from a semester living outside of Kathmandu, and her Spanish was better than mine from a year working in Mexico City. Whereas in my reportorial work I observed and detailed the way immigrants were caught up in the morass of our legal system, she was by their side advocating for them.

I wrote back my last message of the night, thanking her for the link: "Now I can go to sleep happy." Then I threw out a Hebrew good night expression I liked: "Chalomot paz"—literally "golden dreams."

Before I could fully explore my feelings for Talia, I boarded a flight to Berlin. I had been awarded a prize for a radio documentary I reported with a German colleague. When I bounded onto the stage in my new iridescent blue dress, the thin, slightly bent, older German man presenting the trophy had one question for me: *What does your aunt Raya think now of the Germans?* I managed to hide my wince. I knew he would not like my answer.

In the opening scenes of the radio piece, my grandfather's petite and opinionated cousin Raya invites me into a room in her Upper West Side apartment to "introduce" me to portraits of relatives the Nazis slaughtered. They were all from our family's ancestral hometown: Zamość, Poland—which she pronounced Za-MOSHCH. "They create a machinery of gassing a whole nation, a whole people. And they're looking for excuses, they are looking that we should love them, they are looking for innocence," she told me in her thick Yiddish accent and then, eyes reddening, pointed at my great-grandmother. "She was killed by Hitler, and her grandson was killed by Hitler."

For me, that is what Zamość was: ghosts of ancestors murdered after my grandparents, great-uncles, and great-aunts, including Raya, fled to protection and new struggles in the Soviet Union.

I hadn't planned on making a radio documentary about the Holocaust. I hadn't even planned on going to Germany. After a couple of years reporting on immigration for the *New York Sun* in my twenties, I was eager to explore other countries and put the Portuguese I had studied in college to work. I had hoped to go to Brazil or East Timor, only applying for a Germany fellowship on the recommendation of a relentlessly enthusiastic colleague.

Two months in the verdant Berlin summer and I saw a whole new side of the country, a success story of Germany's soft power investments. I returned the summer before I turned twenty-eight on a second, extended fellowship where I was set to investigate the complex legacy of its guest workers, an international extension of my immigration reporting beat. But a more personal story called to me.

The defining narrative for my family was our exodus from Zamość, and I was closer to it than I had ever been before. I began to report on the unexpected echoes of the Holocaust in my year in Berlin. The story just kept pulling me back. The helpful neo-Nazi next door, the rage of my uncle when we visited his first home at a Bavarian refugee camp, my lovely neighbor whose grandfather was active in Hitler Youth. With a German colleague, I had funneled these stories into audio reportage, and now I had returned to receive an award.

It was also a chance, far from the intentional and often frustrating dating scene back home, to flirt with Spanish and German men, bike the canals, and share leisurely coffees. I loved being back in Berlin. But I did not need to ask Raya to know her feelings would never change: Germany was no place for a Jewish girl, particularly one like me who should have long since married a nice Jewish boy.

When I returned home to Los Angeles a few weeks later, I was still thinking about Talia and invited her over for dinner. As I prepared fish in my tiny kitchen, I chatted giddily on the phone. This dinner felt different, I told a friend: "It's like a first date." And yet, I did not consider the possibility that it was one.

We dined on my intimate Echo Park patio, overlooking a blooming garden and sweeping views of the sun setting on the valleys and hills stretching west. Long after we had finished dinner, we lingered into the darkening night. I wanted to hold on to the elation I felt with her. Talia suggested we walk to the Gold Room, a Dodgers' dive bar down a steep set of stairs leading to Sunset Boulevard. Giggly, we ordered the tequila beer combo, drinking more than either of us usually would. By the time we climbed back up the hill, Talia was worried about driving home and asked to sleep over. A New Yorker friend, who had her own plans that night, was already crashing on my living room couch. That left my bedroom. It felt a bit odd, but fun, like an adult sleepover. I made her a place to sleep on my Ikea chaise lounge; I slept alone in my bed.

The next day Talia texted: "Thanks, again, for a lovely dinner plus..."

Once again, I told myself we were just friends. Really magnetic friends.

On our third outing, we met on a packed Silver Lake bar patio. With no seats available, Talia sat on the floor in tight jeans with the cuffs rolled, a small red purse hanging over her sunburnt shoulder. I felt jealousy sneak in as she chatted about lying out too long on the beach with her ex-boyfriend, a medical student.

Close friends of mine had accompanied us to the bar. I had been eager to introduce Talia to them, but we focused on each other, our conversation jumping easily from her afternoon on the beach to a journalist friend and then, somehow, to a Holocaust tour she'd taken to Poland as a teen. This passed my non-Jewish friends by, but I knew immediately what she was talking about.

March of the Living is a trip where young Jews visit concentration camps and reenact the three-kilometer death march from Auschwitz to Birkenau. I had never considered making that trip. I'd visited Auschwitz when I was a teenager, and my clearest memory—other than the piles of sheared hair from murdered people in the exhibit—was the guide informing us that every step was on the ashes of cremated people. I told my father as we left, "I don't think I believe in God." I had no interest in returning, or worse, seeing more camps. Talia, I would learn, was more comfortable than me within the confines of organized Jewish life—president of her local United Synagogue Youth chapter, a counselor at Ramah summer camp—and the program was a natural extension of that upbringing.

Sidestepping the devastation, I asked Talia where her family was from before the war, assuming it would be some shtetl I had never heard of. No ancestral hometown, no matter how harrowing the destruction, is as interesting as your own.

"Zamość," she said.

CHAPTER 1
Peshke and Mottel

Peshke had recently returned from a delightfully independent year in Warsaw learning about all the latest fashions. Back in Zamość, at twenty-two, she surely had been getting not-so-subtle hints that the time had come to settle down and meet a husband.

Why not go to the Purim ball? her older sister Dora nudged. *I have someone in mind you just might like.* Dora, like Peshke, knew what it was like to come back to Zamość after a big adventure. She had left behind their hometown six years earlier in 1927, sailing across the Atlantic to Buenos Aires looking for opportunities with their two brothers. But Dora was miserable in Argentina and returned to Zamość. Now she was active again in the local social scene and believed she knew how to ease her younger sister's transition.

Peshke recognized the earnest young man with light blond hair observing her from behind wire-rimmed glasses. Mottel, the match her sister had in mind, was a couple of years older than her, and lived down the block. While Zamość was a town of around twenty-five thousand people, nearly half of them Jewish, it felt much smaller where they lived in the Old Town. The young people all knew each other, at least by sight. They had grown up meandering together on Shabbat afternoons in the park wrapping the town, even if during the week their paths differed.

Peshke was friendly with one of Mottel's sisters, but she'd never really spoken with him. Not until that night, when they could not stop talking.

The party ended at five in the morning. *May I walk you home?* Mottel entreated.

The couple strolled together toward their neighboring apartments over their families' stores on the square. More than five decades later, when my grandfather retold this story, he said with complete certainty that he fell deeply in love with my grandmother that very night. The date would become known as their special 3s: 3/3/33.

My grandparents were one of many happy young couples in Zamość, coming of age in a modern era of radical politics. Within a decade, thousands of their peers would be reduced to ash.

* * *

What granted Mottel and Peshke the foresight to leave Poland when they did? From my grandmother, I learned that even if you one day feverishly packed a bag, held your parents close not knowing it was goodbye, and miraculously survived, you—and your descendants—might never know what propelled you.

As an old woman, Peshke would ask herself how it was possible that she had so much courage. But on that day in October 1939, ahead of the German soldiers arriving in Zamość, she did not ruminate. Raw instincts drove her to cross the border to the Soviet Union with her beloved month-old baby boy. She raced up the stairs to her apartment knowing she must leave and let nothing, not even her father, stop her.

Don't go! he had cried out to her. *People are dying in the streets! Where will you sleep? There is no place in the synagogues across the border with so many refugees already. Where are you taking your baby?*

To his father, Peshke volleyed back, resolute in her conviction, in her defiance.

Mottel had left days earlier, urging her to wait it out in Zamość. That nothing would happen to women and children and the war would soon be over. But now she felt an urgent need to join him, as fast as she could. She raced downstairs, her baby, Arik, grasped tight.

You will lose the baby, her father shouted after her.

Then her teenage sister, the youngest in the family, chased her down.

I want to come with you! Don't leave me behind! These pleading words would echo over the continents and decades in my grandmother's nightmares.

No, Peshke, then twenty-nine, responded resolutely, imagining Zamość was safer for her little sister. *Stay with Father.*

My grandmother then climbed onto an open-air truck clutching her baby. They bumped toward the border, and crossed the River Bug, into Soviet territory where she reunited with Mottel.

The largest group of survivors from Europe's largest Jewish community would not be those who hid in the forests, posed as Aryans, miraculously survived the concentration camps, or received last-minute visas to Latin America. No, the largest group by far was those who made the brave choice, the lucky choice, to leave their homes in this brief opening in the fall of 1939 and cross to the "other side," into the Soviet Union. For years, many believed they had made a terrible mistake.

CHAPTER 2

Never Forget, Never Forgive

As Talia and I stared at each other in splendid disbelief, goose bumps rising on my arms despite the warm Los Angeles summer evening, my next question came quick: "Was your family also in Siberia?"

To be from Zamość meant your ancestors had evaded the Nazi decimation of three million Polish Jews. And in my family, I knew well the route to survival. First, they fled the Nazis to the Soviet side of the border, where a different murderous totalitarian regime saved them, ironically, via deportation.

"Yes! In a labor camp." Talia's brown eyes flashed in the evening light. To most people it was bizarre that my grandparents had survived the Holocaust in a Siberian Gulag. But Talia appeared to know just what I was talking about.

"Were they also in Uzbekistan?" I asked.

"I don't think so." She groped for details. "They never really talked about the war or Zamość." That they were in Siberia was about all she seemed to know of her grandparents' wartime story, and what came before.

I could not imagine this.

For my family, commemorating Zamość was an inherited duty. Our grandparents told the stories and my parents, and later my siblings and I, did our best to probe and document to preserve their testimony. Among my first attempts was at my grandfather's deathbed, where I'd sat in the hospital asking questions for an eighth-grade research project.

My grandparents' accounts of their desperate flight, years of limbo, and the hardships of starting over as middle-aged immigrants had been woven into my essence. I came back to their stories as touchstones throughout my career as a journalist, and later as a professor. Talia's work as an immigration lawyer had originally drawn me to her. Discovering that she also had roots in Zamość—this place that often felt mythical—charged a breathtaking intensity into our friendship.

When I got home from the bar, I was wired. I flicked on my computer and searched for photos of what was probably my grandfather's proudest accomplishment. He had helped lead a movement to build a memorial to Zamość's murdered Jews in a vast cemetery in Paramus, New Jersey. Among row after row of neat, evenly spaced graves, all shades of gray, stood a stone wall with the word ZAMOSC carved in Hebrew and English letters.

Planted in American soil, the memorial had served as a physical tribute to the boundless loss my father's family had left behind in Poland. It would also become the final resting place for my Yiddish-speaking relatives. At this plot, I'd watched my grandmother try to climb into her husband's grave. Years later, she, too, was lowered into the soil beside him.

I sent Talia a photo of the stark memorial stone bearing the words my grandfather had carefully crafted in Yiddish, relying on my parents to finesse the English translation: "This memorial erected in memory of twelve thousand innocent victims of the city of Zamosc Poland who were brutally burned gassed and slain by the abominable Nazis and their helpers in the years of 1939–1945."

At the time, I did not yet realize the discrepancy in my grandfather's inscription. His numbers of the murdered seem to be inflated. Zamość was home to a bit over ten thousand Jewish residents before the Nazi invasion. About half of them were killed, leaving a number much smaller than what was written on the wall. Perhaps my grandfather's victim figures referred to the broader community?

Either way, exactly how many Zamość residents the Nazis murdered remains a mystery. Despite the German reputation for meticulous documentation, expedient slaughter took precedence in the nearby gas chambers. The Nazis killed around half a million Jews at Bełżec in nine months of operation. Unlike at Auschwitz, almost nobody lived to tell the story—only a handful of the victims are known to have survived to provide testimony.

What is well documented is that most Zamość Jews who survived fled east. My grandmother described their plight as "nothing" compared to the slaughter of their parents, siblings, and other loved ones who had stayed behind. She might have felt that way, but I knew what those who fled endured was not nothing. Deportation and deprivation plagued their path as well. I saw my grandparents as double survivors, first of Hitler's genocide, and then of Stalin's persecution.

Why, then, I had often wondered, was their survival story not featured in the Holocaust museums we visited or the books I read growing up? I found a clue in my grandfather's fervor, and how he directed his memorializing efforts to his murdered parents and loved ones, while not publicizing his own story. "We will always remember them," he had inscribed on the stone. "We shall never forget. We shall never forgive."

* * *

In my apartment, I scanned the martyrs listed on the memorial under the heading לזכר עולם, a Hebrew expression often translated as "for eternal memory." In this personal place, which I visited for paternal family funerals, I saw the unmistakable word "Inlender." Talia's last name carved into the same stone as many Gersons. The memorial listed three Inlender victims: Chaya, Leah, and Tuvia. Trembling lightly as I typed, I sent Talia an image.

Then I kept searching. I found myself newly intrigued by pages of community history and photo galleries, curious to see if they might reveal more intersections in our pasts. But it was getting very late.

Around two in the morning, I sent Talia a final link to an Israeli society for Zamość history and at last shut down my computer for the night.

Hours later, I woke to the blazing Sunday morning sun and a message from Talia: "This is unbelievable." She was even more shocked than I to find her family name on a Zamość memorial. "We know so little about our family."

Inlender is a rare name, and Talia's father was an only child. To her knowledge, the only people who had survived the war on her grandfather's side were a cousin Zyg and his family. They bore a different last name. Another branch of the family had landed in Ireland before the war but spelled their name Enlander. The only Inlenders she knew were members of her immediate family. And yet, here was their name carved in granite.

"I'm still in shock," Talia wrote.

When Talia had opened the page from the Israeli Organization of Zamość Jewry, she'd been confronted with a chilling surprise. A picture of an adorable girl, head cocked to the side, dressed for snow in a warm jacket. The caption identified her as Roma Inlender and described how when Nazis liquidated the Zamość ghetto, ordering the remaining Jews to march twenty kilometers, she paused for a moment to tie her shoes. A gestapo officer shot her that October day in 1942. Her distraught mother requested they shoot her, too. The German officer obliged. The caption went on: "About the Inlender family: one of the richest families in Zamość, also owned a bank. The father contributed a great deal to the community. The whole family perished."

Talia had heard her father's family was very rich before the Holocaust, and something about a bank, so these were likely her Inlenders. But clearly it wasn't true that all of them had perished. Her grandfather, part of the Zamość Inlender family, had survived in the Soviet Union, just like my grandparents. Who were all these people who died? And why did she know nothing about them?

That afternoon, the messages flew between us. Talia told me she had been choked up at her computer. I had been, too, and it surprised me.

My family's story might have been tragic, but it rarely made me sad.

From a young age I adopted an attitude of intense curiosity while preserving an emotional distance, just as I did when reporting. But when I discovered our last names together on the memorial for our murdered ancestors, the inherited loss felt newly raw and personal.

Talia and I pledged that afternoon that we would track down the journey from Zamość that our grandparents had undergone to survive.

"The time to do this is now!" Talia wrote. I knew she was right. All seven of my Zamość relatives who had survived the war together were already dead. Only my aunt Raya, the youngest, who had found her own way in the Soviet Union, remained. Talia had three survivor relatives still alive.

I told her I would meet her that night to get started.

CHAPTER 3

Seekers

Despite our initial urgency, Talia and I soon lost sight of researching our intertwined roots. We became consumed instead with navigating our own unexpected relationship. Within months of meeting, I realized the attraction pulling me toward her was not simply one of a source, or a new friend who happened to have family roots in Zamość. By the time I caught on, Talia, one step ahead of me, had already known the truth.

As a couple, when we shared our common background, sometimes people would exclaim how it was b'shert that we found each other in Los Angeles. *B'shert* is a Yiddish expression for "meant to be," often reserved for a soulmate. It did not always feel so straightforward to us. Secure as we were in our connection, building a future together still felt frightening and disorienting. We first had to release assumptions of lives married to nice Jewish men before we could take in the gift we had received in each other.

So it was with as much disbelief as bliss that on a Friday night three years after we met, I watched our mothers break a plate together, kicking off our wedding weekend with this symbol of our commitment. Talia intertwined her fingers in mine and rested her head on my shoulder. Dozens of friends and family cheered. Then a hush came over the room as our fathers—mine tall and unusually svelte due to a recent heart bypass surgery, Talia's abba a head shorter and rounder—raised silver wineglasses in unison. As they chanted kiddush over the wine together, my father felt moved in a way he did not expect. He told my mother later it was not only about the momentous occasion, but also about our shared past: For the first time someone outside his family matched him in the Zamość melody he had learned from his father. I saw no signs that my boisterous father-in-law-to-be felt that same nostalgic pull. Nachum's eyes danced around the room, immersed in the joy of the moment.

* * *

Not until seven years after we married did Talia and I at last embark on a search for our families' intersecting journeys. We were in a place that could not have been further from the remote Uzbek village and Austrian displaced persons camp where our fathers had been born refugees. And yet it felt at last like the right place and time.

When I first told Talia that my parents owned a house on Martha's Vineyard, she assumed that she would feel out of place in such an elite destination. I shared with her that the Massachusetts island was more than a vacation hot spot for US presidents and movie stars—it was also home to a deep-rooted Black summer community, Brazilian immigrant laborers and entrepreneurs, and the Aquinnah Wampanoag, whose ancestors were its first inhabitants. In Chilmark, Jewish families had begun spending summers on a rural part of the island in the post–World War II years—when "gentlemen's agreements" barred property sales to them in some of the other towns. They read books, played tennis, and sometimes hung out naked on the beach. My mother, raised swimming on the Rhode Island coast, immediately fell in love with this part of the Vineyard when she visited while pregnant with me. Years later, after her German Jewish immigrant father sold his business, she knew just what she wanted to do with the windfall. My parents bought land, and when I was in college, they built a home.

The house was where our family came together for blessed summer weeks of ocean swimming and beach paella bonfires. Talia was the first partner I brought to the island. None of the men I dated lasted longer than six months—and most were fleeting romances in far-flung locales such as Rio, Berlin, and Tel Aviv. Talia was different, and not only because she was a woman.

The morning of her first visit, I led her under the rope with the private sign cutting through to the adjacent Land Bank property. She followed me down the dirt path, keeping an eye out for poison ivy and ticks, then we descended the wooden stairs onto the curve of beach. Talia squealed as she dipped her feet into the water—frigid to her Southern California toes. Then she followed my lead and we swam together, rounding the Great Rock with its black cormorants proudly sunning. Talia stumbled out onto the rocky shore beaming. Terns swooped and an osprey eyed us from above. No longer would I swim alone in the mornings.

* * *

On a summer day with the pandemic still raging, Talia and I settled in at a round wooden table, gray from the rain, isolated enough to allow for intimate conversations outside the West Tisbury Library. To our right was a sculpture garden of oversized mythical creatures crafted in bronze. Bedraggled parents enthused to their children about the joys of reading, while year-round residents complained about the summer residents staying too long.

We started at the beginning of our families' trajectories. I sent a message to a group for descendants of Zamość Jews, providing all the information we knew about our ancestors. Within an hour, Shelley Pollero, a coordinator for Jewish Records Indexing-Poland, sent me a list of births, deaths, and marriages of Gersons and Inlenders in Zamość, dating back to the 1840s. We delighted in this proof of our shared histories linked to the same town. We also finally debunked the theory that "we could be cousins." We were not even third cousins. No common relatives had emerged.

We next turned to excavating and organizing the records we already knew existed. I tracked down more than a dozen hours of VHS and audiocassette recordings that family members, the Jewish Community Relations Council of Greater Washington, and the USC Shoah Foundation's Visual History Archive had recorded of my grandparents decades earlier. While the professional interviews were part of an effort to document the Holocaust, as I listened to them for the first time, I discovered in them just as much about how my relatives loved and lived before the war.

* * *

My grandmother wore a dress jacket that had become oversized as she'd withered in her final years, with a mic clipped to the lapel. She was being recorded for the Shoah Foundation, part of an effort Steven Spielberg launched in the late 1990s after the release of *Schindler's List* to document the stories of Holocaust survivors and witnesses before they perished. For my grandmother, the recording came just in time. She died months later.

"Did you have a special boyfriend?" the interviewer asked her.

My grandmother surprised me, nodding a few times, returning to a youthful entanglement that came before my grandfather. I perceived a subtle eye roll as she momentarily returned to her teenage self.

But when asked his name, my grandmother went dark. She shook her head and stumbled out, "Oh... he's not... he's still in the cremations." The researcher knew what this meant: Her first boyfriend had been incinerated in a death camp's crematorium. My grandmother inhaled deeply into her failing lungs and breathed out sharply. The name of that early crush came back to her from across the span of six long decades. She looked down and touched her chest. "Grynberg, Eryk Grynberg."

He was the younger brother of the woman who had first taught her to be a seamstress.

My grandmother had never told me of this first romance. But twenty-five years after the recording, a wave of gratitude came over me as I watched her reach, with the help of the interviewer, for that searing detail of a man erased. Eryk Grynberg's last record would be the Zamość ghetto census. Even though my grandmother could no longer color in the details, as an adult I could now glimpse contours of her life before the devastation.

* * *

When we returned to Los Angeles, I took the lead in our research as Talia began a demanding job at a new immigration law and policy institute. I called on my journalism background, submitting government data requests and pursuing sources to help me uncover family records.

Among the first experts I contacted was Steven Vitto, a research specialist at the US Holocaust Memorial Museum, asking for help finding documents from our families. He tempered my expectations: "Please keep in mind that the records of Zamość and for this area are not good." Despite the Nazis' reputation for fastidious record keeping, they had not documented people killed where they lived or at death camps like Bełżec. In addition, Vitto explained that Polish Jews who fled to the Soviet Union were often not in the museum's collections since they primarily focused on those who remained in Third Reich–occupied territory and suffered persecution there.

But when Vitto searched for my family records across multiple databases and spellings, he found many matches and sent them to me. Over lunch on a workday at our kitchen counter in Los Angeles, I exuberantly reported back to Talia on the dozens of attachments: testimonials, displaced persons camp records, and reparations correspondence left behind from my grandparents. Talia's brow furrowed.

"Did you ask about my grandparents?" she asked.

"Of course I did." A flash of resentment rose in my chest. Was Talia accusing me of overlooking her family?

Yes, I had put my grandparents first in my research request email, but I had included her family and was now waiting to receive more information. Was I prioritizing my ancestors? Probably. But we also had another problem, which was the real cause of Talia's disappointment. When I asked about the Inlenders, I hit walls. Talia's grandparents had left behind few traces for the next generations to find.

* * *

I hungered for more details about Leon, Talia's grandfather. But the unspoken code in her family had been not to probe. We were confronting a profound imbalance—for decades, my family had documented our Holocaust story in deliberate acts of remembrance, while hers endeavored to leave the terrors behind in a cloak of silence. I had gathered more than fifteen hours of recordings from six of my survivor relatives, whereas I had secured only one precious hour of a Zamość native from Talia's family.

Talia and her older brother Daniel had tried to break through that barrier of silence once, just after Talia's first year of law school. Together, they drove north through neat San Fernando Valley suburban developments to their uncle Zyg's house.

Of the many Holocaust testimonies I had transcribed, this was the only one where everyone laughed, and often. The camera focused on Uncle Zyg—white hair combed back, face flushed from years in the Southern California sun, lanky body relaxed in a velour tracksuit unzipped at the chest. Daniel, from behind the camcorder, zoomed in and out with the excitement of an amateur filmmaker.

Zyg knew how to captivate an audience. One moment he's jumping trains in Central Asia, ducking his head to avoid a wire that decapitated an unlucky companion; the next he's clicking his tongue and clapping his hands to show how he did business with local Uzbeks. He's eating rats to fend off starvation in a Kazakh prison, and then he's at a refugee camp in Germany, shaving his face to pass with fake papers that said he was a prepubescent boy.

Despite being a raconteur, this was Zyg's first recorded interview. He had refused his daughter's entreaties that he submit a testimony with the Shoah Foundation. Even though he was seventy-six at the time and had been a US citizen for decades, he still feared authorities discovering he had forged his age to qualify for a refugee youth program. The anxiety about deportation was not rational, but it was immutable. Still,

Talia convinced him to talk with her, promising his recollections would not be shared beyond the family.

During that same summer, Talia also sat with her then fifty-seven-year-old father and recorded an interview on his birth in an Austrian displaced persons camp, moving to Israel as an infant and the United States as a young man. Their youthful voices transported me to a moment of intimacy shared between father and daughter. Only once did Nachum mention, in a long sentence that reflected his imperfect English, the secret his father, Leon, had held from him his entire life: Nachum was not his only child. He had left behind a firstborn child and wife in Zamość. The Nazis murdered them.

"I didn't know until he was deceased, he actually had already a family... and a kid... and they didn't make it to the other side of the border and they got deceased."

Leon had always been quiet, doting on Nachum and his grandchildren but also removed, by both geography and his nature. Talia spent summers at the home of her grandparents, whom she called by the Hebrew Saba and Savta, north of Tel Aviv, running around dusty parks in sandals, taking the bus to the beach, and bringing home fresh pita from their Yemeni neighbor. She felt particularly close to her grandfather Leon, climbing on his lap and taking walks around the neighborhood holding his hand.

In contrast, his wife, Pepa, Talia's grandmother, her savta, was often brusque. It was she who, after Leon died, told Nachum the secret they had kept from him for four decades: Leon had once had another wife and child. The revelation shocked Talia's whole family. But nobody seemed to press Pepa as to who this first family was, and I could find no documentation.

* * *

The first night I met Nachum, back in 2011, I discovered how different his connection to Zamość—and by extension, to all that was lost—was from my own family's.

"Shalom, Daniela," Nachum practically shouted, adding the extra syllable to my name that comes up in Hebrew—*Dah nee YELL ah*. After I responded, "Shalom, Nachum," and threw out a few more greetings, he enthused that my Hebrew was "metzuyan"—excellent—which I knew was an exaggeration. But when Talia told him, "Daniela's family is from Zamość!" Nachum barely raised an eyebrow, betraying no emotional connection.

I felt deflated and confused. This muted response was radically different from how my own father enthusiastically embraced the news of our Zamość connection when I told him on the phone. But Talia appeared unfazed by Nachum's disinterest. As she jousted with her father in Hebrew, her eyes glowed. She adored him, and she knew what to expect of him.

Now a decade later, listening to the audiotape of Talia's interview with her father, I heard that same adoration in her voice and felt a sharp stab over not having asked him my questions when I still had a chance. Weight started slipping off Nachum's frame two years after we married, but none of us believed that a man so vibrant could waste away at just sixty-eight. After he was diagnosed with pancreatic cancer, Talia had asked me to interview her father, urging me to accompany him to a chemotherapy session. I kept putting it off, afraid to face him with the urgency of capturing his story. When we could not avoid his fate any longer and I finally asked him for an interview, it was already too late.

On a terrible November afternoon at the northern edge of the park where Talia and I had met, we buried my father-in-law in the company of hundreds of fellow mourners. The following summer, we returned in an intimate group to unveil his grave. Talia, stomach unfathomably round, told her abba about all that he had missed. The international news coverage of immigration protests with her at the center, the two lives growing inside of her, and the unbearable sadness of bringing them into a world without him.

While Nachum's grave was inscribed with the words "saba sababa," for "cool grandpa," our twins born months after its unveiling would never know him. Instead, our son, Aviv Nachum, would inherit his name, and together with his sister, Alma Pearl, would years later visit and lay stones on his tombstone's polished surface, tracing their fingers on the other descriptions: "haver nefesh," or "soul friend," and the imprint of a bicycle.

"Why didn't you ask more questions?" I would prod Talia as we embarked on our search, wishing I had more to tell our now three-year-old children about their family history. But I knew I was also to blame for not capturing more of her father, Nachum. Same with Uncle Zyg, who had also passed away, along with the two more surviving relatives in Israel. I was frustrated with the lack of information about Talia's family, but I also knew how easy it was to let the stories of our past slip away—and I was determined to not lose any more opportunities.

CHAPTER 4

Leon's Secrets

More than a decade after Talia and I had vowed to visit Zamość together, we were going at last. I began planning our trip. In late February, I investigated hotel options for a spring visit to Poland, as well as across the border in the Ukrainian city to which our grandparents initially fled. Then, I checked in with a Russian friend, Oleg, to ask what he thought about growing tensions between Moscow and Kyiv. He told me what he saw in the state-controlled media: NATO was expanding threateningly to the east and Ukraine was committing genocide against its Russian-speaking residents. In contrast, in American news outlets, I was reading that claims of ethnic targeting were unfounded and that Putin was falsely using NATO as an excuse to act on his aggressive desire for more territory. Our perspectives differed, but neither of us imagined an escalation beyond border tension.

A few days passed with no news from Oleg, and I assumed the situation had simmered down. Then, on a Wednesday night, February 24, 2022, Russia invaded Ukraine simultaneously from the north, east, and south. Russian President Vladimir Putin proclaimed that his troops would "demilitarize and denazify Ukraine," since "the outcomes of World War II and the sacrifices our people had to make to defeat Nazism are sacred." I had been studying these places and ideologies as part of history. But now I felt like I was in a twilight zone where Putin was blaming these demons from our past for his assault on an independent Ukraine.

By nightfall, the first of hundreds of thousands of refugees had arrived in Zamość, less than fifty miles from the Ukrainian border and an initial stop en route to Warsaw. A welcome point had been organized. The town became a base for the US Army 82nd Airborne Division, and helicopters whirred overhead, offering swift evacuations from Ukraine via Black Hawks and Chinooks.

On the twelfth day of the war, Ukrainian President Volodymyr Zelenskyy vowed from his hiding spot in a bunker, "We will not forgive, we will not forget." In the words of this Jewish man whose own paternal grandparents were murdered in the Holocaust, I heard my grandfather echoed. As secretary of the Zamoscer Progressive Branch, he endeavored every year to find a new way to express not only "never forget," but also to "never forgive." Growing up in the United States, removed from the personal suffering, my generation had dropped the immutability of "never forgive." But now I feared that we had been naive to believe society could progress toward peace and cooperation. This same region, which historian Timothy Snyder termed the "Bloodlands" for its brutal past, had returned to a place of vicious hate and violence, with new reasons for vengeance.

* * *

Talia and I soon canceled our spring trip, but we did not give up on visiting Zamość. Poland appeared relatively safe from Putin's advances. We developed a new plan to travel with our children in the fall for six weeks in Warsaw, a three-hour drive from Zamość.

The pieces fell into place with surprising ease. I had received a sabbatical from my university. Talia set up a visiting fellowship at Warsaw's Centre of Migration Research, which was immersed in the nation's escalating immigration confrontations. Even before the Ukrainian influx, in the past few years, more people had been moving to Poland than leaving it for the first time since World War II. Among them were Arab and African asylum seekers, arriving—and being violently pushed back—at Poland's border with Belarus to the north. Talia would be studying this shift. Meanwhile, I would dive into excavating the little-known history of how Polish Jews survived the Holocaust in the former Soviet Union.

We rented a light-filled loft in a leafy residential district. The director of an English-speaking preschool enthusiastically welcomed our children, offering up four homemade hot organic meals a day, including a daily 11:00 a.m. soup course. Our mental image of what it would be like to live in Warsaw, colored by stark Cold War imagery from our childhood, transformed.

Still, I woke at 2:00 a.m., worrying. Not about the prospect of moving so close to the escalating war in Ukraine. Not about the reports of resurgent anti-Semitism in Poland. Not even because the right-wing Polish federal government was antigay. I was afraid we'd travel across the world and that I would fail to uncover more about the migration journeys of our two families, especially since I had next to nothing to go on about Talia's.

* * *

When I opened the message from the United States Holocaust Memorial Museum, I immediately sensed something was missing. Vitto, the research specialist, had sent records tied to Talia's grandparents. But just a handful of documents were attached. Two revealed Leon and Pepa had registered in Poland after the war as a couple. The rest were International Tracing Service files with information the Inlenders provided in 1957 as part of an effort to secure reparations from the German government.

The first attachments were for Talia's grandmother and Leon's second wife, Pepa. She was the only one of our paternal grandparents not born in Zamość; she came from a town about twenty miles away called Tomaszów Lubelski. The little we knew of the couple's backstory included that Pepa, like Leon, had fled independently across the border to the Soviet Union where they met.

But Pepa's tracing service file stated that she had survived the war in two Lublin ghettos before escaping in 1942. I opened Leon's file, only to find yet another story. When Talia's grandfather would have been in a Soviet labor camp, the document said he was in the "Zamość ghetto" and that he had escaped to the forest.

I felt a tinge of guilt as I realized I was uncovering the lies of Talia's grandparents. Her family was secure enough in the one piece of their story they knew that I felt certain these testimonies could not be correct. And I could imagine that my wife's grandparents, who spoke so little about the war, would not want me to dig up this meager, fabricated record they left behind.

Why did Pepa and Leon lie? More than a decade after the end of World War II, this paperwork was the first step in an application for reparations due to Nazi persecution. But they would not have been eligible since they had fled east and been imprisoned by Stalin. Like many other survivors of Nazi atrocities who didn't fit the strict requirements for suffering imposed by the German government, Leon and Pepa, by then living in Israel, fabricated their wartime history. I imparted no blame for these lies. I soon found that some of my own relatives had done the same. But these false testimonies obscured the historical record of those who fled to the Soviet Union.

I was starting to doubt we'd ever find answers to why Leon had left behind his first family, that previously unknown wife and their child. Who were they? And how had Leon survived and met Pepa?

* * *

Months before we were set to leave for Poland, I contacted a high school teacher named Marek Kołcon. My brother, David, a filmmaker who had recently visited Zamość exploring his own project taking inspiration from our family legacy, suggested he could be a good source. I emailed Marek, asking if he might be able to unearth any information about Talia's grandfather and the family he left behind.

Later that evening, we scrambled to get the twins showered. We were back on Martha's Vineyard for a summer visit. In the kitchen my mother, after stretching out her beach time, was frantically preparing Shabbat dinner for nine guests. I snuck a look at my cell phone and caught a message from Marek. My eyes raced over the words.

"Hi Daniela: I am sending you some information about Leon Inlender and his wife and son. Leon Inlender was a salesman. He lived with his wife Manya and son Kolonimus, born in 1934, in Zamość at Rynek Wielki 3."

I scrolled down, and staring back at me from my phone screen was a boy with dark hair, pouty lips, and big, mischievous eyes. This must be the lost child.

"Talia!" I ducked into the bedroom, where she was wrangling our son into pajamas. "I've got Aviv. You need to look at this." I thrust the phone at her.

Talia stared into the screen. The photo of the boy looked so familiar. Had she seen it before? This was her father's half brother, Kolonimus.

"The child?" she asked. "How did you get this?" Talia trembled, laughed, and shook her head all at once. She felt certain she had seen this picture before. It looked just like a photo of her father that the family dug up after he died: An adorable young boy, he squats near the family's chickens. We look from that to the image of Nachum's half brother, Kolonimus, dressed in a tailored sailor suit. One boy has a part in the hair over to the left side, the other to the right. And yet, Kolonimus looked just like Nachum as a child. Both displayed a full smile, with a bit of mischief in the eyes. The resemblance was startling. This was Talia's uncle, Kolonimus, whose name her abba, his half brother, had never known.

One day, Talia's grandfather Leon must have held his five-year-old son close, saying goodbye, unaware that he'd never see him again. And then, almost a decade later, he would have another son who looked almost identical to his lost child. What was it like for Leon to see that resemblance in little Nachum's eyes? And to hide the horrors that flashed before his own?

As Talia stared at the photo, I pulled my arms around Aviv's squirming body, touching my lips to his forehead. And then I nudged him away. "Go and have a snack with Grandma and Alma." I needed another moment with Talia and Zamość's long-dead. Aviv scampered upstairs to where guests had started to arrive.

Talia scrolled further on my phone. In the second photo, a woman with inquisitive eyes stared back, a hat stylishly perched over her bob, and a white-and-black scarf smartly wrapped around her neck. Serious, sophisticated. She was Leon's first wife: Marja Miriam Inlender, known to family as Manya.

* * *

Later, Marek told me how he'd found these disappeared relatives. First, he identified Talia's grandfather in a list of Zamość residents that the Judenrat, the Jewish council the Nazis created to do their dirty work, had compiled to identify all Jews who'd lived in the town prior to the German invasion. The listing stated that Leon had resided with a wife, Marja Miriam, and a son, Kolonimus.

Armed with those names, Marek had plugged them into the World Holocaust Remembrance Center's Database of Shoah Victims' Names. Entries emerged. The first was submitted by a Khaim Sherf, Manya's brother. The second entry included images submitted by a woman named Adi Shalit, Sherf's granddaughter. They both provided addresses in Israel.

As I heard my mother offering up gin and tonics upstairs, I hurriedly typed into my phone the address of Talia's grandfather's home in Zamość, Rynek Wielki 3. The map homed in on the main market square. My pulse quickened. I knew my grandmother had grown up right on the square, so I plugged in her address. Talia's grandfather lived only a two-minute walk from where my grandparents had lived.

"They must have known each other," Talia said.

Marek's email included another crucial detail. Manya was born the same year as my grandmother, 1910. They were the same age and grew up just across the square from each other. We already knew our families would have likely been acquainted. But this was spellbinding proof of just how close they must have been.

As I bounded upstairs to join the guests, Talia dashed off a note to her family to catch them up on our discoveries before she turned off her phone for Shabbat. Her mother, Tobi, opened her email to find a photo of a boy with her dead husband's face. She started sobbing. Ever since learning of her husband's murdered older sibling, she assumed he or she perished as a baby. "I didn't realize how old he was," Tobi told me later. "When I saw this boy who looked just like Nachum when he was a boy, it just shattered me."

That night Talia couldn't sleep, and neither could her mother. Before the arrival of the photos, they'd felt their loss as two relatives among six million Jewish victims of the Holocaust. It was a tragedy, but vague and anonymous. Now, with the names and the faces, the searing pain of their murders, buried for decades, pierced them.

* * *

The next morning, Talia and I left the house early while our kids and my mother still slept. At a nearby fishing harbor, we swam through the placid water as far out as a buoy with a bell ringing to alert boats of land. Just as we were about to round it and head back toward shore, we thrust our heads up out of the water with the same realization.

"The woman who sent in the photos—the granddaughter of Manya's brother is likely still alive," Talia exclaimed. "Her name was Adi." That was just what I had been thinking. Treading salty water, we exulted.

Then we matched each other's strokes, racing back home with new energy. My thoughts moved quickly.

This Adi, if we could find her, just might know the stories Talia's grandfather had taken with him to the grave.

CHAPTER 5

Finding Adi

"We're trying to track this person down: Adi Shalit," I said in a message to Hagar, a friend in Tel Aviv. "Any chance you can see if you can find anything?"

Weeks went by as we eased into a new elementary school routine for the kids in Los Angeles. We heard nothing from Hagar. My own attempts at locating Adi failed. Maybe Hagar hadn't been able to identify the woman who submitted those eerie photos, our one and only lead to understanding Talia's family history.

Then one morning as I was dressing our children, I paused to scan my phone. Still nothing from Hagar. But a message from Marek, the social studies teacher from Zamość, stopped me. As I opened it, I felt that thrilling jolt again. Each message from him seemed to contain a gift, a revelation about our ancestors' intertwining pasts.

This time, it was a collection of black-and-white photos, eyes staring back at me from over the decades. These were the faces of Leon's first family. I pushed the phone in front of Talia's face, telling her there was more from Marek.

"Let me see..." She, too, momentarily forgot the morning rush. "Wait...I think that's my grandfather!"

Leon appeared youthful and light in a way she had never known him to be. He stood in a park with his hat just off-kilter, overcoat revealing a double-breasted suit and tie, an arm tucked gently behind

Manya's back. She revealed just a whisper of a smile, dressed properly in gloves and head scarf. To her left stood a man we assumed to be the brother-in-law Khaim, who had survived, his arm wrapped tightly around a substantial woman who looked to be his and Manya's mother. To that woman's left, standing apart from the others, must have been the father, with a stern face and a bowler hat.

This did not square with Talia's memories of her quiet and casual grandfather, the chicken farmer, biking around his humid Mediterranean town in a light shirt. Instead, she could now see Uncle Zyg's descriptions of Leon as a young man in Poland: "Dressed sharp, he didn't look like a Jew. He looked like a Pole."

Talia took in the photo, the first she'd seen of her grandfather as a young man before the war. The life that he had tried to erase. We realized that his unspoken losses included an entire extended family.

Talia stared, stunned at the image as our kids chattered at the kitchen counter, spilling their breakfast everywhere. She was far from this light-filled room. Her last memory of her grandfather was at age thirteen, leaving him for a flight to Los Angeles. Leon's eyes had filled as she waved goodbye. Though generally stoic, arrivals, departures, and even phone calls would quickly move him to tears.

Months later, Talia's father boarded a flight to Israel after a desperate call. Leon was in the hospital. Nachum's flight was delayed in Paris; he did not make it before his father died.

Why had Leon walled himself off from sharing his suffering? Why had he allowed, even encouraged, his only living child to move across the globe from him? Perhaps loving a child so fiercely was that much more painful when you knew what you could lose.

* * *

The year Talia was born, 1979, *Children of the Holocaust* was published, a groundbreaking investigation of the intergenerational transmission of survival trauma. In interviews with hundreds of Israeli and Diaspora children of Holocaust survivors, New York journalist and author Helen Epstein found a marked difference between the two groups. Her interview subjects in the United States, like her own survivor parents, tended to focus on recording and commemorating family stories. In Israel, she noticed something different. Epstein found her peers there knew much more about the Holocaust as an attack on the Jewish people never to be repeated, but much less about the personal assaults on their families.

Beginning in 1953, a national day of mourning for the six million murdered Jews stopped the entire nation. A siren sounded, sporting games paused, highways ground to a halt. But, Epstein noted, the individual trauma of survivors, an unwelcome reminder of the ghetto-subjugated past, at least initially, received scant attention. The state had built a national narrative of valiant soldiers and builders, of how Jews rose from the ashes. Even the Holocaust Remembrance Day was selected to coincide with the anniversary of the Warsaw ghetto uprising. These were the Jews who went down fighting.

* * *

A month after we uncovered the names of Leon's lost family members, a message arrived from my Israeli friend Hagar, apologizing for the delay. She'd been busy but now that she finally had a moment to look, the woman who had left the record of Kolonimus and Manya had been easy to locate, and she wanted to meet with us.

Talia and I sent a message to Adi, explaining our connection via her grandfather. She immediately responded: "I'm very, very excited to hear from you!"

We set up a video meeting, and days later a woman with wild strawberry-blond hair and large brass-rimmed glasses popped onto my computer screen.

"Hebrew, English, who is who?" Adi said, laughing and tossing her hands in big motions.

"Shalom! Hello!" Talia and I responded in unison, sitting next to each other in my office shed.

"I'm curious to know everything!" Adi took the lead. "We all are from Zamość, right?"

Talia and Adi, women in their forties connected by their deceased grandfathers, took each other in across the divide. In the early morning Los Angeles sun, Talia sat feet neatly tucked under her on a chair, hair pulled tightly back. Tears dotted her eyes. Adi's effusive face shone under the glow of apartment lights in the Tel Aviv evening.

"I've imagined this moment, also thinking it could never happen," Adi said. She worked as a social worker ensuring health benefits for the last of Israel's Holocaust survivors. In 2009, the Central Database of Shoah Victims' Names contacted her. They were looking to capture testimonies before all the living witnesses died and asked her to encourage her patients to submit their memories. But even as Adi had been invited in a professional capacity, she first searched the archive for her own family story and discovered her grandfather's entries for his sister and her son. This came as a surprise.

Adi had no memories of her grandfather Khaim, who died when she was three, but she had been told he had refused to talk about the family he left behind in Poland. He departed Zamość after he graduated from high school, first going to medical school in Warsaw and then to study agronomy in France. There he was part of a group of students that mobilized against an anti-Semitic professor, and, facing troubles with authorities, found his way to Tel Aviv in 1929.

Eight years later, Khaim boarded a boat back to the European continent with a new document, the words "British Passport" inscribed in gold on the top and "Palestine" on the bottom. According to the family story, he tried desperately to convince his Zamość loved ones to leave on that trip. But the British refused his parents' visas because they had ties to the right-wing Zionist Ze'ev Jabotinsky. These were all the details Adi knew.

Here was his neat, looping script writing the names of his parents, sister, and nephew in the database of Holocaust victims. The submission was dated 1955. That was the year the Israeli government pursued the biographical information of the slaughtered with the fervor of a national census, sending teams house-to-house and broadcasting radio announcements urging citizens to document their lost loved ones. Their collective stories would reinforce what Israel stood to prevent from ever happening again—the destruction of Jews.

When Adi found her grandfather's entries in the victims' database, she knew she had more to offer: photos of Kolonimus, frozen in time as a little boy. As she filled out the form, she remembered there had been one person who had survived, Manya's husband. Sure, her grandfather had been furious with that man for leaving his sister and nephew behind. But maybe he had since had more children, or grandchildren? Perhaps they would come looking?

So, when her phone rang from an unknown number one summer day, she was surprised but not shocked. "Finally!" she exclaimed. "I've found people who care more about this past than I do."

* * *

"We simply did not talk about my father's family—at all." Talia leaned in toward Adi, describing her shock at seeing the photograph of Kolonimus. "My father never even knew he had a brother until after his father died."

Adi told us this was, in her experience as a social worker counseling Holocaust survivors, a common situation. People often found out decades after the end of the war that a parent, a spouse, once had a different family—loved ones who didn't survive.

Talia was still stuck in the shock of realizing what a person you adore can keep from you. "I felt very connected to my grandfather growing up," Talia reminisced. In family pictures, she was always leaning against Leon. When she spoke again, her voice broke. "He had a whole life I didn't know about; it's just hard to process."

Adi looked like she wanted to get something off her chest. "I'm sorry, but my grandfather didn't want to talk to your grandfather." Her words spilled out fast. It immediately made sense to me: Khaim blamed Leon for leaving Manya and Kolonimus behind in Zamość. "I think he was full of guilt that he wasn't able to save his family and he was, you know, completely alone in the world." Adi considered the divide. "I don't know about your grandfather, if he had anyone?"

"He had nobody." Talia shook her head. At least that is what she had always been told. Leon's closest relative had in fact been Adi's grandfather, his brother-in-law. After the war, for four decades, they'd lived fifteen miles from each other. "My grandfather must have known then that your grandfather was in Israel?" Talia struggled to process this manufactured solitude.

"Yes, he knew." Adi nodded. "To see your grandfather would be to remember Kolonimus. Kolonimus completely did not look like our family." Adi then paused, building up to a question it seemed she was unsure if she should ask. "Do you want to hear the story of what happened to him?" I was eager to jump in, but I held back, turning to Talia. She nodded.

Adi told us how as the Nazis rounded up the Jews in Zamość's ghetto to march them to the deportation trains, "Kolonimus had something on his shirt and his grandfather went to clean him. The German soldier yelled at him and then shot both." They never made it to the gas chambers at Bełżec.

For a moment the three of us went silent. My stomach panged, thinking of how impossible it was to get our children to listen to directions; how they were constantly dropping food on their clothes.

But was that truly how Kolonimus had died? Adi said she started to doubt the account as she spoke to more aging Holocaust survivors and realized stories, like this one, often circulated and became memories when they were based on rumors. She also witnessed how true memories sometimes felt like fiction.

"What about his mother, Manya?" Talia asked. "Do you know how she died?"

"Nothing, nothing, nothing. We don't know anything about her."

Adi knew so much more than Talia's family, but what happened to Manya, her murdered great-aunt, remained a mystery to her.

* * *

After the call, I found myself longing for my father. I wanted to share the thrill of these discoveries with him, to lean on him with my historical questions. We'd learned that Leon's first family strongly supported the breakaway Zionist leader Ze'ev Jabotinsky—though Adi and her mother, both social workers who leaned left, distanced themselves from his political legacy. I recognized the name from central boulevards in Tel Aviv and Jerusalem and had a vague recollection that he was linked to a Jewish militant group that would go on to blow up the King David Hotel. My father, who did doctoral research in Israel, could have told me much more about this historical figure. He'd have relished sharing each detail and his perspective, pushing me to think in new ways.

In the liberal Washingtonian milieu of my childhood, my father sliced through norms with piercing questions. He sent me to a Quaker school where I learned about nonviolence, but he often asked how anyone could *not* fight when faced with a Holocaust. He was a hawkish supporter of Israel, but one of his closest friends was a Moroccan Muslim diplomat with whom he worked for years. I yearned to talk with him, but I no longer could.

* * *

When Talia spoke about her abba to the packed funeral home, tears rolled down my father's face. My mother had never seen him so stricken. But even after witnessing Nachum's shockingly early death, he still assumed he would be allotted at least the lifespan of his own father, who had lived into his eighties. So, of course, did we.

"I should have another decade or so, and so how do I want to live?" Dad, in his seventies, pondered this question like a Talmudic text, bringing others into the debate whether we wanted to talk about it or not. Forever the displaced person, he obsessed about the next place to land. In his career, he had consistently searched for the more fulfilling, more consequential position, from professor to US Justice Department attorney to UN counsel to his own practice suing countries for terrorism. Now he turned his focus to real estate, in which he also had big ambitions, fixating on retirement near the Pacific Ocean in a home with a gallery to display his passion project—photography.

Yet it is on an island in the Atlantic Ocean that he will remain. My father's brilliant mind collapsed in the fall of 2019 at breathtaking speed. Within months his heart seized and stopped. Now wild turkeys wander by his tombstone, with his name, Allan Gerson, engraved in large letters. Below is etched a photo he took of a clock in Paris and words he lived by: "Justice, justice you shall pursue."

With every detail Talia and I uncovered, I longed to share the thrill of the reveal with our fathers, to laugh with their joy, to ask them questions only they might know the answers to. I felt a new closeness to both men as I encountered elements of their stories, just as the permanence of their deaths pummeled me with its unrelenting finality. Now four years old, our children would grow up without memories of either grandfather.

Resuming our search after Nachum and then my father died within three years of each other, a new urgency infused the task of unraveling our family's survival story. We wanted our children to one day understand what it took for Talia and me to come together in this world. We set out for Poland to probe how Zamość and loved ones left behind, and their desperate journey to survive, reverberated across borders and through generations.

CHAPTER 6

Motherland

On a Los Angeles September day with a light breeze kissing our skin, Talia, the kids, and I packed large suitcases into our Prius station wagon. My brother then steered us onto the freeway past the downtown skyscrapers and above the homes of South Los Angeles before we turned west toward the airport. We were all giddy with anticipation. Having studied images of the attic apartment in Warsaw's leafy Mokotów neighborhood that would be our home for the next eight weeks, Aviv could not wait for the promised Legos, and Alma, for the tent in their bedroom. Talia longed to explore the adorable wine and grocer below the apartment, and all I wanted was to slip into the lofted soaking tub.

We rolled our four overstuffed suitcases into the international terminal at LAX.

"I can't believe I once spent so much time here," Talia said.

Five years earlier, Talia drove to the airport not to travel—but in an emergency effort to help immigrants. Of the two of us, she had taken the more observant path in Judaism and generally powered down from sunset Friday to sunset Saturday. I tended to keep my phone connected and relayed to Talia alarming news on the morning of January 28, 2017: Muslim immigrants and tourists were being detained and turned away at the airport. Donald Trump, one week into his first term as president, had issued an executive order barring their entry. Talia determined this was an emergency, during which her religious practice would permit her to work. She was one of a small group of immigration lawyers in the city who knew the legal intricacies deeply enough to support those stranded at the airports.

Talia threw on jeans and a blazer, wrapped a scarf from my father around her neck, and grabbed intake forms. At LAX, she found chaos: a student blocked from deplaning, grandmothers and children held for hours on end, and a young woman frantically trying to help her uncle. He had arrived from Iran with a long-awaited immigrant visa, but he was being told he could not enter the country because of Trump's new order. Talia argued with airline representatives and when that failed, she presented a Customs and Border Protection officer with a habeas petition to stop the plane from returning to Iran with the uncle on it. The officer was unmoved.

"This is America," he told her after the plane took off with the uncle.

"This is not my America," Talia shot back.

Talia led press conferences with more than a dozen microphones pointed at her, beaming the story to news outlets around the world. The *LA Times* profiled her. *Slate* showcased her leaning in to counsel immigrants above the headline "This Is Why We Need Lawyers. This Is Why We Have Laws." The courts ruled the travel ban unconstitutional and the uncle returned. Kamala Harris, then California's senator, invited Talia for a meal at a Syrian restaurant with local migrant leaders in the Valley.

Talia was shocked by the attention, but even more so by the lunch's location. Of all the places in the vast city of Los Angeles, the senator's staff had chosen the restaurant her father adored visiting even as cancer ravaged his body. There was no way for Harris's team to have known that Kobee Factory, a hole-in-the-wall in Van Nuys, was where her gregarious Israeli father had become fast friends with the Syrian owner during his final year. This was Talia's first visit to the restaurant since Nachum had succumbed to the disease only months before. She was honored to be there but also felt completely unhinged when the owner, Wafa Ghreir, tearfully embraced her, bridging traumas personal and political.

"For Talia, whose own grandparents fled Poland, whose father was born in a refugee camp in Austria, it was a heartbreaking but inspiring weekend," Los Angeles Mayor Garcetti proclaimed weeks later, honoring her as part of his State of the City address. "Talia said she never felt so ashamed of Washington but so proud of Los Angeles. Thank you, Talia." I enthusiastically joined the packed chamber with City Council members, agency heads, and staffers all applauding for my wife, who stood in her signature blazer, not yet showing the twin pregnancy that had taken hold amid the chaos of the past months.

* * *

Five years later, the airport was back to its usual frenetic pace of international travelers in a hurry, our twin prekindergarteners and us among them. We searched for LOT Polish Airlines. Dozens of blond young people donning a smattering of college shirts marched by. I assumed they were Polish teens returning home from a tour of the United States.

"Would you mind if we went in front of you?" I asked a few of them as we took our place in line. "We have two very restless kids."

"No," a woman leading the group shot back. "We can't be separated."

She was likely anxious about organizing a big group. But my gut reaction was not rational or without prejudice. *Polish people are mean. They're not going to like us. This is not going to go well.* I had not expected this degree of raw emotion.

I heard my grandmother's words in my mind. "Don't go," had been her long-standing mantra about visiting Poland. "They want now the Jews to come back and to build up their economy. They want the money from the Jews." There was no allure for her in the notion of returning to her old home. "It's remodeled, and anyway somebody else has it. For what? For what?"

Just as these thoughts were spiraling, my brother texted a photo he'd taken of us smiling broadly with our bags on the airport curb moments before. He wrote: "Return to the motherland."

Not exactly. Yes, our grandparents were from Poland. But I anticipated no homecoming like those experienced by my students when they visited the native towns of their grandparents from Mexico or the Philippines. For starters, we had nobody left in the town. Nazis had exterminated our extended families in Zamość. Poles had threatened Jews who returned. The Poland we were visiting was where our families lived for centuries, but I had never thought of it as a homeland that might welcome me back.

More Poles arrived at the airport. I grew increasingly uncomfortable, realizing it was not just about one woman's brusqueness. I tried to squash the feelings questioning our decision to spend time in Poland. I reminded myself that two generations had passed. Still, I felt my anxiety rising once more as we boarded the plane.

I texted my brother: "What was I thinking??"

* * *

Many hours and movies later, our kids sat with their heads pressed close to each other and up against the window, straining to catch a glimpse through the clouds.

"Whoa, I see Poland!" Alma shrieked.

Below, they looked out on a green and flat land dotted with red-roofed homes, church spires, and Soviet Bloc architecture.

That evening, we settled in for our first meal in Warsaw. Talia and I grasped large cups of red wine, sitting outside in the brisk September evening with blankets wrapped around us, savoring a spread of delectable Italian food. When we told the charming waiter in his twenties what brought us to Poland, he responded that his grandfather was also from Zamość. A welcome from a landsman?

On the walk home through a regal park, my preconceptions and prejudice against Poland receded as we tossed golden leaves in the air. We'd made it to Europe, and now we had this gift of exploration and time together as a family. Our kids sprinted toward a playground with a train and seesaw. Then Alma made a face at a little girl wearing pink boots and a green full-body rainsuit. The father approached us. I was worried he would be upset, but instead he smiled.

I told him we had just arrived in Poland, and he introduced himself in perfect English as Eliecer. As we watched the kids on the playground, he shared with us how he ended up in this Warsaw park. Eliecer was from Mexico City but had called New York City home for the last twenty years. There, he traded stocks and met his Ukrainian wife. When the pandemic struck, her family suggested a move to their home in Lviv, Ukraine: "Come somewhere peaceful, where the kids can run around." The family relocated. And it was peaceful, for two years.

My attention sharpened at the mention of Lviv. That was the city our four grandparents had fled to in Ukraine, and one I had hoped to visit. But now Eliecer was telling me about how his family had been desperately intent on getting out. Five days after the 2022 Russian invasion, he kissed his in-laws goodbye, not knowing when they would meet again, and took a ten-hour bus ride to Ostrava in the Czech Republic. It was not at all where they wanted to go, but it was a way out of Lviv and that was all that mattered. "We were very, very lucky to find seats in the bus," he told us. Then they took a seven-hour train back east to Warsaw. This was a new Polish narrative, one of welcoming foreigners, especially Ukrainians.

Across the park, a ceremony began honoring the 1944 Warsaw Uprising, with a full band, men in uniform, and patriotic regalia.

Our kids went up and down on the seesaw to the beat of military marching music.

At first, I assumed this memorialization was about the ghetto uprising, the only Warsaw rebellion we spoke of in our family. I was wrong. This was about Poles fighting back against the Germans. I realized I knew next to nothing about the broader history of Poland during World War II. We had arrived as the granddaughters of Jewish victims to learn our history, but we had much to learn about the Polish experience, and how we were tied to it.

* * *

It was already dark when we returned to our apartment, a fifth-story walk-up in a looming Communist-era building. While our new Warsaw home was bleak on the outside, the interior was a light-filled top-floor flat with high, slanted ceilings and dormer windows. The kids went to sleep quickly, tucked beneath animal-print sheets, and Talia nodded off in their room on the hammock perfectly perched on beams between their two beds. For a few hours, we were all at rest, easing into our Poland adventure.

Talia and I went to sleep feeling, as she later wrote in her journal, "We are where we should be, strange as it is."

And then Alma woke her in the dark night.

Long after our daughter returned to sleep, Talia lay on the cozy couch in our living room below lights strung from the lofted rafters and framed posters with sketches of women swimming in Warsaw pools. As her mind spun with jet lag, she had a flashback to sleepless summer nights as a child in Israel when she had just arrived from LA. She would sometimes sneak onto the itchy green couch in the living room without her grandparents knowing. There, late one night, her grandfather Leon had walked in naked to get something from the cabinet. Talia did not tell him she was there. Instead, she just observed him.

"I remember studying his body and wondering even as a young child what it—and he—had seen," Talia wrote that night in her journal. "I can't imagine what he would have thought of us coming here to try to uncover some of what he tried to bury, and was forced to leave behind, all those years ago. We head to Zamosc in three days."

CHAPTER 7
The Book of Memory

Resplendent leaves rained down as we drove southeast out of Warsaw in a Renault station wagon. Poland's Golden Autumn was on magnificent display, an explosion of orange and yellow foliage.

It was during this same glorious season in 1939 that my great-uncle Moishe, a broad-shouldered young man in his early twenties, dodged bombs as he trudged southeast from Warsaw. Desperate to return to his parents and siblings in Zamość, he joined a crush of Polish citizens fleeing mostly on foot from the first terrifying German bombardment of their capital. Uncle Moishe tried to sleep stashed below leaves and tomato plants during the day, walking the road all night beneath a blanket of darkness.

Now, eighty-three years later, we sped past fields of dead sunflowers and bronzed wheat, covering in hours the route that took him days to walk.

"Zamość!" Talia and I cried out in giddy unison as we spotted the first green sign over the highway with our town's name emblazoned in white letters.

* * *

Talia had been the first to recognize that the enticing cover photo on our Poland guidebook was Zamość. We knew the town from pictures, and everyone in my immediate family had visited, including me very briefly as a teen with my parents. My memories were vague, but I recalled it was a pretty town. Still, I did not expect that, beyond the descendants of displaced Jews, Zamość would hold attraction to other visitors.

It turned out the *Rough Guide* authors had a surprising affinity for our town. In the book's breakdown of "twenty things not to miss" in Poland, visiting Zamość ranked number three: "A model Renaissance town, stuffed with the palaces and churches built by the Zamoyskis, one of the country's leading aristocratic families." The author described Zamość as "magnificent" and "elegant," on par with Krakow and Warsaw as a reason to visit Poland.

In 1992, Zamość was even designated a UNESCO World Heritage Site. Once Talia recognized its main square on the *Rough Guide* cover, I started to see it everywhere, from Polish tourism posters to travel tips for Warsaw expat parents. Now I was trying to take in a vibrant history that stretched before our families—and after them as well. But the idea that British tourists would choose to vacation in our ancestors' hometown felt bizarre. After all, we had always known Zamość as a place that had ceased to exist when its Jewish inhabitants were extinguished.

* * *

My elderly relatives' guide to their hometown describes a place where "everything has been destroyed." Each survivor family member, from Buenos Aires to the Bronx, treasured in their home a copy of a thousand-plus-page tome bearing Zamość's name in flames on the cover. Known as a Yizkor, or memorial book, after the Hebrew word for "will remember" and a prayer said to honor the dead, the town's survivors deposited in the massive volume what they wanted to be commemorated.

I introduced this book to Talia when she visited my aunt Raya on our first trip together to New York, eleven years earlier. Raya, dressed in a sweater printed with blooming flowers, was a beautiful woman with delicate features, especially, she would tell me, "after I got my nose fixed." Now her hair was thin, her back stooped, and her eyelids permanently red, but she still managed to maintain a regal air.

Upon entering her Upper West Side apartment, I could barely contain myself: "Talia is from Zamość!"

"Ah, what is your name?" she asked Talia.

"My father's family is Inlender."

"Inlender?" Raya said, straightening up in recognition. "We were neighbors. Across the street was the Inlenders." Could this really be true? I had my doubts, knowing Raya left Zamość as a young girl.

"Inlender was a very fine family," Raya went on, nodding. "A very good family, yes. And they were well off." Talia broke into a delighted smile and locked eyes with me across the room packed with the tchotchkes that had multiplied as my aunt aged. Our relationship felt more b'shert than ever to us, even if I had not shared with Raya the nature of it. I had heard enough of my aunt's lectures on finding the right Jewish man to suspect she wouldn't have found anything meant-to-be about our romance.

Raya wasn't technically my aunt. I'm not even certain she was a second cousin. But I knew my grandparents were her closest surviving family after the war. So, the two of them, each with an arm laced in hers, had escorted Raya, huge smile painted red and big white hoopskirt, down the aisle of the synagogue in New York to marry her David, the jazz-playing Bulgarian love of her life.

Unlike my grandmother, whose fierce battles with a God who'd allowed Nazis to slaughter his chosen people only grew with age, Raya had become more observant. Now she tried to lead us in Jewish melodies. For a moment all three of us sang "Adon Olam," belting out the last line, which translates as, "God, you are with me and I shall not fear."

Then she strode across the room, where, stacked among pictures of dead relatives, she sought out the Zamość memorial book as proof of our joint history. Raya flipped toward the end of the tome and identified the family name Inlender in the Hebrew script listing the murdered. That was the last time I saw my aunt before dementia took her memory, and with it my final familial witness to life in Zamość.

* * *

By the time we'd learned the names of Talia's grandfather's first family, Raya had been dead for six years and her daughters had sold the apartment, emptying it of all her photos and framed clippings. My grandparents' copy of the memorial book had moved with them decades earlier from their apartment in the Bronx to North Miami Beach, where they lived in a condominium complex filled with other Holocaust survivors trying to find ways to enjoy, at last, their final years. After they died, my father, ever the enthusiast about Zamość, had the copy he inherited bound in a special gold casing. Now, my family's book was across the country in DC, but I was not there to peruse it.

Instead, in the months before we left for Poland, I searched for an online version. While unique to Zamość, the memorial book was part of a larger movement launched by survivors from decimated communities across Europe to preserve what they could not save of their towns and villages. The New York Public Library holds a collection of more than 730 volumes from destroyed Jewish communities across Europe. Near the end of the massive database, I found a digitized version of the Zamość one. What's more, it had been fully translated from Yiddish to English. Even though I had seen the book many times, this was the first time I could understand it.

"It has taken a full seven years to gather, select and bring together the pain and tears of our slaughtered brothers and sisters," wrote Wolf Kornmass, a lead committee member in Buenos Aires, where the Yiddish-language version of the book was published in 1957. The surviving Jews of Zamość had connected via letters and local meetings in Argentina, Brazil, Bolivia, Australia, Canada, Israel, and the United States. Then dozens of refugees scribbled and typed furiously on the genesis and life of their lost hometown—the pogroms and the rabbis, theater troupes and libraries, the luminaries and the fishmongers.

On page 520, the memorial book shifted from stories of the life and origins of Zamość to its destruction, with chapter names such as "How a Sabbath-Observing Congregation Traipsed off to God," "Ghetto,

Slaughter, Forest, Majdanek," and "Through Seven Hells." And then the section that could be found in all memorial books: the "List of Martyrs."

I read the names of all four of my paternal great-grandparents: Esther, Chaim, Chaya, and Shmuel-Joseph. Then my great-aunts, Dora and Feiga. All had the same place listed as the site of their murder: Bełżec. Listed among the victims, I also found various Inlenders whose names Talia had never heard: Avigdor, Amatzia, Monik, Rivka, and Salek. Who were they? And why, as I carefully traced and retraced through the list, could I not find the Inlenders I was searching for? No Manya or Kolonimus Inlender were listed among the murdered.

Written before the assistance of computers, and compiled across continents, the list, counting 2,702 names, was admittedly incomplete. "It is certain that this is not the full count of those killed by the Nazi murderers and their servants, the SS bands of Ukrainians, Lithuanians, and local collaborating Poles." From many families "not a single witness remained, who would be able to properly recollect." Then there were the survivors who chose not to commemorate the lost. The book committee lamented, "Literally, hundreds of letters were sent out, to places where all we had was merely an address. Over the course of years, we asked for and demanded material."

To live in Israel, near other Zamość survivors, and not submit a loved one to the memorial book meant you were likely working desperately hard not to remember. It was yet another sign that Talia's grandfather had endeavored to erase what he was forced to leave behind in Zamość. And now we were driving straight toward it, with our children in the backseat.

CHAPTER 8

Origin Stories

We circled a dizzying series of roundabouts, leaving behind modern cement apartment buildings for the stone remnants of Zamość's medieval fortifications. Talia eased the Renault into a spot in front of a blood-orange row house. Across the street, an ice cream parlor beckoned, and just down the block was the apartment where my grandparents lived in their first home as a couple. The setting was as beguiling as it was unsettling.

While I checked in, our kids gleefully explored a play nook. The sleek renovated interiors of the hotel upended my expectations of what Zamość would look and feel like. A menorah perched above our childrens' heads was the only hint I could find of Hotel 77's unique history. I'd booked our rooms after Marek, the high school teacher who'd jump-started my search for our ancestors in Zamość, alerted me that it had once housed the Jewish community's mikveh, or ritual bath. I imagined Peshke and Manya as young women preparing to wed, submerged in the purifying water, bursting with the promise of their futures in this town.

Soon, we would get to meet Marek, who for months had sent us documents, photos, and maps unearthing our past. What else would he reveal that might bind Talia and me to this place, and to each other?

* * *

Our first appointment, however, was with a frequent collaborator of Marek's. In the lobby, a man who would not have looked out of place in hipster Brooklyn—beard, hoodie, shirt decorated with tiny pineapples—greeted me. Daniel Sabaciński ran the synagogue, working for the Polish foundation that preserved Jewish artifacts in places where no community remained.

"All ready?" he asked and then set out the agenda for the evening, which included a tour of the Old City before we met up for dinner with Marek.

As we left the hotel, Talia pointed across the street at a gleaming Porsche with Ukrainian license plates. Daniel explained that in the immediate aftermath of the Russian invasion of Ukraine, the town had served as a welcome and registration point for refugees. Beds had been set up in schools, sports clubs, and private homes. Most refugees stayed only briefly, venturing farther west in search of jobs. But some business owners remained, so they could visit their companies across the border less than fifty miles away. We would soon spot more luxury vehicles—Jaguars, Mercedes—all with Ukrainian license plates.

Beyond convenience to the border, I understood why these wealthy Ukrainians would take up residency in our family's town. Zamość was captivating. As the sun began to set, orange-tinged lanterns flickered on, illuminating restored eighteenth-century buildings.

When investigating my family's story, as I often did in my migration reporting, I'd long focused on the journey and the destination, on the decade from when they left Zamość to when they settled in the United States. But to truly grasp their exile, I needed to probe what our grandparents were forced to leave behind.

* * *

Zamość, nicknamed "Padua of the North," was different from other Polish towns. Nobleman Jan Zamoyski, one of the most skilled statesmen of his time, founded his namesake town in 1580. He hired an Italian architect to construct an "ideal city" in the tradition of Plato. Then, to spur its growth, he invited merchants with diverse backgrounds—among them Greeks, Armenians, and Jews—to take up residence.

In early modern Europe, these diasporic peoples occupied a unique position. They were known for their business acumen but also viewed as "permanent strangers who performed tasks that the natives were unable or unwilling to perform," Yuri Slezkine writes in his book *The Jewish Century*. "Death, trade, magic, wilderness, money, disease, and internal violence were often handled by people who claimed—or were assigned to—different gods, tongues, and origins."

Zamoyski had invited to his new town specifically Sephardic Jews, those tracing their roots to the Iberian Peninsula prior to their expulsion in 1492, since they were highly connected to trading networks. They would, as he'd intended, go on to spur economic activity. These early Jewish residents manifested their success and commitment to the town, building a magnificent Renaissance-style synagogue right outside the main market square.

Zamość emerged as a valiant fortress that withstood a multitude of sieges, but even so, foreign armies often breached its moat and high walls and slaughtered its residents. Most of the Sephardic Jews, along with many members of other merchant minorities, eventually left for more secure and lucrative towns. In their places moved Ashkenazi Jews beginning in the mid-seventeenth century, fleeing deadly anti-Semitic attacks to the east.

Zamość, which prided itself on the peaceful coexistence of its varied residents, tended to be a safer place for Jews. My grandmother recalled being friendly with some Polish Catholic girls at her school and later had Polish clients. For the decade after 1919, Jews filled half the local town council seats. But it was not exempt from anti-Semitism or spasms of violence. In 1920, during the Polish-Bolshevik war, soldiers—either Polish or Cossack, according to conflicting reports—initiated a pogrom, hacking to death a woman, beheading a brewer, and slicing off the hands of a man who bled to death. Though deeply rooted in their exceptional hometown, our grandparents grew up knowing the uneasy balance between tolerance and hate could tip at any moment.

* * *

As Daniel led us toward the centerpiece of Zamość—a massive town square featuring a grand pink town hall with a towering 170-foot clock tower—the evening light dimmed to a cinematic glow. To our left rose the four-story brightly colored grand row homes, the iconic scene *Rough Guide* had selected for its cover. I scanned the houses painted lime green, sunny yellow, scarlet, with white finishes sculpted on the surface like icing, until I found the most beautiful one, a deep cornflower blue.

My grandmother's house. I recognized it from the photos, but it was even more striking than I had envisioned. I then shifted my gaze across the square and tried to place Talia's grandfather's home, but she beat me to it. She pointed across the main square at a light purple building with a restaurant on the ground-level piazza. Taking our children's hands, we followed Daniel across the short distance—perhaps a hundred steps—that had once separated our grandparents' childhood homes. It was one thing to see their proximity on a map, another to sit in front of one building and see clearly across the square to the other. Talia and I locked eyes. We did not have to say what we were thinking. There was no longer any doubt. Our families must have known each other, if only by sight.

Yet, while they were close in terms of physical proximity, other divides likely separated our families. My grandparents, like most Zamość Jews, struggled financially. Even if Peshke's building now appeared beautifully restored, when she grew up there, her family of seven had shared a two-room apartment with no running water, using an outhouse down multiple flights of stairs. Mottel's family was poorer, needing him to stop school and start work after his bar mitzvah.

In contrast, Marek had revealed to us that Talia's grandfather's cousin, Wigdor Inlender, was the wealthiest Jew in town. Her uncle Zyg shared memories of how he rode stunning horses into this square, greeting people, "as if he were a Rothschild." Wigdor owned enterprises stretching from Łódź to Lviv, among them a brickyard, a bank, and a rum distillery. His home boasted the first power generator in town, and a toilet with plumbing. He possessed various other properties as well, one of them this house, adjacent to his own, where his cousin Leon lived.

But even if Talia's grandfather appeared insulated with money, he was not protected from tragedy. Marek had found us records that revealed that when Leon was in his mid-twenties, his immediate relatives died in quick succession. First his older sister. She had moved to the opposite corner of the square to marry and soon had a child, Talia's uncle Zyg. But the next time she went into labor, with the heavy load of twin boys, she perished, at thirty-two. A year later, in 1930, Leon's mother died; the following year, his father.

Perhaps, in his anguish, Leon turned to his neighbor Manya for comfort. The first photos we discovered of them courting were printed in the year of his father's death, 1931. Three years later, in this purple building at Rynek Wielki 3, Manya likely birthed their only child, Kolonimus.

We lingered in front of the house, the bottom floor now a burger joint. An elaborate metal gate barred us from ascending the stairs to the living quarters. Unable to enter the building, Talia and I studied the upstairs windows. We delicately balanced trying to imbue in our children a connection to their great-grandfather's former home, while suppressing the image that flashed in our own minds—the boy just a little older than them that Leon had left behind here. Soon, our kids tired of staring at what was to them simply an old building and were ready to move on.

Alma grasped Talia's hand and together they set off back across the square to my grandparents' side with Daniel in tow. Aviv sprinted after, his shark-printed rain boots lighting up the deep red brick piazza with each step. I lingered for a moment in the space between our two sides of this great market square, marveling at how our families were more hauntingly intertwined than even I had imagined.

* * *

We had just taken a seat at a Georgian restaurant's patio in front of my grandmother's childhood home when Marek rolled up on an electric scooter. From our email exchanges, I had been picturing a recluse who lived in the dust of the past. He was nothing like that. Urbane with white hair neatly cropped, blue jacket matching his eyes, Marek gracefully stepped off the scooter and took a drag of a cigarette. Then, taking a seat next to Daniel on a bench, he faced us across the broad wooden table.

We got the kids settled and sampled local specialties of green stinging nettle soup and kasha with wild mushrooms.

After an exchange of pleasantries, Talia and I were unable to hold back a flood of gratitude. Daniel translated our words of thanks into Polish, and Marek responded with an endearing smile. We had more we wanted to share with them. Talia searched for the photos she had pasted together of her father and his murdered half brother.

"Yes, I know this photo," Marek said haltingly in English, assuming the two boys were the same. But then Talia clarified.

"This is Kolonimus," she said, pointing from one to the other. "And this is my father!"

"Ahhh!" Marek cried, recognizing his mistake and the startling similarity.

He paused to examine closer the two boys' images. "Identyczny, nie?"

"Almost identical, right?" Talia echoed. "To see these pictures together was shocking." Though she'd been laughing only a moment earlier, now tears fell. Marek reached silently for tissues. Into the lull, our kids' giggles floated over to us, a welcome return to the present.

* * *

"We need to take a break for a moment," Daniel said. They had their own work to do. Switching to Polish, he turned to Marek. The following week would mark eighty years since the Zamość ghetto liquidation. Independent of government support, they were organizing lectures and a commemorative march. It would end at the train tracks—the deportation site where, in 2018, Marek had spearheaded a memorial.

Growing up in Zamość, neither Daniel nor Marek could have predicted he would one day be a champion of local Jewish history. Indeed, neither knew much about the people who had once populated half of their town.

Marek couldn't recall any lessons about the history or extermination of Jews at the Communist Zamość schools he attended. Instead, what he and his classmates learned about Nazi crimes was focused on the targeting of Poles. In the Aryan racial hierarchy, they were just one slot above Jews. The month after the Nazis declared Zamość as *judenrein*, literally "free of Jews," they went after their next target: Poles. Heinrich Himmler ordered an operation called Aktion Zamosc, expelling an estimated one hundred thousand Poles from their homes in the town's surrounding agricultural region. The Nazis jammed them into concentration camps, including tens of thousands of children stolen from their parents and kidnapped to be raised by Germans. In December 1942, the Nazi leadership faced a quandary: "Starve the Poles to death, or feed them?" The Nazis determined they would squeeze all the labor they could out of Poles and then make them slowly die off. As a result, unlike the Jews, who were annihilated mostly in gas chambers, the Poles from Zamość tended to perish from starvation, disease, torture, execution, or debilitating labor.

Marek's own grandfather was deported to the concentration camp Majdanek. He survived but returned home to discover that Ukrainian nationalists had burned down his house.

The horrors Nazis and their henchmen inflicted on Zamość Poles were all new to me, a disorienting revelation of the brutal suffering of a people I had known as perpetrators of ethnic violence. I hadn't known that Polish people were among the first groups held at Auschwitz, nor that more than a thousand non-Jewish Zamość residents were deported and murdered there, mostly by lethal injection.

Marek and I were not unique in learning completely different histories of Nazi crimes, prioritizing one group's victimhood at the exclusion of the other. He realized that his version of Zamość town history lacked essentially half the pages. The public school where Marek taught was likely the same one my grandmother had attended. When he discovered that about a third of the prewar students had been Jewish girls, Marek began to pursue Zamość's unspoken past with an intense and dogged focus. With each unearthed Jewish story, told through pictures or documents found in archives, he felt he further extricated himself from a collective amnesia.

Daniel, younger than Marek and growing up in Zamość in the post-Soviet 1990s, had learned a bit more about his town's Jews—mostly that they were exterminated in the Holocaust, but almost nothing of their lives. Then he began working as a tour guide and, like Marek, became hooked on the extensive unspoken local Jewish history. When he heard that the Zamość library, once a synagogue, was to be repurposed and restored, Daniel followed his curiosity and took a job establishing it as a historic and cultural institution.

Though funds were often tight, Daniel was resourceful and creative. When he realized that the sanctuary space lacked a ner tamid, representing the lamp that burned continuously in the ancient temple of Jerusalem, he went to T.J. Maxx and bought a light. A quotidian source for a sacred object, but his passion was infectious.

As Talia and I strolled back through lantern-lit Zamość, fingers grasping the warm palms of our children, I felt relief wash over me that these two wonderful Polish men were carrying this heavy burden of our town's Jewish history. Even after we said good night to Marek and Daniel, making plans to meet again in the days to come, they remained, discussing the specifics of their memorial ceremony into the night.

* * *

Later, in our lofted hotel room with its white paper chandeliers, we sang to our children the two prayers we put them to bed with every night: "Hashkiveinu," calling for a canopy of peace, and the "Shema," a core prayer of Jewish tradition.

When the twins were born, Talia had suggested we chant these as a bedtime ritual. A nightly prayer added a layer of religious observance beyond what I had known, and at first, I was uncertain. To me, the

"Shema" was a prayer I only said in the synagogue, though it moved me more than any other. When I would cover my eyes, as is the custom, and chant in Hebrew—"Hear, O Israel: the Lord Our God, the Lord is One"—I felt an overwhelming spiritual connection to a past bigger than my present. I often sensed my grandfather chanting alongside me, and the generations before him saying these same words.

I had come to love the nightly routine. Now Talia's and my voices met, chanting words that were once uttered throughout this town multiple times a day—at the synagogue down the street, in scattered homes as thousands of Jews woke and before they slept. They were gone, but our voices singing to our children affirmed all was not lost.

CHAPTER 9

Radical Moderns

The next morning, we woke in cozy beds many flights above the ancient mikveh. Talia set out with the kids in search of a playground, and I returned to my grandmother's childhood home to see what else I could uncover in the glare of sunlight. A souvenir stand offered magnets in front of the shop where my great-grandfather once butchered kosher meat. Among pretty pictures of historic buildings, I spotted one with an image of an old religious Jew. And then another. Three different illustrations of Jewish men with variations of a long nose, dark head covering, and a white beard.

I'd heard about these "Lucky Jews." Poles placed the likeness of a religious Jewish man in their house to bring financial fortune. The practice of adopting a "Lucky Jew" dated back to before World War II, when Jews and Poles cohabited, but it had taken off more recently in capitalist post-Soviet Poland. Today, many more homes in Poland likely contain "Lucky Jews" than actual Jews.

Disdain rose in my chest. I'd left our hotel searching for traces of our grandparents' lives here, and instead I found this persistent stereotype. Yet, as much as I pushed back at the timeworn trope of Jews controlling access to wealth, I also recognized an uncomfortable truth. My vision of my ancestors who had lived here resembled the images on the magnets, except with less prominent noses. I had reflexively populated this serene market square with a one-dimensional vision of Eastern European Jews, filled with characters like *Fiddler on the Roof*'s Tevye belting out "Tradition!" But the more I probed our past in this town, the more it became apparent that my grandfather was no Tevye, and 1920s Zamość was no 1905 Russian shtetl, the setting of that enduring musical.

* * *

Long before my grandparents were born, the Jews of Zamość had already prided themselves on being more rational and intellectual than neighboring Jewish communities. They pushed back on the fervent religiosity of the Hasidim that swept through other towns in their borderlands area, defending their values as an early center of the Jewish Enlightenment, or Haskalah. Even as most remained religiously observant, they were open to engaging in the ideas of the community in which they lived.

Zamość was known for producing Jewish luminaries who challenged established norms. One of them had long captured my imagination. The revolutionary Rosa Luxemburg, born in 1871, spent her first years in a home adjacent to where Talia's grandfather lived a generation later. I walked to see the building, but there was no marker for the "She-Eagle that Flew out of Zamość" who Lenin lauded for inspiring generations of Communists around the world. Just graffiti, "We Remember Rosa!" scribbled in Polish over a discoloration in the wall where a plaque once had been.

In my twenties, I had gravitated to the bold radical—nicknamed "Red Rosa" for her politics and the color of her voluminous hair. She left Zamość with her family for Warsaw as a young child, later moving to Switzerland and Germany. There she worked for a global Marxist revolution, advocating for a new social order that would bring equality to workers across borders. When I lived in Berlin, I joined a journalism cooperative just blocks from a square named for her in the former East. I often strolled by its gargantuan people's theater and felt a spark of pride in our common Zamość roots.

If Luxemburg was Jewish Zamość's most famous, albeit errant and rebellious, daughter, then the Yiddish writer I. L. Peretz was its most beloved son. My grandfather once taught classes on Peretz's writing to other Holocaust survivor retirees, but I had not been interested in learning about him then. Until recently, the man with a slick mustache, gleaming eyes, and beautifully tailored suit whose portrait once hung on my grandparents' wall struck me as a relic of a bygone era. I assumed Luxemburg, the female revolutionary, could teach me about the socially engaged life I wanted to live.

But now, at last open to learning about Peretz, his actions emerged as radical in a way different from Luxemburg's. The lawyer-turned-writer took Yiddish, the language of Jewish Poland often derided as jargon, and used it to create literature, interpreting folk themes through a modern European lens. Peretz promoted living a proudly and richly Jewish life in the Diaspora, but one also fully entwined in the culture of the country in which one resided. It was Peretz, I realized, who'd likely had a bigger impact on my life. His approach was part of the tradition I was raised with, and one that Talia and I had embraced for our own family.

* * *

By the time our grandparents came of age in the 1920s, a generational shift had taken hold in Zamość. Luxemburg and Peretz were dead—German paramilitaries had murdered Luxemburg and discarded her body in a Berlin canal, and after Peretz died of a heart attack, one hundred thousand mourners packed Warsaw's Jewish cemetery. The Great War had ended, empires had collapsed, and new countries were being forged—among them an independent Poland, which emerged in 1918 after being erased from the European map for 123 years. Following the treaties at Versailles a year later, the country's Jews were, for the first time, provided citizenship and minority rights, at least officially. Most still struggled financially, except for a few prominent families like the Inlenders, but felt rich in ideas and conviction that they could change the trajectory of their lives.

The year my grandfather celebrated his bar mitzvah and officially became a man in Jewish tradition, 1921, Zamość hosted its first democratic elections for the municipal council. With new rights available for

Jews, the "concept of the proud struggle for equal rights for Jewish citizens in Poland threw down roots among the youth in our city and motivated them to unusual activity," recalled a writer in the memorial book.

With opportunity emerged a jagged generational divide. *Polish is for the street! Only Yiddish in the home!* My grandmother's father raged about language at his children, an attempt to keep a grip on a receding world. The word "Yiddish" translates to "Jewish," originating from the Middle High German "Jüdisch." To be a Yid was to be a Jew. My great-grandfather's ire was against assimilation into Polish society, since he was determined to preserve his distinct religious community. It must have felt like a losing battle. He watched as his children, part of the broader so-called "independence generation" of their country, embraced new liberties.

Zamość's young Jews flocked to wildly divergent social movements, firm in their beliefs they could shape a different trajectory from that of their parents. Whether rich, poor, traditional, or Orthodox, their generation was unified by what historian Kamil Kijek describes as a "radical modernism," engaging with revolutionary political ideologies of the interwar years. Late into the night in kerosene-lantern-lit rooms, Mottel and Leon surely joined seething conversations about their collective future, engaging in a ferocious marketplace of ideas: Was Communism and an end to religion the way to shed their enduring status as permanent strangers? Did power come from the Orthodox party vying for seats in the new Polish government? Should they embrace the "Jewish socialism" values of the Bundists? Or, as more and more youth argued, was the only path to safety and preserving their culture to be found in creating a new Jewish country?

* * *

It was at this time of heady ideas and unprecedented gains for Jews living in Poland that, counterintuitively, a movement to leave Europe behind for the Middle East gained momentum. For decades, the prospect of a mass return of Jews to the biblical land of Israel after two thousand years in the Diaspora had appeared to most as far-fetched.

When Viennese journalist Theodor Hertzl organized Zionism into a political movement in 1897, only a tiny percentage of world Jewry then lived in Ottoman Palestine. Some belonged to communities that had been a continuous thread since biblical times and had persisted after multiple expulsions. Others, known as Lovers of Zion, were recent arrivals from Eastern Europe with aspirations to revive Hebrew as a spoken language and work the biblical land. Even as tens of thousands more Jews began to take up the call of the evolving Zionist movement, they remained a small minority of the population. And the Ottoman Empire, which had ruled the territory since 1516, did not support the formation of a Jewish state.

But in the first quarter of the twentieth century, Zionism gained a transformative foothold with a world power. In 1917, Great Britain's foreign secretary, Arthur Balfour, wrote to Lord Rothschild, the head of the Zionist Federation of Great Britain and Ireland, "His Majesty's Government view with favor the establishment in Palestine of a national home for the Jewish people." The only reference to the 94 percent of the population that was Arab was that "nothing shall be done which may prejudice the civil and religious rights of existing non-Jewish communities." This letter, which would propel Zionism into a real possibility, most likely came out of not only sympathy for the Jewish cause, but also Lord Balfour's personal connection to the evangelical belief that the Jewish return to Palestine was part of God's plan and biblical prophecy, as well Britain's desire to reduce Jewish immigration to their country and to gain secure positioning in the Middle East.

While a breakthrough for Zionists, not all Jews celebrated. Sir Edwin Montagu, secretary of state for India and the only Jewish member of the British cabinet, wrote in a secret memorandum of his disdain for the movement and confusion over its specific aims: "I assume that it means that Mohammedans and Christians are to make way for the Jews, and that the Jews should be put in all positions of preference and should be peculiarly associated with Palestine in the same way that England is with the English or France with the French, that Turks and other Mohammedans in Palestine will be regarded as foreigners, just in the same way as Jews will hereafter be treated as foreigners in every country but Palestine." His criticisms of the potential for displacement were a minority, however. Five years later, as the French and British carved up the former Ottoman Empire territories, the newly formed League of Nations granted London a mandate to govern Palestine, which would include implementation of the Balfour Declaration and establishment of the "Jewish National Home."

In the borderlands around Zamość, known as the Kresy, Zionism pulsed with new energy. Russian leaders, facing arrests and crackdowns following the Bolshevik Revolution, had relocated to the adjacent and more open Poland, bolstering the movement. Meanwhile, in the wake of World War I, the belief in national self-determination, at least for Europeans, had risen to the forefront. Just as Poland had received its state, other peoples who were previously part of the German, Russian, and Austro-Hungarian Empires were getting their own independent countries. Now the potential glimmered that Jews, too, could govern themselves.

The Zionist movement expanded as alternate immigration options for ambitious Eastern European Jews contracted, and rising anti-Semitism made clear that while they may have Polish citizenship, the minority protections granted at Versailles were fleeting. Polish Jews by and large were barred from the United States—racist laws passed in 1924 had ended the great wave in which millions of Eastern European Jews entered. Some, like my grandmother's siblings who moved to Argentina in 1927, looked to Latin America for its economic opportunities at a time when jobs were limited for Jews in Zamość. But soon, Mandatory Palestine became the most sought-after option, and Poland the primary source of Jewish immigrants.

* * *

By his early teens, my prodigious grandfather was already a local leader and dedicated Zionist, a political persuasion of his own choosing. He had seen enough in his young life to be convinced that only in a Jewish homeland could he be safe. World War I erupted when he was six, and

Zamość passed violently from Austrian to Russian control and back again. Mottel's parents furtively packed their three children into a carriage and fled east to a Kyiv raucous with revolt. He would never forget how the upstart Vladimir Lenin established the world's first socialist state, impressing him as a young boy with the power of people's movements.

Along with witnessing tremendous political transformations, Mottel learned how his Jewish life became a target during periods of instability. The nationalist movements of Ukrainians and Russians collided in the aftermath of revolution and turned on Jews. Mottel watched as Cossacks ruthlessly grabbed an elderly religious man by his beard, tying his long facial hair to a horse, which then galloped around the streets as the man's mauled body trailed behind. He heard the wails of Jewish mothers as they bolted from burning homes ahead of looters. "The scapegoat was always the Jew," my grandfather stated in a recording made at the end of his life, invoking a lesson learned early and repeatedly.

The ensuing savagery would shatter scales of destruction and atrocities committed in previous pogroms. Within years, more than one hundred thousand people would be murdered. My great-grandparents must have foreseen that they would soon be in extreme danger, fleeing back to Zamość with an eight-day-old baby boy in their arms.

Back in his hometown and growing up in the newly independent Poland, Mottel began to envision a different future. One that wasn't Communist—but that held many of the ideals he had seen firsthand—and where Jews could safely determine their own fate. While as a teen he worked during the day as a warehouse bookkeeper, his passion was reserved for his evenings and the socialist efforts popping up in Zamość. For Mottel, it was natural to pair his political ideals with a move to Palestine to build a Jewish homeland.

Many nights, my grandfather, with his sixth-grade education, led lessons about the workers' movements of the world and taught Hebrew and Jewish history. He took on leadership roles in the bookkeepers' union. He participated in the Maccabiah Games, a competition and celebration of Jewish physical prowess, the antidote to the weak victim. And he joined a movement dedicated to working the land and developing agricultural settlements in Palestine.

In the memorial book I found a photo, taken in the 1920s, that I recalled my grandmother showing me as a child. Dozens of adolescents stared back, looking sharp in jackets and ties, dark hair coiffed with center parts. The girls wore dresses and flapper hats. The only child with blond hair, who looks younger than the others, is perched in the center of the front row, hoisting a sign. That sweet boy is my grandfather. The sign, an interpreter revealed, announced a fund-raiser for a youth branch of HeHalutz, Hebrew for "the Pioneer." My focus sharpened. I had recently learned of the Zamość branch of that Zionist group. But I had read about how Talia's family, not my own, played a pivotal role.

* * *

Wigdor Inlender, the richest Jew in Zamość and a cousin of Talia's grandfather, apparently had a soft spot for the workers' movement, despite his capitalist prowess. He agreed to lease HeHalutz a few acres he owned on the outskirts of town. In turn, these "Pioneers" called their training camp Avigdoria, taken from Wigdor's given name, Avigdor. Soon, the socialist Zionist youth of Zamość flocked there on Shabbat for long discussions over meals, as well as to sing in Hebrew and dance together. For one year, a particularly hardy group lived completely off the land.

Avigdoria was one of among more than two hundred training communities across Poland where young people, inspired by the neighboring Bolshevik Revolution, communed and adopted physical trades from which Jews had long been restricted in Poland. More familiar with crafting shoes, tailoring, and keeping books, they learned to plant crops and chop wood. But facing visa limitations as the British support for a Jewish homeland in Palestine waned in the face of Arab opposition, most only made it so far as tilling Polish soil.

Did Leon also work the land at his cousin's property? Did our grandfathers dance together or debate politics late into the night? It's impossible to know. Leon left no trace of his thoughts, and the Zionist movement was highly stratified. While his cousin Wigdor supported these socialists, or at least leased them his land, Leon's wife, Manya, and her family backed a right-wing militant group.

Its leader, Odessa-born Ze'ev Jabotinsky, was merciless in his portrayal of Eastern European Jews—describing his native brethren as "ugly, sickly," a belittling opposition to the "ideal image of the Hebrew with masculine beauty, stature, massive shoulders." But it was in Poland, not Palestine, that he initially found his strongest supporters. The family of Leon's wife, Manya, were among them. Her grandniece Adi had told us about this during our revelatory video call, but I lacked the context at the time to appreciate what it meant. She also shared pictures of Manya's brother and father attending the 1931 Zionist Congress in Basel as proud members of Jabotinsky's new Revisionist Party, named for promoting a revision to expand Jewish land acquisition to both sides of the Jordan River. A few years later, when the far-right leader determined that it was untenable to work with the General Zionists, Leon's wife, Manya, was listed as a founding member of the Zamość chapter of a women's group to support his new break-off organization.

Which way did Leon lean? Just as I found no records of Leon consorting with my grandfather's leftist Zionists, neither was there a mention of his presence among Jabotinsky's backers. Did he join the Zamość Zionists who would gather for talks with topics such as "The Revival of Eretz Israel," "The Jewish Village," and "Ploughing the Fields"? While they focused on the movement's gains, they also must have addressed Arab protests deploring the Zionist initiative, as news spread of increasing attacks on Jews with knives and clubs, and of fire being set to their agricultural fields.

Most of the Zionist movement initially believed that there was a peaceful way forward where Jewish migration to Palestine could also benefit the existing Arab residents and gain their favor. On the far left, Hashomer Hatzair advocated for a binational state based on Marxist class struggle, envisioning Jewish and Arab workers united against capitalist oppression. Groups like HeHalutz, the pioneer movement that had trained at Avigdoria in Zamość, saw themselves as bringing modern techniques and cooperative settlements that would benefit everyone in the region.

Jabotinsky was steadfast in his derision of these ideas, calling out the Left as hypocritical "Arabophiles," delusional in their beliefs that Arabs would ever consent to Jewish self-determination in Palestine in return for greater prosperity. "Our Peace-mongers are trying to persuade us that the Arabs are either fools, whom we can deceive by masking our real aims, or that they are corrupt and can be bribed to abandon to us their claim to priority in Palestine, in return for cultural and economic advantages."

Jabotinsky believed he knew the answer to inevitable Arab opposition: military might, forging a virtual "Iron Wall" of force. Like any indigenous people, he argued in a 1923 essay, existing residents would resist settlement if "they possess a gleam of hope that they can prevent 'Palestine' from becoming the Land of Israel." Zionists, in his estimation, needed to squash that hope. "It is utterly impossible to obtain the voluntary consent of the Palestine Arabs for converting 'Palestine' from an Arab country into a country with a Jewish majority," he wrote, noting he also believed "it utterly impossible to eject the Arabs from Palestine."

The more I learned about these charged debates, the more I longed to talk with my grandfather about where he fell within them. Did he consider the existing Arab population's perspective in Palestine? Did he worry that his dreams of a socialist Jewish state could be regarded as an attack on their own dreams of self-determination? These questions would go unanswered. My grandfather died just after I turned thirteen, and I had never asked him about his early Zionism. I also wished I could talk with Talia's grandfather Leon, or at least find some record, to get a sense of where he'd stood. I started to wonder if he had been a Zionist at all as a young man in Zamość.

Even as they endured financial hardship and anti-Semitism, most Jewish youth held tight to the belief they could build lives at home in

Poland. In the last Zamość town council election before the war, held in 1939, the anti-Zionist Bundists, who advocated for Yiddish culture and that Jewish liberation should be achieved in the Diaspora—dominated the Jewish vote. Five out of six elected town council members were from the party, though they would never have a chance to serve.

Zamość's wide-ranging Jewish political activity had been silenced generations before I wandered the square in the serene and picturesque town, mostly empty save the buzz of Polish tourists on golf carts. How would my grandfather's radical dreams have shifted if he had known then that all his study and organizing could not stop the growing tide of fascism? If he had known about the bloodshed that would follow the founding of the State of Israel? These being impossible questions to answer, I turned instead to the fickle nature of luck.

The Yiddish-speakers who once dominated these streets spoke of "Yidishe Glikn" or "Jewish Luck," an entirely different concept from the stereotypes now hawked to tourists in the "Lucky Jews" magnets. "On the simplest level, it is bad luck," historian Eliyana Adler writes. Yet, like so many Yiddish expressions, "Jewish Luck" contains "layers of meaning." Outcomes that at first appear to be bad often reveal fortitude in unexpected ways. As Adler asserts, it would be hard to find a better example of Jewish Luck than what awaited the youth of Zamość who fled to the Soviet Union with our grandparents.

CHAPTER 10
The Pendulum

Daniel raced our kids over Zamość's ramparts and through its vaulted passageways to a wooded idyll of fountains, meandering trails, and a lake. We recognized it immediately from the photos of Leon's first family. This was where Talia's grandfather had once strolled with his wife and in-laws. Now Aviv scampered up a perfect climbing tree. Nearby, children tossed leaves in the air, burying each other in piles of gold. We had always seen our families' pasts in shades of gray, but this place burst with vibrancy.

To us, looking back at their young lives in the 1930s, desperation and horror loomed in every corner. To our grandparents, it must have been a thrilling time of not only ideas and social organizing, but also young love and beginning their families.

Two weeks before Adolf Hitler was appointed chancellor in neighboring Germany, a rabbi married Leon and Manya on January 12, 1933. Surely, with their wealthy families, a glorious party took place, and perhaps they even went on a honeymoon.

The marriage had been planned for at least nine months. Marek uncovered a prenuptial agreement in the archives. Its language was legalese, reminiscent of our own. "On March 30, 1932, Lejba Inlender, son of Kelman, bachelor, age 27, and Marja Szarf, daughter of Szloma, age 22, both residing in Zamość appeared before the notary," reads the agreement with its formal Polish spelling for Leon's and Manya's names. "They testified that Lejba Inlender and Marja Szarf intend to marry. They enter into an agreement that the property each of them currently owns will be the separate and exclusive property of each of the future spouses."

Then Marek shared details that made us question the little we knew about Leon. First, Manya had paid the notary. And the agreement only listed her belongings: wardrobes, beds, quilts, cushions, tables, chairs, clocks, sewing machines, a gramophone, fifty records, a piano, carpets, furs, and cutlery. She possessed a relative fortune in a town where most Jews were poor.

Among the sparse details Talia inherited about her grandfather's life was that he was wealthy before the war. But why did this prenuptial agreement protect only Manya? Perhaps Talia's grandfather, in the little he shared, told just part of the story.

We took stock of what we knew: Leon's parents were dead by the time he was preparing to marry at twenty-seven. He lived with Manya and her parents, in a building his wealthy cousin Wigdor owned. But of Leon's personal finances, we had no real evidence. Had Manya's father been intent on protecting his daughter's assets from an orphan connected to a successful family, but with little of his own? As always, more questions arose about Leon than answers.

* * *

Daniel and Marek guided us on rented bikes, the kids in a trailer, to a residential area removed from the center of town. There, on a Zamość playground, Alma spun a giant globe while Aviv manipulated the hands of a brightly colored clock. With them distracted, Marek told us about the children who'd occupied this space nearly a century before.

He held up photos of teens all wearing hats, the boys in chaps, girls in knee-length skirts, standing on a sepia-toned version of the stairs up to the school. The structure in front of us, bluntly renovated during Communism, was once the pride of Jewish Zamość. Marek had found photos of Manya and her brother Khaim performing chemistry experiments inside this progressive and coeducational institution, the town's first Jewish secondary school.

The Humanities Gymnasium also served as a community space, and on a date my grandparents would still speak about years later with the same spark, their special "four threes," March 3, 1933, they met at the Purim Ball in the auditorium. By then, Mottel and Peshke were surely aware that Manya and Leon, across the market square, had married only two months before.

In my grandmother's collection was a photo from their courtship, likely taken in the same Zamość park where Leon strolled with his first family. Mottel wore a dress shirt and glasses. He looks much more robust than I ever knew him to be. Peshke is airy in a V-neck summer dress, hair still full and dark. Young people delighting in each other's company, they sit with their shoulders and legs touching, a departure from previous generations' mores separating men and women before marriage.

Their courtship lasted much longer than either would have liked. Mottel's older sister was still single, and protocol demanded she wed first. After four years of dating, Peshke gave Mottel an ultimatum: *Marry me or I'm moving on.*

His sister got engaged just in time, releasing Mottel and Peshke to wed in 1937. Unlike Talia's grandparents, there was no prenuptial agreement as neither brought wealth to the equation. A small ceremony was held in the bride's two-room home, spilling over to the other apartments that shared their floor. Peshke sewed her own dress, white with tiny flowers and meant to last for many summers. She finished the look with an elegant hat. They danced, sang, and feasted. Then Peshke moved a block away into an apartment with Mottel, the newlyweds full of promise for what their life together in Zamość would bring.

* * *

Their home looked right over the Salt Square, where in Zamość's early days merchants traded the valued mineral that gave the area its name.

During our grandparents' time it was steps outside the center of town, hectic with horse-drawn carriages, the occasional motorized vehicle, the chatter of merchants, and brisk foot traffic. Now the location was the same, but it was very quiet. I touched my hands to the cool exterior of the building.

Peshke and Mottel, I imagined, once sat upstairs at their new dinner table. He had the Yiddish newspaper in hand and was reading aloud, aghast at the Kristallnacht pogroms across Germany during which more than fourteen hundred synagogues were burnt and rampaged. My grandparents both had read *Mein Kampf* when it was released more than a decade earlier. In it, Hitler described Jews as the "personification of the devil," powerful and destructive forces to be destroyed for subjecting Aryans to their financial control. They must have asked, what more would he and his Nazi supporters do?

Weeks later, did my grandparents push their concerns aside and join nicely dressed couples, swirling and dancing in a local Zionist club? Arie Fialkow, a young emissary from Palestine, captured the scene in a letter he wrote home about a 1938 visit to Zamość. Despite the buzzing radio and upbeat feeling, he sensed something sinister brewing. "The Jews of Poland have a feeling that everything happening to the Jews of Germany will happen to them eventually...an unavoidable destiny, a dark pathos," Fialkow wrote. "If the Land of Israel was open for Jews to immigrate that would be the solution." But by then, for Jews who sought to leave Europe for Palestine, it had become increasingly difficult.

The year after Fialkow visited Zamość, the British issued a white paper limiting Jewish immigration to seventy-five thousand over the next five years and stating that it was not "intended that Palestine should be converted into a Jewish State against the will of the Arab population of the country."

The Jerusalem-based Jewish Agency, the de facto Zionist government, issued a scathing response that the British were severely restricting entry at the "darkest hour of Jewish history." They argued: "Arabs are not landless or homeless as are the Jews. They are not in need of emigration."

The Arab Higher Committee for Palestine released an equally furious response that the white paper permitted any Jewish immigration at all: "Palestine should not contribute to the solution of the world Jewish problem. If the British Government sympathizes with Jewish refugees, why should our country suffer for it?" London, after years of making conflicting promises, courting Arabs and Jews, had infuriated both sides.

For the 3.3 million Jews in Poland, the results were dire. It meant that legal avenues to Palestine, along with Western countries, were mostly closed to them as Hitler secured his ruthless power.

* * *

One Sunday, Peshke was sewing with a neighbor when an officer knocked on her door. He issued a citation for working. She was furious. Zamość Jews, unlike their Christian neighbors, whose holy day was Sunday, refrained from labor on Saturday. Of course, there were rumors of those who broke that tradition. Talia's uncle Zyg, never one to hold back from a good story, suggested in the video testimony that Leon and Manya would open the back door of their specialty cheese, chocolate, and halvah shop on Saturday for gentile customers. But as a rule, the Jewish Sabbath was observed. Two days off for a small business owner was more than Peshke could afford. She worked on Sundays, and for years, the authorities had looked the other way. No longer.

You better pay now, because if you go to a trial, who will they listen to? the officer threatened. *To you, a Jewish girl, or to a policeman?* She paid the twenty-five złoty, which to Peshke at the time felt like a fortune.

Soon after, strolling one Shabbat winter evening with another couple, Peshke wrapped herself tight in her new sealskin coat. Mottel traded furs and selected for his wife the best cut, which she had tailored in nearby Lublin. For the night out, she topped her outfit with a black hat and a fringed veil. As Peshke walked out onto the cobblestone roads of her town, she was feeling particularly stylish. Then cold muddy water sloshed toward her. Poles hiding behind a horse and buggy laughed viciously.

Enraged and humiliated, the two young husbands raced to the police for protection. Instead, they faced accusations. *Don't start with them,* the police reprimanded. *They wouldn't do it if you didn't bother them.*

Anti-Semitism was whirling with breakneck speed from Germany, pulling Poles into its funnel. Hitler had annexed Austria and threatened more to come. But the prospect of a war in Zamość still felt far-fetched.

"It was just harder with anti-Semitism from the Poles," my grandmother said emphatically. "But it didn't enter any mind there could be a war."

Plus, Mottel and Peshke had a joyous distraction to occupy their minds. Their Arik, a perfect little boy, was born on July 30, 1939. As they celebrated their firstborn's entry into the world with a joyous, crowded bris, dictators to their east and west secretly plotted the destruction of their country.

CHAPTER 11

Rainbow Square

Our kids' favorite place in Zamość was what they called the "rainbow square" for its pink town hall and the adjoining row of boldly colorful houses, among them the cornflower blue one where their great-grandmother grew up. The twins had long understood that having two moms was special and readily explained to any kid who voiced confusion that we were a "rainbow family." I sometimes worried they might feel lacking without a father. But, so far, two moms marked a positive distinction in their eyes.

Now this colorful square also seemed part of their unique rainbow heritage. They saw only the bright colors and missed the shadows that took our breath away.

Before we arrived in Warsaw, we'd been warned we could face homophobia we'd been shielded from in Los Angeles. Poland was consistently ranked at or near the bottom of European countries for gay rights and Zamość was in one of the most conservative regions.

Knowing this, I'd been surprised to discover the Zamość synagogue had recently hosted an LGBTQ movie night. With no Jews left to pray, the building now had a broader community mandate. The former sanctuary was a memorial center and events space, and Daniel was in charge. A group of high school students had asked him if they could host the event. Unlike the town's government-affiliated cultural spaces, the synagogue was independent and free to welcome LGBTQ youth, so it did.

I had asked Daniel to arrange a meeting with the group, and on our final Zamość afternoon, he ushered us into the magnificent Renaissance synagogue where for more than three hundred years Zamość Jews had worshipped. That the structure was saved from the Nazis, along with our mikveh-turned-hotel down the street, could be seen as a series of small miracles. First, the head of the Judenrat, the Jewish council the Nazis created, contacted a Polish industrialist who deployed furniture-making carpenters in the synagogue. Upon retreating, the Nazis intended to burn the whole sacred building down, but the Red Army's advance rushed them out. After the Germans left, Poles looted the synagogue for any artifacts. All that remained of the structure were the walls and the ceiling. For decades after the war, the building was a public library.

But now the Zamość synagogue had undergone a major restoration and was one of the first sacred buildings that the Polish government returned to Jewish communities. As I stepped down the stairs to enter the former sanctuary, Daniel explained how even in Zamość the synagogue had been subject to Polish-Lithuanian Commonwealth regulations that no house of worship could be higher than a Christian church. The early Sephardic settlers' solution was to sink the ground floor in order to build a regal, high-vaulted sanctuary. With its majestically crafted stucco finishes and gleaming marble floors, I could see why my grandfather always longed for this congregation, packed on High Holidays with worshippers swaying with an unmatched fervor. Now the sanctuary is a sparse memorial space.

Daniel led us into the old women's section, where my grandmother and Manya likely once prayed. Perhaps they even whispered with each other while their husbands worshipped with the Torah in the adjoining sanctuary. Almost a century later, five young people all dressed in black shirts awaited us. Some had extensive tattoos and piercings. Others were clean-cut and unadorned. They refused to be photographed or recorded, for fear of repercussions, but did not hold back in telling us what it was like for them to live in Zamość.

"This is the worst place in a terrible country to be LGBTQ," one said.

"There is no Pride here," another chimed in.

Talia introduced us as a married couple, and something unfamiliar, but not unwelcome, stirred inside me. The first time I had heard a woman refer to her "wife" was fifteen years earlier when I was living in Germany. Abi and I were both American fellows on the yearlong German Chancellor Scholarship, paired with Russian counterparts in a post–Cold War cultural diplomacy initiative. With gay marriage not legal in almost all of the United States, I was still becoming accustomed to the idea that two people of the same sex could wed. I never imagined it was a description I would come to use daily for my own relationship. It took me a long time to even admit that I could be attracted to a woman, to Talia.

* * *

Two months after we met, my friend Jen accompanied me to Talia's birthday party. I worried she might suspect something. But what was I concerned about revealing? I pondered this question, unable to give words to what I was feeling. As a birthday present, I gifted Talia a copy of one of the many cookbooks my mother authored, *Jewish Cooking in America*, and inscribed it to "My Zamosc buddy, and much more."

The following week, Talia invited me to her parents' house for Shabbat dinner, driving me over the Hollywood Hills to their suburban San Fernando Valley cul-de-sac. In the pastel glow of a late-summer evening, we joined her parents and three couples from their tight inner circle outside, opposite the kidney-shaped pool. The air was fragrant with sweet orange and lemon blossoms, mixed with grilling meat. We mulled around a table set with a white paper tablecloth, candlesticks, and a challah. Then, with Nachum enthusiastically leading, we wrapped our arms around each other and sang "Shalom Aleichem," or "Peace

Be Upon You," to usher in the Sabbath. I swayed with Talia's family, moved to be part of their community.

That night, I slept over at Talia's, despite the easy six-minute drive from her apartment to my home. For the first time, thrillingly, I wondered: "Could anything happen between us?"

Nothing did that night, but a few weeks later Talia sent me an email saying that we needed to talk. She had not been fully honest with me. I knew instinctively what Talia was implying: the overwhelming pull I felt in her presence, the sparks that emanated from her touch.

I left my shared small office at the community news site I edited and walked down the carpeted stairs to the bathroom. Blessedly empty. I took a breath, looked in the mirror, my heart racing. *Can I really do this?*

Talia came over the next night. I made caipirinhas, mashing limes with sugar, hoping the alcohol might ease the tension. Talia, who usually arrived with a big smile and face glowing, was now more reserved in a dark blue hooded sweatshirt, her brown wavy hair pulled back in a tiny bun at the nape of her neck. But she did not shirk away from the topic.

"Okay, so there is something about my dating past that I left out." Talia launched in. "In college, I dated women."

As soon as I heard those words, my heart began to race. I knew what she was going to reveal, and I was both terrified and delighted.

"That was a long time ago, and since then I have only dated men." Gathering herself, she looked directly at me. "But then I met you, and I could imagine a relationship with you."

Emotions ricocheted through me: thrill, relief, and angst all at once. I suggested that we move to the couch and there, for the first time, we kissed. After so many years of touching the rough faces of men, to caress a woman's smooth skin was at once familiar and foreign, tantalizing and destabilizing. If I felt this was something light and unusual, perhaps I could have savored the novelty of a romantic adventure, but this kiss felt weighty.

By the time Talia came over next, I'd rehearsed my lines. I really liked her, but I just was not into women.

"I have a lot of good friends." Talia debunked my argument without a pause: "What is between us is more than a friendship."

We were lying on my bed—in retrospect, not the best place to tell someone you're not interested in dating them. She put her hand on my stomach, and with the sensation of her touch, I let go of the idea that I was not attracted to women, that I was not attracted to her.

Later, we took a walk together through the eucalyptus groves of Elysian Park. When we looked for an outside table at Fix Café, I spotted the tall guy with wavy hair whom I'd brought as my date when I first met Talia. We laughed about the coincidence, and I realized she had given me what he could not. I felt at ease in Talia's presence, enough to let in just a bit of the reality of what was happening: I'd found someone who made me feel more secure in myself, more alive in my world.

* * *

Just months after the US Supreme Court made same-sex marriage a right, Talia proposed in the park where we had first met three years earlier. She presented me with printed pages. "As I hope is obvious, I love your daughter," Talia had written to my parents, asking their blessing to marry me. "Despite how unexpected our relationship was at the start, it seems impossible to imagine a future without her now." I cried my first tears of joy and knew the answer was of course yes, I wanted to spend my life with her.

Still, as our wedding day approached, I kept to myself a profound anxiety. Privately, or among close family and friends, I felt secure and supported in our relationship, but would I feel awkwardly on display with so many people watching our nuptials? Would people judge me as large next to Talia's small frame, gawk at the novelty of seeing two women kiss?

I need not have worried. On the scorching September day of our wedding, when we grabbed each other's faces and our lips met, I knew only pure elation. We stamped a glass in unison and skipped down the aisle to cheers. Then we danced a sweaty, raucous hora that lasted more than an hour, culminating in a parade threading through the Elysian

Valley hills, with stops for spiked lemonade and brownies, to a reception at the craftsman bungalow we'd lived in for a year.

Many people had bravely fought a fierce decades-long battle for the right to marry. Couples loved in hiding and lost their partners before they could be recognized by the courts and public. Our fortune was immeasurable. We received the right to marry like a wedding gift, with immense gratitude, at the perfect moment.

Now, seven years married, Talia was unequivocally my wife.

But in the days since we'd touched down in Poland, I'd found myself selectively circumspect, guarded about our relationship. Not here, though. I relished Talia stating in this synagogue that we were married, connecting our story to this group of queer Zamość youth.

* * *

"To us, Zamość stopped existing," Talia said while sharing how marvelous and bizarre it was for us to be in their Polish town.

"Why?!" a shocked chorus greeted her statement.

All younger than twenty-five, their Zamość reality had not begun to exist until the twenty-first century. We tried to explain that in our minds, this place effectively went dark in 1942, when the ghetto was liquidated.

While we were talking, a tourist strolled into the sanctuary, taking in the exhibit of the traditions of the extinguished Jews. In the corner, our kids scribbled furiously on black scratch paper to reveal the rainbow design beneath. I glanced out the synagogue window at the precious café across the plaza. On its patio, facing us, patrons ate tiny pastries, sampled homemade halvah, and sipped macchiatos.

In the crumbling women's section of the synagogue, Talia transformed into her tenacious attorney self, probing the threats faced by these young adults, who revealed to us they were all trans, and what legal protections they could access in Poland.

Later, Aleksy, the informal leader of the group, told me how the synagogue had played a role in them uniting. He had just begun exploring his trans identity and was eager to meet other queer youth in a safe space when he was invited to the movie night. He knew the synagogue from the outside but had never entered. He was confused. Why would this house of worship, even if there was no Jewish community in town, open its doors to them?

That night, around thirty people showed up and claimed a space at the synagogue, chatting in groups and then taking chairs into the sanctuary and pulling down a screen next to where the Torah was once read. I had a hard time imagining our grandparents accepting LGBTQ Polish youth adopting their sacred house of worship, but I felt proud that the synagogue had made this space for them.

This was not what I expected to discover in Zamość: a place that bridged our families' intersecting pasts with an unexpected present. These young people had introduced us to their dynamic, if highly challenging, reality. As we prepared to return to Warsaw, I felt energized by new connections to Zamość and from witnessing how Marek, Daniel, and Alexey honored its decimated Jewish history while nurturing new forms of resilience and community.

CHAPTER 12

Stay or Go

As I coasted along a path through one of Warsaw's many verdant, enchanting parks on my way to the city center, I spoke aloud to myself the Shehecheyanu blessing. I sometimes said these sacred words to mark a moment of elation, expressing gratitude for a God who "has granted us life, sustained us, and enabled us to reach this occasion." This was an unexpected one.

At this moment, my life was everything I had ever wanted. Dancing with the kids in our attic apartment in the morning light. Transporting them via this Dutch cargo bike to their own adventures at preschool. Enjoying a few moments over coffee and pastry with Talia before we separated to pursue our own research for the day. And now pedaling through this city of sinister shadows but also unexpected delights, with its secrets to uncover, some of them intimately tied to my own story.

Amid my blissful reveries, I got all turned around on my unwieldy bike and arrived late to my meeting at the Jewish Historical Institute. My path dumped me on a sidewalk between a tall modern building, all gleaming windows and reflection, and a drugstore. Where was I? Heart anxiously racing, I spotted an old building with Hebrew letters on the side. Relief washed over me.

I locked my bike and huffed up the stairs.

"I'm here to see Anna," I breathlessly informed the attendants.

"Which Anna?"

I did not remember her multisyllabic Polish last name and didn't have it written down. Silently, I berated myself for not being more professional.

"Genealogy, please?" That, miraculously, seemed to do the trick. The attendants directed me to a far door beyond burn marks that spread along the floor like an oil spill. In 1943, this building, then Warsaw's Main Judaic Library, caught fire when SS Commander Jürgen Stroop ordered the dynamiting of the neighboring Great Synagogue and the torching of this building. It was the final hurrah upon the liquidation of the ghetto, celebrating that the Nazis had beat out the uprising and exterminated those who remained, burning, shooting, or sending them to Treblinka and Majdanek. Stroop then documented the victory in a photo album of the destruction sent back to Berlin with the caption: "There is no longer a Jewish quarter in Warsaw."

Eighty years later, the burn marks remained. I stepped gingerly over them. On the other side, I found the door to which I'd been directed with a key in it. I turned the key, but the door did not budge. I tried again. This time, it did the trick, and I opened the door onto a large room with two desks in the far corners.

"Were you trying to lock us in?" A petite woman with a purple scarf wrapped around her neck, and a Kermit-the-Frog green sweater, greeted me with a playful glint in her eye. She gestured to a seat. "What brings you here?"

I sat down hastily across from her, apologizing for being late, and then let anxious words spill out about my family search. I was thinking of Manya, Talia's grandfather's first wife. What had motivated her to remain with her son in Zamość when she knew the Nazis would soon arrive? I knew that about half the town's Jews had stayed behind, and most assumed it would be safer for women and children, but still, I could not stop wondering about her.

I was rambling, and I assumed Anna was thinking, *Who is this messy American woman, and why is she wasting my time?*

She stopped my internal dialogue. "We need to know a little to understand what they did."

I told her I had no letters; no testimonies that would reveal more about Manya. Anna said there were many ways to collect historical details and build a narrative of the people that preceded us. She could help. I exhaled, releasing the pressure to track a linear journey.

For approaching a quarter of a century, Anna Przybyszewska Drozd had sat in that chair at the Family Heritage Center and, with her colleagues, unraveled countless mysteries. Sometimes, she said, she found clues in a newspaper article from the time. Sometimes it was via vital records. As a genealogist, she unearthed the lives of murdered Jews and those who survived for family members who flew in from places as disparate as Israel, Argentina, and Australia. She also helped Poles who wondered if a relative they'd always assumed was Catholic perhaps had a Jewish past.

Anna took out a notebook with graph paper. She started to map my family, and played with a narrative: "It's early in the war. You don't know to go or not to go. You have a little child... Five is an age."

Oh yes, I knew five was an age, thinking of my almost five-year-olds. "I have a granddaughter that age," she offered. And then, wordlessly, we both considered: What would it take for us to pack up and leave home with no sense of when we could return? To the east of us, at that moment, Russia was bombing Ukraine relentlessly. In Warsaw I saw refugees at makeshift support centers, cutting dresses in a boutique, caring for our children at the nursery school.

Anna shook her head. "I wouldn't go. Not now, at this age."

Would I have the strength and foresight to take my child, my children and go? I liked to think so, but then again, I had never been tested.

We found no new relatives, no documents that day, but Anna exposed me to a new approach for investigating the details of the story. We may learn the context, find all the records accessible, and we still will not know what made a person decide to go or stay. You have to deploy your imagination, she seemed to say, to put yourself in their shoes, to comprehend what drives those very small, seemingly random choices with generation-defining consequences.

* * *

"The day began as a beautiful, clean, and bright day." So commences the destruction of Zamość, the final section of the memorial book.

"Already in the early morning hours, on the Zamość streets... pockets of people were standing about, not like on normal days. The question on everyone's lips was: 'What's new? Will there be war?'"

As people gathered, I tried picturing Manya getting little Kolonimus dressed and fed. At the nearby Salt Square, my grandmother may have lingered at home, nursing her month-old baby. Peshke, Manya, and the other residents of Zamość did not yet know on that beautiful morning of September 1, 1939, that Poland was already under attack.

Three days later, German planes circled over the Zamość market square, raining down machine-gun fire. Then bombs exploded on the train station. When there was a break in the assaults, Peshke and Mottel held tight to their baby and hitched a ride to the countryside. They knocked on the door of a farmer, who rented them a room, and they tried to calm their child and themselves.

For a few days, the farmer tolerated them. But then he got word German troops were approaching.

If they see a non-Jew helping a Jew, they will take away everything, the farmer told Mottel. *Please, I want you immediately to leave. You, your wife, your child to leave my house.*

It was already after dark. The only option was to return to Zamość. They entered a transformed place. More bombs had hit the poorer part of the town, killing dozens. Refugees had begun to arrive from western Poland who told harrowing stories of how they had evaded Nazi "death machines"—planes, which swooped very low, over the unarmed masses on the roads, and sowed death, shooting from machine guns at women and children. Polish appointed officials had evacuated, and the police readied to join them. Everyone was anxiously waiting for the day that the Germans would arrive.

It came soon. In the middle of the night of September 12, 1939, the Nazi occupation of Zamość was announced with a deafening clamor of tanks. By the following morning, the Jewish new year, armored German carriers and motorcycles joined the tanks parked in neat lines in front of the pink town hall. The Wehrmacht soldiers marched the streets in heavy boots, striking the cobblestones with a deafening syncopation, bayonets hoisted high on shoulders.

Heil Hitler! the soldiers announced themselves at the door. *Where is your husband?*

Peshke's steely resolve activated for the first of many times in life-threatening situations to come. She lied: *He is in bed; he is very sick.*

Miraculously, that seemed to do the trick. In the days to come, Mottel would leave the house with his younger sister running ahead of him, checking the way, ensuring he was hidden from soldiers who were beating and rounding up men for forced labor.

Less than two weeks into the Nazi occupation of Zamość, Peshke was looking out at the square from the safety of her building's front entrance when she overheard shocking words. Yiddish was close enough to German that the Jews could communicate with the soldiers, and one of her neighbors had started to ask a question.

Don't talk German now, a soldier shot back. *You better learn Russian. Our Russian comrades are coming here now.* Soon, the Wehrmacht officers drove off in their motorcycles and armored vehicles.

All over town, residents gathered around the radio to hear the news of a great backstabbing secret pact: Stalin to their east and Hitler to their west had joined forces as conspirators in the destruction of their country. Occupation was not new to Zamość's citizens. For much of the history of Poland, a buffer between east and west, the nation had weathered relentless attacks. But this was a new level of deceit.

Two ideologically opposed and ruthless regimes had turned on Poland to advance their common goal of empire building. Warsaw and Moscow meticulously carved the country in two. The Germans had led the attack from the west, but weeks later the Soviets struck from the east, revealing their secret Nazi-Soviet Nonaggression Pact. Zamość fell within Eastern Poland, placing it under the control of Moscow.

* * *

Why, then, did so many of the Jewish youth of Zamość celebrate the news that the Red Army was coming? The afternoon its soldiers arrived, Mottel darted out of town to welcome them. He was Communist leaning and relieved by the shift in power, and not only because Hitler's army was departing. The hope was as poor Jews they would receive work and equal rights.

But as Peshke watched the Soviet soldiers march to the main square, she could not believe her eyes. She had imagined the Red Army as a glorious force. This was no such thing. Soldiers wore mismatched shoes. Coats were ripped. A piece of string hoisted up pants. Peshke had received her first unsettling revelation into life under the Communist revolution.

Still, when a red flag was raised at city hall, four houses down from her apartment, perhaps she believed life in Zamość was about to improve. And the Soviets did bring one positive change: For the first time, it was the Polish anti-Semites, not Jewish youth, who needed to fear the authorities.

Days later, a Red Army soldier again climbed the city hall stairs, indicating an important announcement: *The border will now be the River Bug.*

Could they have heard right? Zamość would change hands for the third time in a month? Once more their town would be under German control? How could this be?

Zamość's Jews took to the cobblestone streets, debating whether to leave with the Soviets or remain. But Mottel did not equivocate or consider a noble stand for Zamość.

He grabbed a knapsack and said to Peshke: *You know I must escape. Don't worry. Nothing will happen to women and children. Besides, this won't last long, maybe a month or two. England and France are coming to help Poland. I will try to stay nearby. So, when the war stops, I'll come home right away. In the meantime, take care of yourself and the baby. There is enough wood and a new sack of flour in the closet.*

Mottel kissed their baby boy goodbye, held Peshke tight, and told her once more, *Remember, don't worry.*

* * *

But Peshke did worry. And days later when a Red Army soldier again climbed the steps to the city hall and the crowd hushed in anticipation, she was listening. *Anybody who wants to go with us, across the border, they can go with us. But no belongings.* Peshke decided at that moment she could not wait. She would carry her baby out of Zamość on a Soviet truck.

I like to imagine Esther, Mottel's mother, did not protest when she heard that her only grandchild would be taken from her. After all, she knew what it was like to have to follow your instincts and flee with young children. Instead, I picture her directing Peshke in a steady and determined voice to take a moment, sit down, and listen to what she had learned about how to survive on the run. And perhaps that is why, in the hours between when Peshke revealed that she was taking her baby across the border and when she jumped on the Red Army truck, she frantically packed her most valuable wedding gifts, which could be traded for bread, as well as family photos and her sewing machine.

The Red Army soldiers barred Peshke from bringing anything but her infant on their truck, but she knew others would be following and could bring her the supplies. Indeed, days after Peshke left in a rush with baby Arik, her brother-in-law Moishe rented a horse and carriage from a villager. The twenty-one-year-old youngest Gerson sibling climbed the stairs of the cornflower blue apartment and hoisted Peshke's sacks onto his burly shoulders. He settled them into the wagon, along with his father and three sisters.

One person was still missing.

If I leave, somebody will take the house away. Esther, his mother, was adamant in her refusal; she needed to stay for all of them. She had already fled twice and refused to do it again. *I'm too old now to start over again. Go! What would they want with an old woman? Here are a few dollars from a relative in America; here is a ring. Now just go and wait out the hard time.* They followed their mother's instructions and left her behind in Zamość, her home emptied of her five adult children and husband.

* * *

"When the war started, nobody"—my grandmother said, pausing to conjure that moment when she left—"nobody could imagine this could be something like this. He calls it a Final Solution?" The absurd prospect of a systematic Nazi death machine in 1939 provided her pause. They knew Hitler despised Jews, that his supporters burned their synagogues and businesses, but who could imagine systematic murder? Had they known what was to come, they all would have left. Just about everyone in Zamość could have escaped to the east. Unlike the Western countries and Palestine, the Soviet Union was one place that had opened its borders to hundreds of thousands of Jews. Even more could have joined them, if only they had known.

"My parents and my sisters and thousands more, thousands more," my grandmother said, trailing off into the abyss of loss.

Among the masses who determined it was safer to stay was Talia's grandfather's first wife. Even after we returned from our sojourn in Warsaw to our routines in Los Angeles, we puzzled over Manya's choice. I kept hearing echoes of the advice Anna, the genealogist in Warsaw, had provided: Collect the historical record, analyze what you know, and then follow your instincts to find your way within the story.

Ruminations about Manya's fatal decision-making process followed me and Talia into bed, and we woke up with theories. Perhaps Leon had begged his wife to depart with him, but she was petrified to leave behind her wealthy parents. Or Manya may have begged to go, and Leon said he was sure it would be safer for her to stay.

I wondered sometimes if we were getting any closer to uncovering what dictated her fate, or just attempting to comprehend an unfathomable past. To try to reassure ourselves that, faced with the same odds, we would not make the same unlucky choice.

* * *

After weeks of theorizing, I returned to the one record from Talia's family we had of the time: Uncle Zyg's tape. There, I was shocked to discover a clear testimony that Talia had not remembered, and that I had let slip by. "Your grandfather went with us," Zyg said of Leon. Then he added, "The wife didn't want to go. She had a father and mother." Her loyalty to her parents dictated at that insecure time. Our instincts had been right all along, or perhaps the truth lingered in the depths of our mutual memory.

In contrast, Uncle Zyg's father did not waver in his decision to flee Zamość and to bring his whole family. During the German army's first occupation, officers had arrested him. Badly beaten and hungry, he was released when his wife offered a ransom for the remaining goods in their store. Upon hearing the Germans were returning, he immediately got a horse and carriage to transport his family members—wife, children, and his nephew, Talia's grandfather—over the border.

Leon's wife, Manya, and baby, Kolonimus, were also offered spots, but she made the fatal choice to remain with her parents. Almost at the very end of the interview, Uncle Zyg shared a detail that now made much more sense to me. "Your grandfather's wife with the kid was on the border, she was ready to go, he wanted to bring her over. And then she changed her mind."

One decision, two lives. From our perspective, it was so clear: "Run! Cross the border. As fast as you can!" we wanted to shout to Manya across the years. But from her point of view, whatever uncertainty waited for her and her child beyond German territory was more dangerous than remaining with her parents at home in Zamość.

CHAPTER 13

Other Side

In the neon glow of New York's JFK Airport, I hugged the kids and then Talia. We were in a transit terminal, all bleary-eyed after an overnight flight from Los Angeles. They were about to board a small plane to Martha's Vineyard, where my mother would be waiting next to the tarmac, ocean breezes whipping through her short black hair. Later that day, I would begin the long, winding journey into Ukraine, to a war zone.

I was on the trail of the one place we knew where our four grandparents had landed at the same time. In the winter of 1939, about seventy miles southeast of Zamość, they were all refugees in what is today Lviv. It was another piece of the string connecting me to Talia, and I had hoped to travel there together. But the closest we got was driving to the Ukrainian border near Zamość, glimpsing its wheat fields stretching to the horizon. We did not consider putting our family at risk.

While adventurous, I knew my limits. As a young journalist, I had reported from drug dens and false-document mills. But I never wanted to be a war correspondent. Living in Israel during the second intifada and New York during September 11, I had felt the fickle breath of luck and had no desire to get closer.

Until now. Lviv had become the hub of the biggest displacement of Europeans since our grandparents fled their homes. Millions of people had spent the past months moving through the same location that had once been our family's refuge. And Lviv, itself, did not appear to be particularly unsafe despite the war. Russia seldom targeted Ukraine's westernmost major city.

And so when an opportunity emerged to visit, I seized it. Talia was accepted to a migration studies conference that would take place in Warsaw at the end of June. We could both travel then. First, Talia would shepherd our children to my mother, and I'd head to Lviv for a couple of nights. Then Talia and I would reunite in Warsaw. The timing was going to be tight, but I thought we might just be able to make it work.

Hotel rooms were plentiful. Disregarding the warning on my booking site of, "an increased risk to customers' safety in this location," I reserved a four-star stay at a very affordable price.

I tried to pack as lightly as possible, in part because of damaged back nerves that had made three of my right toes go numb, but also because I needed to make room for an unfamiliar item: chest seals. A Ukrainian interpreter, who shifted from ferrying Jews around on heritage tours to transporting medical equipment to soldiers after the Russian invasion, requested I bring him these first-aid devices. They could keep someone's heart beating and lungs breathing if a bullet struck.

When my anxiety mounted a week before leaving, a *Wall Street Journal* correspondent in Ukraine reassured me via text that Lviv, so far from the front, was essentially safe: "Really, missile strikes are the only risk, and it's a low risk. I'd get an app called Ukraine Air Alert before going in, which will notify you if there are air raid signals (which you can't always hear). But I really think you'll be fine."

I also believed I would be fine. But as I walked off alone toward international departures, I thought of Talia's grandfather, who must have believed he was leaving Kolonimus for a relatively short trip. Then Alma called me back for another hug. I held tight to her one more time. At what point after you've left your child behind do you realize the finality of your goodbye?

* * *

Four flights and two nights after I left Los Angeles, I touched down again in a flat and green country. All airspace had been closed in Ukraine since the outbreak of the war. Entering involved a constellation of trains, buses, and automobiles. Even the US president took a ten-hour night train over the Polish border to meet with his Ukrainian counterpart in Kyiv. I needed a place to rest for the night before crossing the border, and Zamość was one of the closest Polish towns to Ukraine. I landed in nearby Lublin. The terminal was tiny; fewer than thirty people walked off the small commuter plane with me.

The wind whipped over the grass and pulled at my shirt, a fresh greeting to Poland. A bearded figure bounded toward me in a t-shirt with Van Gogh's *Starry Night* printed on it. It was Daniel, who had guided my last trip months earlier. He had generously agreed to pick me up at the airport, an hour from his home in Zamość. I gave him a big hug.

We drove off into the broad blue sky, past high summer fields ripe with tobacco and hops growing on long vines. Daniel described how, at the outset of the current war, this two-lane road had become an international thoroughfare with hundreds of thousands of Ukrainian refugees inching along the highway en route to Warsaw. In the opposite direction, trucks packed with weapons and military gear drove toward Ukraine.

Our small car rattled along, dodging potholes. Just as my exhilaration began to wilt, Daniel turned off the main road, navigating the roundabouts, passed the old moat, and pulled up to the now familiar hotel built over the mikveh. This time, arriving in Zamość felt a bit closer to a homecoming.

* * *

"Why do you want to go to Lviv?" The question came at me repeatedly in my brief interlude in Zamość. With a war going on, why would I cross the border? Daniel, Marek, and now the woman driving me to the bus station, where I would catch a ride to Ukraine, all posed the same question. They told me how in the past they loved visiting nearby Lviv, the sophisticated city with a rich Polish history. But they had not been since the war began.

I stared out the car window, as we headed out of Zamość. Aleksy, the organizer from the queer young people's group I'd met in the fall, sat behind me in his mom's Volvo SUV. A few weeks earlier, I'd asked him if he could provide a ride. He offered up his mother, reminding me how young he was even as he had maturely explained his complex situation as a trans person and led others in doing the same.

His mother asked again why I'd possibly want to go to Ukraine now. "It's quite dangerous," she chided, searching for the right words in English to capture the terror of having war break out so near to their home.

Aleksy jumped in: "In my school we had a few refugees. Once there was a huge noise. The refugees jumped under the table."

Withdrawing from their questioning and my own, I took in Aleksy's mother driving next to me: blond hair pulled back, a jean jacket, long red fingernails. Very polished and feminine. I asked how she handled her son's coming out and transition, his crossing over of a different type of border.

"It was very hard," she said carefully. "I worried life would be hard for him."

I thought of my own mother's reaction when I told her about Talia and recognized that she, too, worried I'd chosen a precarious and potentially painful path.

* * *

Talia and my mother's first meeting had occurred under less than auspicious circumstances. It was not for lack of planning. Not long after we started dating, my mother planned a visit to me in Los Angeles. I invited two friends and Talia out to dinner at a Thai restaurant, thinking if my mother first got to know her before I told her about our relationship, she would be more receptive to it. Then minutes before she was set to arrive at my house, a plump rat plopped out of my swim bag and skittered into the kitchen of my apartment. My mother, adventurous and otherwise unflappable, despises rats. When she arrived at my house, the rodent, dripping blood from a failed attempt to trap it, was still on the loose. Realizing it would not be caught that night, I told her we needed to go. Immediately. Then I drove us in my aging VW convertible, heart racing, toward Hollywood, where I had arranged that dinner with two friends and Talia.

"Do you have any friends who are gay women?" I asked on the drive, trying to suss out exactly how shocked she would be to discover that her daughter was dating a woman.

"No, not really." Her tone shifted. "Do you?"

"Of course," was my stilted response.

The truth was that my close gay friends were men, and my decision to reveal my affection for Talia often felt like a step into the unknown. But I wasn't going to let my mother know that.

We were the first to arrive at the strip mall restaurant. The tables bustled with Thai families, hipster foodies, and waiters deftly navigating the crowded aisles with sizzling spicy dishes held high. As soon as the two of us sat down, my mom asked a variation of the same question.

"So, do you have many lesbian friends?"

Was she concerned? Did she suspect something?

The words flew before I could think, ruining the choreography of our carefully planned introduction: "Mom, I'm dating Talia."

The blood drained from her face.

Moments later, Talia walked in, arriving on time as always.

Under normal circumstances, my mother is famously curious, warm, and chatty; the best of anyone I know at connecting with all types of people. That whole night, she barely looked across the table at Talia, focusing instead on my friends who joined us. I tried to remind my mother that Talia was my Zamość friend she had heard so much about and ease them into conversation. Nothing worked. Talia sent me a text message under the table: "I don't think your mother likes me."

I felt terrible, but also empathy for my mother, who was already exhausted from flying across the country and distressed by a rat, when she suddenly discovered her adult daughter was not what she thought she was. By the time my mother left town, she had tamed her shock a bit, going out with me and Talia for a drink, and conversing warmly with her. But still she made a request: "I think it's best that you wait until I return home to talk with Dad. So I can be there to support him."

I agreed. The truth was we were both worried about how my father would respond. But when I finally told him about Talia, he surprised me with a story: "I once had a girlfriend who left me to date a woman." Not something he'd ever mentioned, and he seemed to take the news in calmly. Still, he voiced one concern. He outlined an "opportunity cost" theory. If I pursued the relationship and ever wanted to have children— I'd get Talia, the opportunity, but I'd not be able to have kids, the cost. I countered that a lesbian couple on our street had just had a son.

After I hung up, flying high now that my father knew the truth, I felt compelled to see Talia immediately. Even though I was late to dinner at a friend's house, I drove instead to her apartment. We celebrated my father's reception, and that of her own parents. They already knew me and had taken in stride the nature of our relationship when Talia told them over breakfast the day before. Her abba, usually so forthcoming, gingerly inquired, "Can I ask questions?" He knew Talia had serious relationships with men. Now he wanted to know what had led her to date a woman.

As we began to navigate the outside world together as a couple, we breathed easier with each reveal, each perceived barrier crossed. A few weeks later, when my father met Talia on our first joint trip to New York, he immediately started intellectually sparring with her about the law, connecting over their shared passion.

My mother's dismayed reaction appeared less about me dating a woman than concern about others' responses—her mother, brothers, close circle of friends, and particularly my dad. But once she saw that we would be okay together in the outside world, my mom wholeheartedly opened herself to our relationship, and to Talia. When my dad privately told her he was disappointed he would never toss a football to a son-in-law, she set him straight: "But you never threw a football in your life." And when I questioned my feelings for Talia early on, it was my mother who counseled me not to throw away our extraordinary connection in search of a vision of perfection that did not exist.

As Aleksy's mother now drove us on the two-lane road toward Ukraine, I thought about how hard the transformation of expectations had initially been for my own mother and considered how challenging it must have been to embrace a trans son in one of Poland's most conservative communities. Other parents would have demanded he keep the name they had given him at birth or prevented him from getting hormones. But Aleksy's mother found a way to accept that she had two sons, not one.

"I'm lucky to have my mother," Aleksy said, and I could feel the strength of their bond. I, too, knew what a gift it was to have a mother who supported you to be your truest self, even if the journey was not always an easy one.

* * *

We pulled up to a desolate lot about thirty minutes from the border, just a few miles from the site of the death camp at Bełżec. Just one woman sat on the ground waiting, her bags sprawled around her, packages of butter and coffee peeking out the top. The bus schedule was printed on yellow paper and nailed to a dilapidated wooden sign. Pigeons gathered at the base. Rain began to fall as the gray low-lying cloud layer closed in around us. Could a bus crossing an international border leave from this godforsaken place?

I excused myself and crossed the empty parking lot to use the grimy bathroom of a small restaurant. When I returned, more Ukrainian women had appeared and Aleksy's mother spoke to one to confirm I was in the right place. The bus approached and I hugged them goodbye, not wanting to let go. Though I had lined up interpreters to support me in Lviv, I was nervous I'd been too cavalier in my planning. Had I made a mistake thinking I could cross the border alone? What if something happened during the journey through Ukraine?

I climbed onto the ragged bus. The temperature rose with each new passenger. I sat alone, a pit in my stomach beginning to burn.

"Does anyone speak English?" I turned around and asked the women in sweatsuits and white sneakers chatting around me. They looked back, pausing just a beat before continuing their conversations in Ukrainian.

Then sweet words came from behind me: "I speak a little." I swiveled around and faced a middle-aged woman with strong features, neatly turned out with blond hair pulled back and blue mascara lining her eyelashes.

Maria told me that, like many of the women on the bus, she was returning from a stint harvesting Polish strawberries. "Ukrainian women love to work; we aren't afraid of work." That was particularly helpful right now, since prices had skyrocketed, and men were not permitted to leave the country.

I resettled in the seat next to her and we moved on to the outlines of our lives. "Do you have a husband?" she asked. I hesitated. I had read that Ukrainians were increasingly open to gay people, but acceptance was far from universal. Easier just to lie and say yes. But I had a good feeling about Maria and took a chance.

"I have a partner; I am with a woman." I was careful with my words, not sure she would understand or if I would provoke her by saying, "wife."

A spark flicked in her eye. "Ooh." She seemed more intrigued than judgmental. I said a silent prayer of gratitude.

The driver announced in Ukrainian that he would be coming to collect our passports. We examined our respective documents, different countries but the same shade of dark blue.

"US, you are very lucky," she told me. "You don't need visa to many countries. You have the door opened." With the last word she rotated her hand in a sign of welcome.

I often recognized my good fortune at holding an American passport, never more so than when interviewing immigrants who could not risk leaving the country to visit dying parents. I had won this citizenship game by so many twists of fate. When my grandparents crossed the very border we were now approaching, running away from Zamość, they could never have known that their fleeing east would, in a convoluted way, lead to their descendants holding on to passports in the West.

* * *

At the outset of the Second World War, crossing the border from Poland to the Soviet-occupied territory was called going to the "Other Side," or "Yener Zayt" in Yiddish. Learning this term called to mind the Mexican immigrants I reported on for years, covering their journeys from their village in Puebla to their newfound homes in Brooklyn. They also spoke of crossing to "El Otro Lado," or "the Other Side," recalling how that once relatively easy journey—wading over a river, paying a coyote smuggler a small fee to cross the desert, or jumping over a wall—had become more treacherous and expensive.

When Peshke, Mottel, Pepa, and Leon crossed to their Other Side in the fall of 1939, the border between Poland and the Soviet Union was easy to traverse for the Jews who took the chance. During that brief opening in 1939, hundreds of thousands of Polish Jews entered Soviet-occupied territories. Within weeks, border patrol tightened and very few refugees could slip through.

More than eight decades later, the border to Ukraine loomed on the highway with the familiar signs of land barriers: Guards. Checkpoints. Traffic.

"We are lucky, no buses in front of us," Maria said. I relaxed a bit. I'd been thoroughly warned about the hours-long wait I should anticipate.

We grabbed our passports and filed off the bus, inhaling the cooler outside air before shuffling into a small border post. Inside, I stood alongside the Ukrainian women. I was now part of the collective journey, the banality of communal waiting—for a line to move, a stamp to be issued.

First step completed, we got back on the bus, now waiting for official admittance into Ukraine. After what felt like an hour, the guard returned with our stack of passports. He exited and the bus lurched forward.

I'd anticipated being gripped by excitement upon entering Ukraine. But the warm bus, the women talking around me in a language I did not understand, the forward movement, lulled me into an overpowering sleep.

Maria tapped me. We had arrived at her town. Out the window I saw a horse-drawn carriage and trucks.

She left me with a few words of advice: "Go to the cemetery where all the heroes are being buried." Then she stepped off the bus and a broad-shouldered man with a crew cut enveloped her in a hug and grabbed her bag. I was on my own again, but now I was not concerned. Maria, like a guardian angel, had helped me cross, and I knew a driver from my hotel would be awaiting me when the bus arrived in Lviv.

For months I had feared that something would go wrong—the war would escalate, I would get sick, the four flights and the bus trip would get delayed—and I would not make it to Ukraine. But now I was here, and a jolt at last ran through me as I took in the urban landscape out the window. Bikes, buses, and trams competed for space on the roads with cars. Ukrainian flags waved yellow and blue from seemingly every building and car. A billboard featuring an older soldier welcomed me into the city limits with a sign: "Thank you for the opportunity to speak Ukrainian." How different this was from the multiethnic Lviv our grandparents entered as refugees, where Yiddish, German, Russian, and Polish, as well as Ukrainian, were all spoken. I was now wide awake, eyes roaming the streets, eager to step into this contested city.

CHAPTER 14
The Ones Who Run

If I can live to May, I'll be able to go outside with my child. I'll be saved.

Long before I entered Lviv, my grandmother recited these words in the same city on bitter winter days as she caressed and bounced her baby boy in a room packed with refugees. Through long nights, lying next to Mottel, she tried to find peace as the room reverberated with the snores and grunts of her father-in-law, four of her husband's siblings, two of their partners, three cousins, and a rotating cast of friends from Zamość. But all those breathing bodies could not thaw her toes or soothe her nerves.

Peshke and Mottel had first reunited months earlier in the fall of 1939. Not in Lviv, but in a small town fifty miles east of Zamość, on the other side of the River Bug, the revised border between the German- and Soviet-occupied zones. Already skilled in accounting, Mottel soon revealed a knack for black-market dealing. He had found them a corner of their own on a church floor, and their baby was healthy. Like most, they assumed it would just be a few months until the British and French vanquished the Germans, and then they could return to their home in Zamość.

But political forces beyond their imagining redirected their course. Weeks after Peshke's arrival, the Soviets proclaimed a shift in policy: "Bezhenets," as refugees like them were called in Russian, were henceforth banished from border towns. The Soviet government feared they posed a security danger and made them relocate farther from the border—farther from their families back home in Zamość.

Mottel and Peshke, baby Arik in their arms, rented a truck with other refugees. Or maybe they took a train? In one of the many tricks of memory that colored our family's recollections, my grandmother remembered one detail, my grandfather another. Either way, by January 1940 they had entered a city with greater suffering, the one they called Lemberg in Yiddish, and Lwów in Polish. By the time they arrived, the signs likely read Lvov in Russian and Lviv in Ukrainian. Call it what you choose; the city was overrun with refugees.

* * *

"Bezhenets" was the only Russian word my grandmother uttered in hours of testimonies. It is generally translated as "refugee," but that isn't an exact fit. In English, "refugee" traces its roots to the Latin word "refugium," indicating someone who seeks sanctuary, a refuge. But in Russian, "bezhenets" translates to the action of motion, "the one who runs." It's no accident that the word deeply imprinted upon my grandmother's psyche. For seven years, my grandmother was running in the Soviet Union. And the Communist regime, with its aim of total control of its population, had little tolerance for people who ran unless ordered to do so, no matter the terror that propelled them.

Moscow blamed bezhenets who had sought refuge during World War I for blocking military movements, spreading diseases, and draining coffers. When Stalin took power in the 1920s, intent on the Communist State building capacity to instantly mobilize for war, he created checks to ensure that when the next battle came, bezhenets would not cause problems. In 1937, Moscow shifted refugee administration from the humanitarian Red Cross to the political police, the dreaded People's Commissariat for Internal Affairs, or NKVD.

Did my grandparents know that they should fear the land where they sought refuge? That Stalin, in his quest to create a "workers' paradise," employed mass killings and deportations against his own people? Did they know of the more than one million slaughtered in the Great

Purge? Of the three million who starved to death in the man-made famine in Ukraine? Or the 1.7 million farmers, or kulaks, deported to the hinterlands so that farm collectivization would move forward unencumbered? Probably not. Despite the proximity, they likely knew very little about Stalin's mass extermination of real and imagined political opponents as he cemented his ruthless hold on power. The Supreme Soviet masterfully controlled information.

Peshke and Mottel entered Lviv assuming they would find a refuge. Red Army soldiers, after all, had given Peshke a ride over the border, presumably because they wanted to protect her from the Germans. Initially, the Soviet Union opened its doors, one of the only places in the world where Polish Jews could move. But within months, Mottel and Peshke—and somewhere else among the hundreds of thousands of others recently arrived in the city, Talia's grandparents—would find they had entered no workers' paradise. For the refugees, the bezhenets, the Soviet Union would come closer to hell.

CHAPTER 15

City of Lions

The Leopolis Hotel, taking on the Latin name for Lviv meaning "City of Lions," provided me with a sumptuous welcome: deep turquoise velour chairs and sofas, luxurious purple walls, and gleaming wooden banisters. To my left, a library beckoned.

"Where's the bomb shelter?" I asked the young clerk who checked me in.

"Your bellhop will show you," she said, with a flip of her long, dark hair. I realized only after the bellhop left me alone in my well-appointed room that I had forgotten about my question. I let go of my anxiety for a moment, taking off my travel shoes and feeling the cool floor on my toes.

I had made it safely to Lviv. My whole being tingled with gratitude. Now I had just two days to explore the place where our grandparents landed during the last war this city had endured, one that fundamentally transformed it and its inhabitants.

* * *

"Lwow was one of the loveliest Polish cities in the sense that it was a merry city. Not so much the people, but the city itself. Very colorful, very exotic, it had none of the grayness of Warsaw, or even Krakow," described the Polish futurist poet Aleksander Wat of the city he moved to in the fall of 1939. That would all soon change. By the darkening months, Lviv was no longer a merry city. "The Soviets had barely arrived, and all at once everything was covered in mud (of course it was fall), dirty, gray, shabby. People began cringing and slinking down the streets. Right away people started wearing ragged clothes," Wat recalled. He had been among a prolific group of Polish Jewish intellectuals whom the Communist Party recruited, promising good working conditions and opportunities to study. Most were not so fortunate. "There was a multitude of refugees. People had nothing to live on, terrible hardship."

Lviv in the winter of 1939 was not just overcome with the burdens of housing refugees. The city itself, still reeling from successive occupations by German and then Soviet forces, underwent an excruciating transformation from capitalist to Communist, from a constitutional republic to a dictatorship. Meanwhile, it was once again caught in the crosshairs of empire building. Lviv had, like Zamość, endured shifting rulers: Austro-Hungarian, Polish, and more. After World War I, the city had briefly been the capital of the Western Ukrainian People's Republic. But its Polish residents, who were then the majority, pushed back. Warsaw recaptured it in 1920.

Now the city was Soviet, and Moscow placed great hopes on Lviv, an initial case study of Communism's global destiny. Within ten days of occupation, almost one hundred informers had been recruited. Everyone was under suspicion for violating the workers' revolution. Newly arrived Russian government workers tore down Polish street signs and statues and replaced them with giant busts of Lenin. Movie theaters showed propaganda flicks with the capitalists and their spies as the villains, and the Communist commissar as the hero.

As state-controlled trade struggled to take form, residents went hungry. Refugees, even if they arrived wealthy, were reduced to beggars when, without warning, the Polish złoty was withdrawn from circulation. There was no bread to be found and food lines were everywhere. Ukrainians, Poles, and Jews shared their misery. The only ones exempt were the Russians, with their matching drab haircuts, who had relocated to run this new, supposedly more just, society.

While more than seventy shelters had been set up to house migrants, by the time Mottel, Peshke, and baby Arik arrived that frigid winter, there may have been no beds to be found. Officially, Lviv's prewar population of roughly 330,000 had jumped by more than 50 percent. Observers at the time believed it had tripled. Somehow, my grandparents secured a room with a kitchen and no heat, where often more than ten relatives and friends slept. It was freezing, but at least baby Arik had a roof over his head.

One morning, determined to get meat to sustain his son, my grandfather Mottel left their room at 4:00 a.m. Already people were standing huddled in the dark, biting cold.

No more meat today, the shop owner announced just as the sun started to illuminate the furious, famished faces lining the street. How did my grandfather then return to his wife and howling baby and tell her they needed to endure another starving day?

* * *

"You will need to eat," was the first thing my guide and interpreter Inna told me as she steered me down the old town streets to Lviv Croissants, a regional chain. I ordered orange juice mixed with coffee, a local drink I found more pleasing than I expected, and a tuna-on-croissant sandwich. We took seats facing each other at a café table on the well-trafficked pedestrian road, older than most in these youthful streets.

Signs abounded of a nation again at war: *God Save Ukraine* graffiti, guards with machine guns in army fatigues. Yet the food was plentiful, and the atmosphere felt secure and even upbeat. Street musicians played patriotic songs to enthusiastic crowds, but also ones about love. I had been prepared for the famed beauty of this city, but I had not expected Lviv—at war—to be bursting with life.

Inna told me that she once guided droves of tourists around Lviv, a city that had been about half Polish and a third Jewish before World War II. Many tourists visited to try to uncover their heritage. After the Russian invasion, though, the flow of vacationers and ancestry tourists stopped.

Inna pivoted to guide a different type of visitor: Ukrainians who had fled their homes. They slept in theaters, libraries, schools. Inna's job was to ensure that migrants safely exited the country and joined their millions of compatriots who had already left for the European Union. It was not easy.

"Ukraine is bleeding," she said. "You want to help people. But helping them leave the country is difficult."

* * *

Inna led me down streets lined with massive trees and elegant buildings built under Austro-Hungarian rule. Above the others loomed a corner four-story Jugenstil stone structure with Art Nouveau touches: arched windows, a protruding round tower, and a two-tiered cupola on the top. A red banner swathed the base—the logo of a large Ukrainian fast-food joint serving up a ready supply of borscht and varenyky, potato dumplings. Flanking the entrance stood two sculptured knights. This building had been one of the city's most fashionable addresses a century earlier.

I stared in wonder, wishing Talia could share this moment with me. According to property records we had dug up, her grandfather's cousin Wigdor Inlender and his wife, Sura, had owned this refined building in the 1920s and used it to house one of his companies, distributing seventeen kinds of Count Alfred Potocki's liqueur, rosé, and rum throughout Poland. Wigdor, as far as I could tell, could easily have fled Zamość and come to this outpost of his enterprise but must have believed he could handle the Germans.

The inveterate businessman knew how to grease wheels. During World War I he had got on well, even hosting a German field marshal during the occupation. Like him, most of Zamość's better-off Jews remained in town, intent on protecting their property and rightly concerned about how they would be treated as capitalists in the Soviet Union. But Wigdor took the Nazi threat seriously enough that he sent his wife, who was sick with cancer, across the Soviet side to Lviv, along with three of his four children. I imagine they likely landed in this building.

Did Leon also move to an apartment here? Did he stand transfixed at this place of beauty in the chaos of Lviv under war? Had he opened the door with a key that his wealthy older cousin had placed in his hand as they parted ways?

If the building served as a haven for Leon and the rest of Wigdor's family, the respite did not last long. The sophisticated stores and liquor outfit would have been easy targets for nationalization. Throughout the winter of 1940, the Communist government rapidly seized privately held businesses. They eventually took control of all the stores in Wigdor's building. The fine restaurant on the ground floor named Renesans (Renaissance) was soon replaced with a waiter cooperative canteen, "Dining Room Number 9."

One day in that brutal Lviv winter, Soviet officers in double-breasted business suits likely knocked on the door and announced that they were taking the property from the Inlender family for *being a landlord and exploiter*. Weeks later, relocated to a cold floor somewhere, Leon might have walked by the apartment and spotted an NKVD agent through the window, a Soviet secret policeman and his family in the apartment enjoying his cousin Wigdor's fine furnishings.

Leon must have wondered, What next? He could not have known then that he would never see his wife or child again. Nor could he have imagined that his next wife, a much younger fifteen-year-old named Pepa, was finding her way as well in this city of refugees.

* * *

In the week of mourning after Talia's grandmother Pepa died, a small brown book with yellowed paper surfaced in her bedside table. My mother-in-law, Tobi, found it. She could not decipher the words, but she sensed this was a rare keepsake and brought it back to the United States. As we started to research years later, Tobi dug it out of a box in the closet. The handwritten notes on the brittle paper were in Polish, Yiddish, Russian, and German. There were dates and places. At last, a chronology and map from Talia's grandmother to push us along the journey. And one of those entries was from Lwów in January 1940.

Pepa must have taken her autograph book from her bag upon arriving in Lviv, the city she called by its Polish name. She added more than a dozen new names in one winter week—connecting with classmates from her hometown who had relocated and meeting new people. Even in war, she was highly social. Yet, when we had the book translated, we learned these were no frivolous messages. To read the words that friends and acquaintances inscribed in that second week of January 1940 was to sense her youthful innocence rapidly diminishing.

"To Kind and Beautiful Pepcia: Almost everything is simple. Love God and Homeland. And don't forget me," inscribed a Falek.

"Companion in my plight," Sulamit wrote in solidarity.

And a Moshe provided sage advice: "Life is full of suffering, but we need to overcome it and get stronger and get better."

It was an incredible artifact, and yet all we knew of Pepa's life in Lviv were these morose aphorisms and poems. I craved a fuller picture of this woman than what Talia's family had told me: Pepa was born in Tomaszów Lubelski, the town twenty miles due south of Zamość where I'd caught the bus to Lviv. She was petite and opinionated, preferred men to women, and made clear her preference for Talia's older brother. That detail I had heard, with a laugh that held some sadness, many times.

In my mother-in-law's closet, we found photos capturing Pepa as a spirited adolescent, leaning on a bike, lounging in the green fields or diving in the lake, always surrounded by friends and often with a young man's arm draped around her. But while the images projected a carefree youth, we now knew she also suffered loss. Pepa's father had died at forty-seven.

Two years later, at the age of fifteen, Pepa faced war. When the Germans attacked Tomaszów Lubelski, they tortured Jews. Pepa must have known she needed to get out while she could. One brother left on his own, eventually joining the Red Army. Her mother at some point took her younger brother and sister and fled with them to the Soviet Union. But not Pepa.

Why had Pepa ventured forth alone as a young teen? And how and when had she and Leon come together? I asked these questions of Talia's relatives, but nobody knew the answers. One cousin suggested I speak with the former caretaker for Pepa's now-deceased younger sister. The aide, who was Ukrainian, recalled details of a tragic history that had been lost to Talia's family. Pepa, she told me, had gone to Lviv at the outset of the war to help care for the baby daughter of an older sister. She was not alone, but with her family, nurturing her niece.

* * *

Somewhere else in Lviv, my grandparents battled furiously to keep their baby son alive. "My son, my small son, my little son gets sick," my grandfather cried, his voice breaking. After more than three decades in the States, he still mispronounced his English "s" as a strong "zh." Despite lack of food and disease, their baby Arik had survived to feel May's warmer air, answering Peshke's prayers. Bread was now sold in stores in Lviv. Stalin began bestowing favor on this western outpost so it could showcase the success of the workers' revolution. But just when Arik was supposed to improve, his cough roared back. A Jewish doctor from Zamość visited their apartment, diagnosing diphtheria and giving the baby an injection.

Days later Arik seized in his worst attack yet. Perhaps Mottel was off trying to buy food or selling in the black market, which would explain why Peshke set off alone with her baby boy to the Jewish hospital, only to find no doctors available, no treatments to inject. Arik's lungs struggled, the cough ever more tortured, until he stopped making any noise at all. His mother's sobs echoed in the hospital's halls.

Two nurses forced Peshke to leave. They could not tolerate her anguish; they needed to attend to other suffering.

By the time Peshke, wild with sorrow, returned to the family's room, she was unrecognizable to her husband. Weeks before turning thirty, my grandmother's hair had gone completely white. Peshke's father had been right. She would lose the baby. Arik was dead.

* * *

The former Jewish Hospital, a hulking Moorish Revival–style brick building with a tiled dome, was now a maternity ward. Taped to the brick wall surrounding it was a sign for Bomb Shelter 8.

What was left behind, if anything, of this baby—my uncle—who had died here before he had a chance to grow?

My grandmother left a clue: "We buried the child."

Behind the hospital, Inna led me to a cemetery. When the Nazis later occupied Lviv, they used Jewish gravestones to pave roads and blew up the pre-burial house. Even if Mottel and Peshke made the unusual decision to mark a baby's life at a time when many small children died, no grave site would remain. As a light rain cried down, I traced the pile of engravings marking the names and lifespans found in the rubble, most of them indecipherable. It was a haunting cemetery, with elaborate postwar Jewish tombstones, some enclosed by cages to protect against vandalism, but I found no remnant there of my uncle.

Inna and I left on another streetcar, crossing the city to a different place of burial, the one Maria, who had helped me cross the border into Ukraine, had pushed me to visit. In this one, well-maintained with freshly uncovered soil, a sea of blue and yellow beckoned. This generation's military dead from Lviv were being interred, boldly marked as heroes. One man, head bowed, burly shoulders tucked forward in grief, walked holding the hands of two small children. Different cemeteries, different casualties of war. I tried to make space in my heart for both the dead heroes and the forgotten in this City of Lions.

CHAPTER 16
Return

I woke at 2:00 a.m. with a jolt. Had an air siren gone off? Were other guests scurrying to the shelter? The room was silent. Perhaps I had just heard people stumbling to their rooms. But wasn't it after the midnight curfew? Trying to silence fears that permeated my semiconscious state, I curled into a fetal position in my bed.

A few hours later I rose to a perfect Lviv day. On the elevator down to breakfast, I noticed a room service menu offering up classic cocktails. I almost missed the note in delicate letters on the bottom: "Dear Guests, please use the stairs during air alarms and curfew."

I asked the clerk again where the shelter was. She pointed down the hall.

"Would you go there, if the siren rings?" I asked.

"Honestly, I don't go," she told me. Perhaps living under constant threat inured her to the risks? Or her way to cope was to intentionally ignore? Either way, I didn't have time to check out the shelter.

Inna, my guide, was waiting for me in the lobby.

As I followed her brisk steps toward the streetcar, she told me how her job assisting refugees had transformed. Months after departing, millions of Ukrainian refugees began to return to their towns and cities. Though Russia's bombardment had not ended, they missed home enough to decide a familiar bed was worth the threat.

Among the carloads of citizens returning had been a minivan driven by the father of my precocious Ukrainian student research assistant, Yuliia Zhytelna. She had watched, terrified, from California, as her family fled to Poland, and then, months later, returned to their home in Kyiv. "Ukrainians are different from other immigrants," Yuliia said of their brave move to me. "They love their home so much that they always want to return."

At that moment, I didn't tell Yuliia—who had spent more than a year separated from her family—what I was thinking: that longing for home does not make Ukrainians unique. It makes them just like almost every other refugee. The ability to return is what distinguishes her family from many of the world's tens of millions of displaced people. My grandparents also wanted to return to their Polish homes during World War II—and they almost got their wish.

* * *

Come back, parents, wives, and siblings urged in letters. Loved ones who'd remained in Poland sent word that they'd been forced to wear ten-centimeter-wide yellow armbands with a Star of David embroidered in blue thread to mark them as Jews. That Germans beat old men in the streets for not doffing a hat in time to an officer, another new requirement. But in Zamość, at least, they remained in their homes and most continued to run their businesses.

In the miserable one-room apartment in Lviv, my great-grandfather Chaim made up his mind. He'd already lived once as a refugee in Ukraine. He did not want to languish away from his home and his wife any longer. Besides, what could the Nazis do to a man already in his sixties? He gathered his children and revealed his decision: *I'll go back. I have a home; it's quiet there. I'll be with your mother.*

Wherever governments create borders, smugglers emerge—profiteers in the illicit business of guiding the desperate. One of them was a cousin of my grandfather. He shepherded refugees across the militarized demarcation line between the German- and Soviet-occupied sections of Poland.

The cousin offered a spot up to Chaim. Two of my grandfather's sisters also clamored to join him. But he only had room for one Gerson.

I'll take you next time, he promised the young women. I imagine they were disappointed. They would not know for years that he surely saved their lives.

My great-uncle Moishe was working by then in a Soviet furniture company, and my grandfather Mottel was trading goods on the black market. Together they secured for their father a few złoty, which were still being used as illegal tender, to support his return. But the money did not make it back to Zamość. The Germans robbed and beat Chaim when he arrived at the border, pummeling his body until he could no longer walk; he crawled on the ground to return home to his wife.

* * *

After Chaim departed, Mottel was at the Lviv apartment when a friend shouted tantalizing news: *Everybody who wants to go back to Poland can go back!*

The Communists offered the refugees a choice: Become Soviet citizens or return to Nazi-occupied Poland. Some asked for more options—temporary rights, a transit passport. But for Mottel and his siblings, as for just about all the Jews they knew in Lviv, the choice was clear. They rejected the offer of Soviet citizenship.

When I first heard my grandfather report that "almost all, I would say 95 percent of the Jewish population registered to go back," I could not believe it. Had I misunderstood? I listened to his voice again. Yes, my serious, astute grandfather explained the choice like it was the most natural thing in the world: His family, and basically every Jew he knew, signed up to return to Nazi-occupied Poland.

Why would they ever do that?

* * *

Shortly before I left for Lviv, I received a family recording that contained the answer I had been searching for. My brother shared the video he had shot almost eighteen years earlier of Dad and his cousin Sol interviewing my great-uncle Simon during his final days.

"Why didn't you want to become a Russian citizen?" Sol asked Simon, whose name we pronounced the Yiddish way of Shim'on.

My elderly great-uncle took his time to find the words, his hands shaking. He told the story of a friend's cousin, a loyal Polish Jewish Communist, who after crossing the border to the east was deported to the hinterlands of the Soviet Union, never to be seen again. The cousin's wife told Simon's friend when he found her in Moscow: "Run away. Go back to Poland. Run anyplace. Don't stay here." Other Communists he knew in Zamość had also been beaten and arrested upon arriving in the Soviet Union. "I was afraid. I was very afraid of what was going on in Russia. I knew what was happening."

My brother kept filming as Simon hobbled off to the bathroom with his walker. Dad and his cousin, framed by the bright Florida light streaming through the blinds, sat for a moment together on the couch. Then my verbose father, whom a *New York Times* writer once described as "rabbinical and elegant," uttered just one word: "strange."

But to our grandparents at the time, petrified of being stuck in the Soviet Union, returning to Poland must have felt like the only choice. They had glimpsed the truth of the Communist "paradise." Mottel's younger sister Chuma had, earlier in the fall of 1939, accepted official Soviet calls, which were closer to demands, to relocate to the interior. At first, when her group of young people landed at a small town near the northern border with Finland, they were welcomed like kings. But within a couple of weeks, the conditions degraded precipitously as they slaved in a factory with scant food. Chuma defied Soviet protocol and relocated to Lviv with a beau who was also from Zamość, my great-uncle Simon. Remaining indefinitely in the Soviet Union was not an option.

The urge to leave escalated when fellow Polish citizens, once welcomed, began to disappear in the winter of 1940. Aleksander Wat, the futurist poet, was arrested in January as the NKVD went after intellectuals. Our grandparents may have woken to shrieks in February's icy early morning hours when the security services rounded up families at gunpoint, delivering them to the train station. In April, the NKVD viciously knocked on doors again, arresting Polish citizens who were military leaders, farmers, and other perceived threats to Soviet social order, along with their wives and children. Sentenced as prisoners or exiles, they were shoved into trains headed toward the dreaded east.

* * *

In May 1940, Nazi officers drove into town and parked in front of the Lviv villa where I now stood. After a half-hour ride on the streetcar away from the city center, Inna and I had stepped off onto a broad and quiet road with stately villas and blooming gardens. I wanted to walk on the streets where Peshke and Mottel, Leon and Pepa once stood, to see if I might better understand the choice they made, which felt unfathomable in retrospect.

All day long Polish citizens, Jew and gentile alike, waited their turn in the adjacent park, documents in hand, hoping to retrace their steps across the border to the west into Nazi territory. This scene repeated itself in towns and cities across the Soviet-occupied borderlands. At a different registration point, a German officer turned to a crowd waiting and demanded: "Jews, where are you going? Don't you realize that we will kill you?" The Nazis at the time had been considering plans to relocate Jews to Madagascar or deeper into the Soviet Union. They were trying to get rid of Jews, not bring them back.

Soviet authorities were also watching, appalled that their generous offer of citizenship would be broadly rejected. Nikita Khrushchev, who then presided over the integration of the formerly Polish territories, recounted in his memoirs an official's report to him: "I was shocked to see that most of the people in line were members of the Jewish population. They were bribing the gestapo agents to let them leave as soon as possible to return to their original homes."

One June day, the German commissioners stepped into a freshly cleaned car and departed for the west. Many refugees began to wonder aloud about the terrifying prospect that had been nagging inside their heads: Was this a German or Soviet trap? Or had the two powers teamed up, as they had before, this time to destroy Poland's citizens who chose to return?

* * *

The answer came days later in the inky hours. On a June night when Lviv residents had been told to remain home with the lights off to train for an air raid, the streets burst with Soviet military trucks, headlights strobing and racing toward the refugees' homes.

Four men forced Peshke's door open. *All of you need to come with us immediately!* they barked at the mess of family and friends sharing the floor.

Our grandparents had been tricked. The refugees realized then the mistake of providing the NKVD with their real names and addresses. The dreaded secret police had come to collect them. In revealing their willingness to leave, Stalin declared them unfit to be Soviet citizens, a security risk. They could not return to Zamość, nor could they remain in Lviv.

My husband is not here. I can't go. Peshke, resolute once more, stood up to the NKVD agents and Communist Party members who'd arrived with an order, demanding they depart immediately for the train station.

Word had flown through the refugee community with rumors the NKVD might come and target men. So, on the June night that the officers arrived at the door, Mottel and two of the other men in their group had slept at the furniture factory where they worked. Peshke refused to leave without him.

Had this gutsy woman really been my grandmother? When I knew her in her old age, she always seemed so meek, warning me not to run in the hot sun lest I overheat, blowing on my food excessively so it would not burn me. When she moved into my childhood home to live out her final years, I grew resentful of her timidity and of the shadow of suffering that followed her. But in her youth, I now saw she'd been a remarkably courageous woman.

Peshke did not waver: *This is where my husband is, and if you bring him, I'll go wherever you send us. But alone, I'm not going.*

Mercifully, while other families were divided in the evening raid on their homes, this soldier allowed my great-uncle Simon to fetch my grandfather and Moishe.

My grandmother launched one more battle.

I want my sewing machine; without my machine I'm not going. Peshke defied the order that they take just one suitcase with them to the train tracks. *With my sewing machine, I will not starve to death.*

My great-uncle Moishe told it differently: By the time he had returned from the furniture factory in Lviv's gray predawn hours, officers in dirty trucks had swarmed the streets surrounding their apartment. *Everybody out.* Moishe defied the orders and ran back through the streets of wailing children and the forlorn elderly to grab the sewing machine and then sprint with it under his arm to catch up with the open truck where the rest of the family was huddled.

Whichever story is correct, by the time Mottel and Peshke and their six family members waited by the train tracks, the sewing machine was safely with them. Hundreds more distraught refugees shared their misery: a lawyer, a child dressed beautifully as if to go to synagogue, mostly Jews, but also some Poles. Neighbors brought food. All wanted to know: *Where are we going, and why are we being taken away?* But surely, they knew by then that when you were forced to report to a train track in the Soviet Union, your destination was the frozen wastelands of Siberia.

They had learned an indelible lesson of Soviet existence: "No such thing as a refugee; either you are a citizen or a spy." In refusing to become citizens, they had become enemies of the state.

CHAPTER 17

Territory of Terror

The sun filtered through soft clouds, lacing the Lviv air with a thick humidity. Then a train rattled. Sweat trickled down my back. On a different June day, NKVD officers had forced our four grandparents to stand by these same tracks, in dreadful anticipation of the moment when they would be forced into the idling cattle cars.

Inna, my guide, led me into our destination: the Territory of Terror. A patio featuring gargantuan felled metal statues of Communist leaders greeted us; these stern larger-than-life figures lay on their sides, fierce in their magnitude even if now powerless. Inside the museum, we peeked into a bedroom exhibit, the scene of so many nighttime arrests as the NKVD rapped on the door with rifles ready and caught victims in their beds, permeating the intimacy of homes, demanding that people like our grandparents pack up in the night. The adjoining space depicted a different type of place to rest, barracks with beds—a symbol of the Nazi terror when they occupied Ukraine the following year, making the region an epicenter of mass violence with a spectrum of camps: death, concentration and forced labor, prisoners of war.

At the age of forty-five, I took in for the first time my grandparents' deportation to Siberia in the same commemorative space as that of their loved ones who were sent to a Nazi death camp. I had visited major Jewish Holocaust memorials and museums in the United States, Israel, Germany, and Poland. But the tortured route to survival my grandparents had taken via imprisonment in the Soviet Union, long on the margins of the historical record, tended to warrant a small plaque at most.

Not here. At the Territory of Terror, their persecution was preserved as part of this borderland city's history of repression on all sides. The museum documented the dual deportations during World War II: initially east to Soviet prisons and the forced labor of Siberia, and later west to Nazi death camps. Our guide to the museum, a lithe refugee from Odessa with a single long dreadlock, argued it made logical sense to tell the stories together: "The wagons are very similar, the conditions are almost the same."

* * *

The Territory of Terror had started small, in 2009, as a local city initiative without a fixed space. Six years later, Olha Honchar became its director. Despite being just twenty-four years old, she had vision and broadened the museum's mission to commemorate victims of totalitarianism that local histories had often overlooked. Along with the Ukrainian experience in Lviv during World War II, it now told the stories of its other former residents—Jews, Poles, and more.

Probing the legacy of Soviet repression took on a new weight in the current war. A common message in the giant blue museum visitor book conflated the past with the present battle: "Glory to Ukraine. Glory to our Heroes. Death to our Enemies."

When Inna translated the words for me, I raised my eyebrows and said, "Wow," with a nervous laugh.

"I know we are not very polite sometimes," Inna responded. "We are treated as a crazy, aggressive people now." Western European visitors sometimes urged her to have a coffee with Russians and work out their differences. That was not going to happen. Inna emphasized the motives behind her resistance: When someone threatens you with extermination, you do not invite them to sip coffee; you fight back with all your might.

In the visitor book, we also often came across versions of what

Ukrainian President Zelenskyy proclaimed at the outset of the war: "We will not forgive. We will not forget." It brought to mind a visit with my uncle, a liberal Berkeley psychologist, to his birthplace in a Bavarian refugee camp that he had left more than five decades earlier as a two-year-old. "Sometimes I just want to kill them all," he said of the Germans around us. No matter that a renowned local artist who had preserved the camp history had graciously welcomed us. The experience of being threatened unleashes an animal instinct to fight that does not end when the threat recedes. As my uncle knew from experience, and as an expert in intergenerational trauma, the imprint is passed down between generations.

Here in Lviv, I saw how fresh wounds were being imprinted on Lviv's residents, beginning the cycle anew. The museum director, Honchar, told me that before the Russian invasion her mission had been for people to leave convinced "never again." But since the war she had resolved, "It's impossible. Life looks like pain. Maybe it's the nature of humans that we keep fighting each other."

Honchar now saw her battlefield as an intellectual one; her mission included preventing Russians from erasing the Ukrainian experience. At the Territory of Terror she brought to life in gory detail how just about every Lviv family had been a target over the past bloody century. Honchar still hoped that presenting the history would break a light through the cycles of violence. Pain is universal, she stressed, and preserving this history could connect people rather than divide.

While that was true, I also knew how competitions among those who had suffered could play out. Even in my family, there was a hierarchy. On the lower end was the horror of being forced into trains to a far-off place they called Siberia. When my grandmother shared her saga, she made sure to add that it was "not worthy of any comparison to the plight of our people and my family in Zamość." But the Polish deportees under Stalin had also suffered, and I was intent on seeing for myself what happened to them—a history I had not found commemorated along side Hitler's atrocities before this Lviv museum.

* * *

"Did you ever see a cattle train?" my grandmother asked my younger sister in the video. Merissa looked around twelve at the time, likely fulfilling a family history assignment for school. Earnest and giggly, my sister shook her head. My grandmother continued, "They took out the cattle, and they took people who were registered as Polish citizens." I wondered how my sister's teacher responded to the unexpected and graphic history that followed.

In a red train car meant for a half dozen cows, iron bars sealed my grandmother in with more than thirty refugees. The Soviets were already masters at forcibly moving people at the outset of World War II; the Nazis would soon learn from them. Old men hid their tears as the wheels lurched forward; three small children comforted each other. A wife howled for a husband left behind. Even in their misery, my grandparents realized they had one advantage: All five Gerson siblings and three of their spouses were together.

Armies of lice attacked fresh skin. Provisions rapidly diminished. A Soviet officer thrust a pail of watery vegetable peel soup into the train car just once a day. At seemingly random intervals, the wheels ground to a halt, the sliding door unlatched, and the refugees could jump off to relieve themselves on the tracks. Guards surrounded women, men, young and old as they squatted, propriety stripped. Then, without warning, the train would lurch forward again, the prisoners scrambling for the doors, terrified they might be left behind, alone, a fate worse than continuing.

For weeks our grandparents traveled in a moving prison, with each stationmaster instructing the conductor to keep going. They chugged past the rich black earth of Ukraine, with the distressing sight of farms lying fallow. They saw Russian people working the fields without shoes, but only rags and rubber tied to their feet. Any last remnants of hope for the Communist promises of equality that my grandfather once cherished were demolished.

Some suffered deprivation aboard the train even worse than that of my grandparents. "It was packed so tight that we could only sleep standing," Tina Jaffe, who had been twelve at the time, recalled. "I looked down at what I was standing on, and there was this body of an old lady. I was standing on it, not knowing. And I started screaming, screaming. And they couldn't stop me from screaming." The old woman's body was tossed out of the train, along with more to come who died of heart attacks and sickness.

Everyone survived on my grandparents' train, but during the weeks-long journey into the unknown they were not certain they would make it alive. The hunger, the filth, the anguish were constant companions. The guards refused to tell them where they were going; perhaps they did not know. As hundreds of trains chugged along the Soviet expanse, the northern summer sun glimmering through the wooden slats gave an eerie glow for all but six hours of the days that streamed together. "We went oh so far away." My great-uncle Simon pictured the desolation after they had crossed the Volga River. "We saw only woods, woods."

* * *

Meanwhile, back in Lviv, the Jews allowed to remain in the summer of 1940 were surely convinced they were the lucky ones. At compulsory meetings, the Bolsheviks ensured they had no doubts: *This is how we annihilate the enemies of Soviet power... You will never see again those that we have taken away.*

Soon letters arrived from remote provinces thousands of miles away with the pleas of deportees for food supplies, blankets, and clothes. Once more, those who remained in Lviv anguished at the fate of loved ones—and felt fortunate that they had evaded the NKVD clutches.

But just over a year after our families were deported, on June 22, 1941, German bombs hailed down once more on Lviv. Hitler, intent to destroy what he believed was a Judeo-Bolshevik conspiracy to the east, had launched a surprise attack on Stalin. The führer's plan: to create lebensraum, living space for Germans on the lands of Slavs whom he planned to murder. Despite reports of millions of soldiers deployed to attack, Stalin could not believe the affront from his former ally in destroying Poland. In shock and denial, he retreated to his dacha.

Nazi soldiers, with the support of Ukrainian nationalists, soon marched on Lviv, sweeping through the Jewish district with a furious intensity aimed at eliminating residents whom they accused of being part of the diabolical Judeo-Bolshevik conspiracy. One witness described them "driving out all Jews found regardless of sex or age onto the street, where they arranged them into a four-sided mass and then squeezed them tighter and tighter, murdering them by stabbing them with knives or by hitting them with rifle butts, clubs, and even with their fists." In a days-long bloodbath, German police squads, assisted by the Ukrainian auxiliary police, recorded shooting thousands of Jewish men.

Another witness, who wrote under the name Stanisław Różycki, described with precise and excruciating detail how Lviv's surviving Jews went into hiding, and how soon hunger took away all other thoughts. "We have ceased to care about anything else: whether they will take us to perform forced labor, deport us to a camp, beat us up, execute us, throw us out of the flat, or rob all our property—to hell with that."

Those who once felt grateful they had been saved from deportation to Siberia now questioned their luck. "Fortune is a strange thing," reflected Różycki, who later somehow found a way to get his testimony out of Lviv to the Warsaw ghetto. There, he deposited it with the Ringelblum Archive, a clandestine effort that documented the Holocaust as it happened. Years later, his handwritten notes, buried in a tin box under bloodstained earth, were uncovered. But no details emerged of who Różycki was or his fate. Just his unparalleled testimony on the unpredictability of luck in the borderlands remained. "We had done everything to avoid deportation but now many of us—scarce survivors—regretted not having been deported back then."

* * *

Among those trapped in Lviv under the German occupation was the older sister of Talia's grandmother Pepa. Who had she been? And why had she not been deported like Pepa? Now that I knew a little of the history, I assumed that she and her family had moved to Lviv earlier, before the war began and were automatically provided Soviet citizenship at the time of annexation. They would not even have been provided the false offer to return to Poland and were not subject to deportation.

I looked for details in the first family records we'd acquired more than two years before. A genealogist had sent us birth dates for Pepa's siblings, starting with a Sura Blima Fajl.

That must have been her name, Sura. In the crush of initial family details, I'd overlooked this older sister to Pepa who had not survived. And I found more: In 1937, Sura, at the age of twenty-five, married a Szlomo Wajnstok, also twenty-five.

These funny-sounding Yiddish names I'd glossed over earlier now captivated me. I plugged "Sura Wajnstok" into the victims' database at Yad Vashem. Up popped a handwritten testimony about a Sara Feil who married a Szlomo Weinsztock—clearly Pepa's sister and her husband. The author, who now lived in Canada, revealed that they had been "killed by Ukrainians at place of work." He also provided a name, Rebecca, for their small daughter, who would have been six. And then, he added another little girl I had not known existed, a Devora, age five. He wrote that the fate for both girls was the same: "deported, place unknown."

The stark words about one anonymous child who was now two girls, a little Rebecca and Devora, iced through me. If this testimony was correct, three years after Pepa was forced onto a cattle car headed east, different officers, wearing swastikas, packed her nieces into other boxcars headed west. Did these orphans face a Nazi deportation train to Bełżec's gas chambers on their own? Did anyone put their arms around them as they faced death? Did they hug each other? Words uttered by another Lviv child victim that I'd read on the wall at the Territory of Terror flashed in my mind: "God, I'm so young…I didn't even live. Why do I have to die?"

* * *

That evening, in the waning summer sun, I leaned on one of a series of stone slabs that reminded me of tombstones. They were part of a memorial erected in 2016, at the site of the Nazi-demolished Golden Rose Synagogue, to ensure the story of the more than one hundred thousand extinguished Jewish lives was not lost. For some, such recognition of the extermination of a people who once constituted one-third of the city remained a radical move.

"The Soviet system never commemorated the Holocaust. One reason for this is that once you define and identify one genocide, you can recognize other genocidal crimes," wrote author and Lviv native Victoria Amelina in the essay "Nothing Bad Has Ever Happened." "Decades of Soviet education and censorship ensured that even after the USSR collapsed, many in Lviv failed to realize the striking proximity of the Holocaust."

Now, the slabs blended in as a part of the lively nighttime landscape. A cello played a romantic melody to which small children danced at the adjoining pedestrian plaza. Young people drank and smoked on the ledge surrounding the monument. Few seemed to take in the engravings that spoke of this vibrant city's harrowing past. Still, I was grateful for the memorial's existence.

Amelina demanded more from her fellow Lvivians, urging them to join her in reckoning with the sinister elements of their city's deeply layered history: "The stories of the dead and the monuments commemorating them aren't meant to end a conversation, but rather to launch one." But her courage in facing the past was not enough to protect her from the violent present.

The day I visited Lviv's memorials to past reigns of terror, the Russian Federation killed the thirty-seven-year-old writer. Victoria Amelina had stopped at a restaurant in Eastern Ukraine with visiting international writers when a missile exploded, leaving her body sitting in a chair, pale and lifeless.

Words she had written now felt like a parting gift for her beloved

Lviv: "No city is doomed to be haunted forever. We break the spell not when we banish the ghosts, but when we invite them to breakfast."

* * *

As I packed my suitcase the next morning, doleful melodies filled my room.

"Is that a mass?" I asked the clerk at checkout.

"It's for our men. For our dead," she responded. "Sometimes there are five funerals in one day."

All day, I realized, she worked at the front desk of this posh hotel, welcoming visitors while hearing mothers mourn beloved children's lives cut short defending Ukraine.

I asked my driver to wait a moment—I wanted to pay a tribute before I left. I walked toward the gathered crowd and discreetly took a place in the back of the Baroque church filled with Ukrainians standing with bowed heads. Near the altar, I could just make out a woman crying, a casket, flowers.

After a few moments, I left the church, feeling too close to a communal loss that was not my own. The military band—a phalanx of young men dressed in green, hoisting brass instruments—soon followed me out. To their plodding beat, a parade of mourners flowed: clergy in dark robes, and then the coffin shouldered by six soldiers. A bereft young woman grasped the wooden box. It was all impeccably choreographed and desperately sad. The pain and instability of unrelenting violence masked by the lively streets of Lviv hit me. I hurried back to my driver, not wanting to miss the bus that would carry me away.

For four and a half hours we inched forward at the border. First, Ukrainian guards checked the luggage three times. I was told it was to confirm there were no men evading military service. Many more inspections and hours ensued to ensure passengers had the right to enter the European Union. Then, finally, we crossed to the Polish side. Our passports were stamped.

The bus then retraced my route past the death camps of Bełżec where our ancestors' ashes had decomposed into the earth, past the Tomaszów

Lubelski of Talia's grandmother's childhood and Zamość with its Rainbow Square. I thought of all the refugees who had searched for safety over the past century across these lands, all the births, bloodshed, and mass murder that had occurred, obscured now by an enchanting green in the evening light.

After ten hours on the road, it was nearly midnight when Talia welcomed me to the high-ceilinged prewar apartment we'd rented for her migration conference. Unwittingly, I'd selected a place in the former Warsaw ghetto adjacent to what had been the SS headquarters. That night, our sleep was restless. We tossed in the stuffy summer air as we found our way back to each other, and to a city that had unexpectedly delighted us the previous fall.

In the morning, the air raid siren app I had downloaded for Lviv lit up on my phone: "Proceed to a shelter." I had neglected to turn on the volume when entering Ukraine, and to delete it when leaving. A Russian Kalibr cruise missile fired from the Black Sea had demolished a residential apartment building and killed ten people in the early morning hours. It was the deadliest attack yet on Lviv. When I saw the news, I realized, with a catch of my breath, that I had never located the shelter in my hotel.

CHAPTER 18

Sybiraks

"When you're near the tank you just go—bomb!" The museum researcher demonstrated to our kids how to strike a Soviet military vehicle. Talia and I met each other's eyes. *What were we teaching our four-year-olds?*

Then I looked down to the iPad screens they clutched. "Whoa, you did it, Alma!" I exclaimed. "You hit a tank!"

On our initial visit to Poland, we had taken a side trip two hours northeast of Warsaw to a gleaming cement-and-steel institution recently opened to commemorate the deportation of Polish citizens. Unlike my dreadlocked guide at Territory of Terror in Lviv, the researcher waiting for us at Białystok's Sybir Memorial Museum wore close-cropped hair and a dress shirt. Marcin Zwolski graciously bought the kids a cake with whipped cream and raspberries in the café and dug out iPads with the game our kids were now playing, resisting a World War II Soviet invasion.

The game started with a vocabulary lesson. Deportation: "A repression that consists in forcing people to live in a distant place." And then Gulag: "A system for forced labor camps in the Soviet Union." With the basics down, the games began, and our kids were now immersed in trying to bomb Red Army tanks.

Marcin then led me into the exhibit, climbing up into a replica of a Soviet cattle car like the ones our families were forced to ride to Siberia.

Entering an immersive rendering of what I'd tried to imagine for so long put a spring in my step. The topic was stark, but I felt like I'd just received a profound gift: an entire institution that took this elusive history seriously enough to re-create it.

As I ascended with Marcin to the second floor of the Sybir Memorial Museum, the temperature plummeted. A stark maze of enormous sculptured letters spelling SYBIR greeted us. Marcin explained that in Polish the word represented the concept of Siberia, versus the actual geographic boundaries. "It means all the places where Polish people were sentenced, were deported." Sybir could be Kazakhstan, the Arctic Circle. Now I understood why our family members, even though they technically were deposited across the border in the Ural Mountains, always described where they had been deported as simply Siberia.

* * *

For weeks that stretched with each miserable minute, our grandparents had prayed to be liberated from the reeking train of terror. But when the wheels screeched to a halt at last and the door was flung open, they stared outside bewildered. As far as they could see, a smothering blanket of emerald taiga—boreal forests of towering pine and firs, hemlocks and spruces—covered the swampy earth. NKVD officers barked in piercing Russian to exit the cattle cars: *Now!* The deportees clutched their one suitcase and jumped down into a natural prison, walled in by the forest on three sides and an icy churning river on the other.

Just as Peshke and Mottel plummeted to a new level of despair, NKVD officers drove up in trucks, ordering the refugees to jump in. Then they took off into the woods. Every four miles or so one of the vehicles slowed at clearings with filthy barracks—large shacks, really—and deportees were ordered: *Get off; this is your new home.*

When it was my grandparents' turn to exit the truck, a few haggard, emaciated people awaited them. The settlement's residents looked the refugees over and then concluded: *Oh, you're not going to survive here. Only stronger people survive here.*

This beleaguered welcome committee knew from experience. Their group had been bigger when they had been dumped in the middle of this forest prison years earlier, after Stalin deemed them a danger to Soviet society. They had been among the more than 1.7 million deported farmers, derided as kulaks or wealthy peasants for allegedly resisting the collectivization of property. In 1929 Stalin began to ship them to these new "special settlements," forcibly removing entire groups of people as he endeavored to reorganize society.

Two years into an exile they were told would last a lifetime, did they know that they were captive in the biggest prison complex in the world? In the 1930s, Stalin merged the constellation of special settlements with preexisting camps and penal colonies. This terror complex was called the Gulag, an acronym for the Russian name: Main Administration of Corrective Labor Camps. Or, as the Soviets called them: "concentration camps." Some 18 million people would be forced into the Gulag, at least 1.6 million of whom would perish during their imprisonment.

In my grandparents' settlement, many of the initial prisoners in the decade since their arrival had surely starved or died of rampant diseases; others were transferred to even more remote outposts, leaving behind the shacks they had built for my family to occupy. The NKVD officers welcomed them with a tinge more optimism than the existing residents: *Most of you will survive, because you will get used to it, but if not, you will die like dogs. Long live Lenin, Marx, Engels, and Father Stalin.*

* * *

My grandparents soon stumbled around in rags. "Freezing and hungry, we were beside our wits, barely holding on to survival and starving with hunger, typhus, dysentery," Peshke recalled. But they survived. In their Gulag settlement, unlike many others, nobody died. "The air keeps you alive. I never got a headache there," my grandmother often told me.

The barrack where my grandparents and their siblings slept on beds of rotten boards consisted of a single room with a hole in the middle to be used as a toilet. "The first night that we were there, we were overcome by large rats and mice scrambling across our bodies," my grandmother recalled. "Lice and insects were everywhere."

A commandant's refrain, delivered to prisoners across the Gulag, soon dictated the rhythm of their days: *You must work. That is the basic law of Soviet life. He who does not work does not eat. Your salvation lies in labor. If you are weak, then work will make you strong. If you are ill, work will make you healthy. You have nothing else to do but work, and if you do not work, you will perish.*

On their first day, the men were marched deep into the forest until the commandant stopped and shouted: *Let's work!* An officer grabbed an axe, chopped a massive trunk just above the ground, and carved out a notch. Then he and a comrade picked up a shared saw the size of a small man and worked back and forth on the other side of the great tree. When it was almost at the notch, they hacked away with the axe again until the trunk toppled with a tremendous thud in the endless forest. The urbane Polish refugees—many of whom as storekeepers, teachers, and tailors had never previously hoisted an axe—looked on in awe and terror at the task they were now told to perform.

For Mottel, my grandfather, who passed along to me a petulant back, the work was torturous. Despite the "Pioneer" training he had received in Zamość, he had no talent for physical labor. One day he took out an axe and thrust it down on his foot, slicing his heavy shoe instead of the branches. Blood oozed.

Mottel was soon relegated to the women's brigade, which the NKVD agents walked to the grassy banks of the river and instructed to make haystacks to prepare for the winter.

This labor was less taxing physically but featured its own particular afflictions.

On the first day, an officer had lashed out with his scythe, seamlessly cutting the grasses in perfect rings.

Okay, now you do it, he commanded. My grandmother, expert with fine stitches, maneuvered a scythe almost as large as her body. Instead of perfect rings of grass, she scraped her own skin. The blood that trickled from legs and arms saved work for the swarming mosquitoes.

For their eight hours a day of required physical labor, plus additional time marching with heavy equipment, their group of eight was rationed one small loaf of bread made from straw mixed with flour. The siblings entrusted Peshke, the dressmaker, to use her tape measure to cut it into sixteen equal allotments. One day, she realized she could spirit off an extra slice and hide it from the others. At lunchtime, instead of relishing her measly extra portion, she collapsed.

What has happened to me?

She was starving but could not eat. That night, she placed the piece of bread on the rough-hewn table in their barrack and admitted her thievery.

* * *

Hunger was a plague throughout the settlements. Reports circulated of highly observant camp inmates who refused to eat food that was not ritually prepared, only to starve to death and be buried among the giant forests. Other religious women who had never so much as touched meat not cut by a shochet, a kosher butcher, broke down and skinned dogs to eat; some ate horsemeat. Prisoners of all levels of observance recalled foraging once the snow melted in the woods, collecting berries, wild nettles, mushrooms, and nuts.

Diseases ravaged bodies. Lack of fat caused a phenomenon of "night blindness"; dysentery abounded with its bloody diarrhea, or boils, and with the added trauma that body lice infested the swelling.

Prisoners were forced to work in freezing temperatures, marching out and back under the stars in winter. When they reached their worksite, someone would make a fire for the commandant, but the heat was not enough to stave off the cold. Toes and fingers were lost to frostbite. Only when touching a tool meant skin freezing to the metal would they receive an occasional reprieve.

Whatever Stalin hoped to gain from their captivity, he was not getting a financial return. An NKVD confidential report on "labor use of special settlers" found the refugees drained more resources than they produced: "A significant part of this contingent has an unscrupulous attitude toward production, is difficult to master, and labor productivity is quite low." Yet the party's answer was simply to insist the settlers work harder. Every so often the head of the camp would call all the prisoners to meetings and repeat to them the demoralizing mantra: *Don't dream of going home. It will not exist anymore. There will never again be a free Poland.*

* * *

On this, the Soviets were wrong. Poland held free elections again in 1991, and thirty years later, in 2021, its government proudly opened the Sybir Memorial Museum. Marcin told me that instrumental in advocating for the museum were "Sybiraks," people who had spent time in Siberia. Were my grandparents Sybiraks? Why, then, had I never heard the word before?

I asked, "Are there associations of people who were in Siberia?"

"Oh yes, one main Sybirak association, but they have of course many other associations."

Later I was welcomed into a Sybirak social media group upon sharing my grandparents' history but soon noticed that the names of other members tended to be Polish. I had long assumed my grandparents' deportation to Siberia was directly linked to the Nazi persecution of Jews. But the museum walls brought to life how of the more than 330,000 Polish citizens that Stalin deported to the Gulag during World War II, less than a quarter were Jewish. Even though the total number has been the subject of debate, with the Polish government in exile and some experts historically providing significantly higher overall numbers, from my research I learned there is no question that Jews were a minority of the Polish citizens the Soviets targeted.

Most of the gentile deportees were Catholic Poles. Their so-called crimes included being active in the military, landowners, or academics. For these Polish Sybiraks, many of whom were deported in the dead of winter, the Gulag was the nadir of a community's experience. Chances are, if they had been allowed to remain in Nazi-occupied Poland, most would have survived. Those Sybiraks who returned after the war confronted a Communist government that would not tolerate them freely sharing what they had suffered in the Soviet Union. As soon as they could, they ensured this terrible history of Siberian deportation was not forgotten, erecting hundreds of memorials across Poland connected to religious Catholic iconography, and most recently, backing this museum.

When the Sybirak group I joined planned an initial visit to the Sybir Memorial Museum, it chose Rosh Hashanah, one of the holiest days of the Jewish year. I realized these groups were not made primarily for, or of, Jews.

The reason for the divide ran deeper than the historic animosity of Poles for their Jewish citizens to one of historic perspectives. "There are two points of view," Marcin said in summing up the different attitudes. "When Polish people are talking about deportations, they are talking about suffering, about death, about all these tragedies. When Jews, Polish Jews, are talking about these deportations, they are talking about that they survived, because of these deportations."

As we thanked Marcin and departed the impressive building, our kids raced ahead of us toward the tracks that intersected the structure. The museum's site was intentionally located where trains departed east to Siberia in 1940. I saw another, parallel, significance in these tracks. Three years later, in 1943, the Germans jammed thousands of Jewish mothers and children into other trains, likely traversing these same tracks to Treblinka's death machines. Faced with that alternative, for our families, the legacy of exile and forced labor in Siberia would always be a most brutal salvation.

CHAPTER 19

Index of the Repressed

"Why did I wait so long?" I bemoaned to my friend Larisa on a call to her home in Siberia. I was finally ready to make the journey to the site of my grandparents' deportation. But I feared I had missed my chance. Larisa had offered to be my guide ever since we met as German Chancellor Scholars in 2006. Our backgrounds could not have been more different. I had left behind a tiny apartment over a bar in Brooklyn, Larisa one on remote Lake Baikal. I was single; she was married and had an eight-year-old daughter. But we instantly bonded over late-night swims and river bike rides.

Larisa was also the first person I'd ever met from Siberia, and I was eager to learn from her about life there. When I looked up where my grandparents had been kept captive, a province called Sverdlovsk, she offered to accompany me there. Only later did I grasp Siberia's immense scale. Sverdlovsk lay just beyond Siberia's western edge in the Ural Mountains, while Larisa lived two thousand miles to the east near the Mongolian border. No matter. I felt certain that one day I would visit Larisa's home and together we'd travel to the place my grandparents had endured forced labor.

Back when we met in 2006, the arc of history appeared clear. The Berlin Wall that had once separated us collapsed during our adolescence; the Cold War was over. Democracy was ascendant. Everywhere we toured in Germany, the government buildings seemed to be made of glass, reflecting the ethos of our time: transparency.

Now, in the 2020s, it felt like history was rewinding, with authoritarianism renewed and new walls built. Since Russia had invaded Ukraine, Sverdlovsk's capital, Yekaterinburg, had been linked to a series of arrests of Americans on wildly trumped-up and invented charges. Each felt startlingly closer to home than the last.

First, basketball star Brittney Griner, who played for the local team in Russia's premier league, was arrested at Moscow's International Airport after a small amount of medically prescribed hashish oil was found in her luggage. A Russian court sentenced her to a penal colony for nine years. Months after she was released in a high-stakes prisoner swap, the Russian secret police apprehended *Wall Street Journal* reporter Evan Gershkovich, the first journalist arrested on charges of spying for the United States since the Cold War. Then a beautician who worked with a friend in LA was arrested upon arrival to visit family in the city. Her crime? Treason for donating $51 to a pro-Ukrainian cause. That this string of arrests had a connection to Sverdlovsk was likely a coincidence. But it no longer appeared safe for me to travel there to investigate the region's legacy of Soviet political prisoners.

* * *

If I could not travel to Russia myself, I had an idea of someone who might be able to help me. In Warsaw, I had met a recent exile from St. Petersburg, Tatiana Kosinova. For more than three decades, she had broadcast a history of human rights abuses in the Soviet Union that Memorial International, the organization she worked for, revealed. The Nobel Peace Prize recognized the group in 2022 for their "outstanding effort to document war crimes, human rights abuses, and the abuse of power." But Memorial's staff was increasingly unsafe at home. Putin openly targeted the organization, accusing it of falsely blaming the Soviet Union for Nazi crimes. Just months before the Nobel recognition, the supreme court of the Russian Federation had shut down Memorial International. Many of its leaders like Tatiana, who were opposed to Moscow's full-scale invasion of Ukraine, and feared for their safety at home, had left Russia. They scattered to Poland, Lithuania, Israel, and elsewhere around the globe.

These activists and historians knew well what was at stake with a return to the silencing of dissent and the obfuscating of political crimes. While international tribunals exposed and prosecuted Nazi criminals within months of the end of World War II, Stalin had kept on killing and imprisoning. Even after he died and his successor decried those tactics, there was very little public reckoning.

It's not that nobody tried. Activists affiliated with Memorial had begun secretly tallying lists of victims and collecting stories before officially establishing an organization in 1987. By the time the Soviet Union collapsed and archives were opened, they had moved on to complex databases documenting state-sponsored terror. Memorial eventually succeeded in reviewing the files of about three million victims of repression, working in partnership with other activists, among them a group in Poland called KARTA Center.

Author Mikhal Dekel, who in her book *In the East* tracked down her Polish Jewish family's deportation to the Komi Republic, alerted me to a digital database where victims' records now lived. But even after my friend Larisa helped me try variations of our grandparents' names, the results came up empty.

The former coordinator of Memorial Society's Polish Program, Alexander Guryanov, explained to me why: The three million names in the database covered only about a quarter of the victims of Russian political terror. Archives did not generally freely release documents. In the case of the deportation of Polish citizens, limited financial resources had prevented the group from accessing all files, including documents held in Sverdlovsk, where our grandparents had been deported. And following the brief window of relative transparency and reckoning in Russia, researching victims of political repression had become much more difficult. I worried I'd hit a dead end.

Still, Tatiana urged me not to give up. While the government shut down Memorial's international arm, many local offshoots still operated.

Sverdlovsk, the province where our grandparents were deported, was one of them, although among the worst-off in Russia. Following the invasion of Ukraine, officials evicted Memorial from the Yekaterinburg office where they had worked for seventeen years. When organizers tried to move their library and archives into the Yeltsin Presidential Center, dedicated to fostering democracy and named after the Russian president who helped orchestrate the dissolution of the Soviet Union, the building was torched.

Tatiana, months later, wrote to me from Warsaw that while "tensions persist," her colleague Alexey Mosin was running the local office and had no plans to leave. "I hope he will answer and help you."

* * *

"Daniela, good afternoon!" Alexey responded with a warmth that transcended electronic communication. "I'll try to find the information... Send me all the data you have."

I offered to pay Alexey for his help, not realizing that would violate Russia's foreign agent law barring financial support from abroad. He quickly clarified: "Out of the question: We will be immediately closed by a court decision. We help free of charge."

After I sent over family records, I received no response for weeks. On social media, Alexey had seemed to defy fear of government persecution, sharing campaigns for jailed colleagues and posting photos defending Memorial in court. When he grew quiet there, too, I worried he had been imprisoned.

At last, Alexey's name popped up in my inbox. It turned out he had been busy planting his potato crop at his dacha. I was relieved that he was free, and now I felt convinced he could teach me about the captivity of my family. The mention of potatoes clinched it: Those hardy tubers had been key to their survival in Siberia.

* * *

I knew the story well from family lore. My great-uncle Moishe had returned to the Siberian barrack, eagerly grasping his wages. A carpenter, he had crafted a desk for the NKVD commandant. As compensation, he was paid in potatoes.

Moishe directed his siblings: *Half of these we're going to eat, and with the other half, I'm going to make a garden.*

They had little food, and hunger always lurked. Why was Moishe slashing at the frozen earth and burying half of the potatoes?

His siblings may have thought their youngest brother was crazy, but when the green buds emerged at the very beginning of summer, and, months later, they yanked the tubers out of the ground, they were the most delicious potatoes they had ever tasted. Gorgeous, big potatoes. They planned to cultivate more, preparing for next winter in this place NKVD officers swore would be their home for the rest of their lives.

You will never get away from here. Here you will have children; here you will stay.

* * *

Decades after my family left Siberia, could their records remain? Alexey believed so. He told me where we could find our documents: the Ministry of Internal Affairs archives. My stomach clenched. This agency of the Russian government, which ran the secret police under Stalin, now oversaw all law enforcement. Alexey warned that it was extremely difficult to get them to release information. We needed to strategize.

I turned to a Russian writer named Elena who, appalled by the invasion of Ukraine, had left behind her Moscow apartment and her parents and resettled in California. She would interpret for us.

We were still situating ourselves in my Los Angeles backyard office, the bright morning sun not yet warming its dark corners, when a white beard and face framed close to the screen popped up on my computer. In Yekaterinburg, it was night, twelve hours ahead. Alexey stroked his golden cat while above him Ural religious icons kept watch. I shared a map of where our family was deported to in the surrounding Sverdlovsk province, and he told us to wait. Then he reemerged with a magnifying glass held close to his screen. "Aha!" Alexey exclaimed. Talia's family's hell was not too far from his dacha, his family retreat outside of the city, a "wonderful place." How bizarre that he could feel that way. But I realized a warm cabin to retreat to, food, and medicine could transform a natural prison into a respite. Unable to travel to Russia, at last I felt, via Alexey, that I was getting close to the Gulag years.

Our grandparents' deportations sent them, along with some 10 percent of refugees deported that June of 1940, to the same province, Sverdlovsk. My grandparents landed about five hours' drive due north from the capital and Talia's two hours east. Knowing that they could have ended up in wildly different parts of the vast Soviet hinterlands in any one of thirteen provinces where Poles were deported, this seemed another symbol of the invisible string that connected them—and us. Just as my grandparents were chopping trees and slashing grasses in the endless taiga of Sverdlovsk, Talia's grandparents, Pepa and Leon, were doing the same.

* * *

Even in Siberian forced labor, the youthful Pepa found diversion. Within weeks of arriving, she took her autograph book out from her bag and handed it to a Russian man. He sketched colorful caricatures of Siberian men, with bulbous noses and feathers in their green wool hats and left an affectionate inscription in the little book: "To my beloved Pepa from Vasya." Who was this Vasya? Did Pepa have a flirtation with a Russian farmer who had been deported earlier? Did a bored NKVD guard, with an artistic bent, take a liking to her?

Whoever he was, the illustrator also left us a gift: the address, Achitskiy Sector, Quarter 59, written in Russian and dated July 23, 1940. Talia's uncle Zyg, in his recording, identified the same Achitskiy Sector as the place where his family was forced to relocate in Siberia. In doing so, he confirmed the story Talia's family told, that this place of captivity was where Leon and Pepa met. I wanted to know more. How did their budding relationship overlap with his first wife, Manya, left behind in Zamość? What attracted Pepa to this married man nineteen years her elder?

On these delicate matters, Talia's grandparents were predictably elusive. In Pepa's autograph book, I found no new clues of their relationship. After the Russian flirtation with Vasya, the recollections return to stark notes. One entry, written by a friend on September 12, 1940, shared the morose words of a Polish poet.

> You won't always recognize sadness, even when tears are flowing. Sometimes in your soul you feel your life is broken even though there is always a smile on your lips.
> Forever in Russia, Ural, For a kind and sweet Pepcia

Soon after, Pepa stopped collecting signatures and poems in her little brown book; many blank pages were never filled. Though she carried it with her for the rest of her life, dying with it stashed in her bedside table, something had changed in Siberia. Perhaps she had found her first real love and shut the book? Or she considered it a memento of her girlhood, which had so abruptly concluded?

* * *

Two weeks after Pepa's final entry came the holiest day of the Jewish calendar, Yom Kippur. Polish Jews, months into a sentence they were told would last a lifetime, wrestled with how to honor their faith. In the forests and in barracks filthy with stove smoke, they gathered in groups of at least ten men and tried to decipher the direction of Jerusalem. As was their custom, they wanted to face what remained of the twice-destroyed holiest of holies, the temple that Jews dispersed to the ends of the earth, like them, had prayed to return to for thousands of years.

A Russian corporal—watching his diminished charges chant, sway in unison, and then refuse food—muttered: *Strange people; they work, fast, and pray; very strange people indeed.*

In Leon's settlement, the commandant discovered the men praying and furiously barked at the refugees to return to their barracks:

You go home. There is no God. Get home. Get the hell out.

Though they ceased to recite their communal prayers, many of the undernourished prisoners fasted, a silent protest, an affirmation of belief in a power beyond the Supreme Soviet to determine their fate.

* * *

Eight decades later, Alexey was relentless in his fervor to expose Sverdlovsk's political history of forced labor, false imprisonment, and murder. He had been in court the day he spoke with me and Elena, appealing for the third time a decision that his Memorial Society branch had violated the foreign agent law. "They will do anything to liquidate us, but our goal is to keep working no matter what." Defiance sparked from his eyes. "All those years we've been warning that if we don't start actually learning from our collective past," he told us, "the history might repeat itself."

Now Alexey felt he was living that predicted nightmare, a return to his nation's oppressive past. He was no longer permitted to teach history since Memorial had been deemed a danger to society. Instead, he focused more on his potatoes. "Not the greatest harvest this year, but I think it's going to be enough for winter," he said when we spoke later in the fall. "You never know what will come next, so the family needs to have a food bank."

His mother-in-law, then ninety-seven, still remembered being deported at the age of three to special settlements. His great-great-grandfather faced an even more dire fate. The NKVD arrested him, at the age of eighty, in 1937. The family never saw him again. Alexey began to search for what happened to this relative he never knew and discovered buried in archives that he had been falsely accused of participating in a "counter-revolutionary fascist organization of rebel churchmen." He was shot dead one month after his arrest. Uncovering what happened in his own family drew Alexey to memorializing other victims of political repression in the USSR. "It is difficult to work with these documents, but it is necessary," he concluded. "It is necessary to know, to remember, to talk about it."

"What do you think my chances are of finding our grandparents' records?" I asked.

"It will be very hard now," he told me. "The most important thing is that you preserve your desire to know your family history—then you will absolutely find what you're looking for."

Someday he would introduce me to Yekaterinburg, he promised. I flushed with gratitude for this courageous potato-farming historian and his faith in my search. After the call, my interpreter, Elena, and I lingered in my garden, feeding off the energy from Alexey. Every day, she told me, she weighed the risks of returning to Moscow. Elena had not seen her parents for more than two years. Her longing for a home to which she did not know if she'd be able to return was palpable.

* * *

I printed out a letter to the Sverdlovsk secret police archives requesting our grandparents' records and biked to the post office. "We don't service that place," the mail clerk said as she looked up from her computer, startled to see my destination denied. Neither of us were aware the United States had cut off mail service to Russia.

Undeterred, I asked my friend Larisa to print out the letter and send it from Siberia. That took a few days since a minus-forty-degree cold spell had "dead-frozen" her car battery. About a month later, a message in Cyrillic letters from Russia's Ministry of Internal Affairs thrillingly landed in my inbox. But when I read a translated version of the message, my enthusiasm dimmed. To protect "personal secrets, family secrets and other information about citizens," they required notarized documents. Somehow, despite the postal embargo, I would need to get certified paperwork to Yekaterinburg.

* * *

Talia drove us straight from Aviv's soccer game to a San Fernando Valley strip mall for a third attempt at submitting a request. As we walked up the stairs above a smoke shop to Tarzana Notary, she shared her doubts about my plan to pay hundreds of dollars to an Uzbek woman who specialized in Russian documents. I had not yet told her we would also need to hire a courier to whisk our application in someone's suitcase to Moscow, from where it would be mailed to Yekaterinburg and the Sverdlovsk office of the Ministry of Internal Affairs. But we had gone so far, I did not want to stop now.

Tarzana Notary translated our documents into Russian, secured official seals, and took our fingerprints. Then the Uzbek owner handed the papers off to an older man with a ticket to Moscow. Weeks later, another message arrived with a subject in Cyrillic. Contact number two had been achieved. But, again, an obstacle. This time the archives wanted a local designated representative. Alexey emailed a photo of his passport picture, and I paid yet more money to a notary to take our fingerprints, translate a letter indicating power of attorney, and get it lodged in someone else's suitcase to Moscow and then mailed across Russia.

Months later, as I began to fear we had invested all of this for nothing, we received a third and final email from the Sverdlovsk State Ministry of Internal Affairs. They had found a photo and certificate of Talia's grandfather and would send it to Alexey. No other relatives were mentioned. Still, a surge of hope pulsed through me.

* * *

Weeks later, Alexey wrote to me that he had received an envelope from the Ministry of Internal Affairs. They had identified records for Leon, Peshke, and Mottel in their "personal files of people registered in the special settlements." He scanned the contents and sent to me the first papers I had documenting how our grandparents were deported on the same NKVD order on June 10, 1940, along with some seventy thousand other refugees.

Upon opening a photo attachment, I faced the eerie stare of a gaunt man, right eye wandering to the left. He had a dark quilted jacket wrapped around him, hair cropped short. I had expected Talia's grandfather, but this man resembled someone else. I sent the photo to my uncle, who wrote back immediately: "Looks like my dad! But too severe." No, I told him, this *was* his father, Mottel. He's almost ghostly in the image. For the first time, my uncle could witness his father's suffering.

Days later, Alexey wrote. He had found another photo that had been stuck to the envelope. In a quilted jacket that matched my grandfather's, Talia's grandfather stood leading a sickly looking horse. Both undernourished men wore what Russians called a telogreika, a body warmer, which Moscow deployed for Red Army soldiers and Gulag prisoners alike to keep them from freezing in subzero temperatures.

The documents sent via suitcases across the world, the interviews and translations, the hundreds of dollars, all felt worth it to be able to stare into the eyes of these imprisoned men and confront a past that always felt ephemeral.

This was a history that should have sent shock waves through the public, warning about the state's unchecked power and abuse of the individual when it viciously pursued a class of people. Instead, these carefully documented photos and records had been stashed in the archives for decades. In a sharp contrast to German Holocaust records, whose digital files were now accessible almost anywhere to me and countless scholars and descendants around the world, these documents were behind walls of bureaucracy and government embargoes. They were unreachable to all but the most persistent and fortunate.

And we were still short the answer to one question: What could Pepa's records reveal? Alexey encouraged me to keep up the search. But I was out of money, and drive, to delve further into this labyrinthian system. Any records of Soviet abuses against Talia's grandmother, like millions more, would remain closed to history.

CHAPTER 20

An Outstretched Arm

Only my grandmother would dare to question my father when, in his deep professorial voice, he proclaimed the Passover seder's passage: "The Lord brought us out of Egypt with a strong hand and with an outstretched arm."

"What outstretched arm? Feh," a frail but determined voice scoffed.

More than thirty guests looked up at my father expectantly. He loomed over a long table laden with stacks of matzah, a gnarled horseradish root my mom pulled from her garden, and five types of charoset she made with ingredients tracing the Jewish Diaspora—from bananas to dates to the Ashkenazi apples, nuts, and wine. Dad had no words to respond to his mother.

Instead, he moved on to the symbolic four questions, starting with the wise child: "What are the laws that God has commanded us?"

I had always assumed that the reason for my grandmother's rejection of the two-thousand-year-old redemption story was the slaughter of her parents and sisters that she had left behind in Zamość. But now, as I delved deeper, I realized that she felt God had abandoned her as well.

Peshke had shared her deepest moment of despair with her children. I recalled a story my uncle Sam had told me. Trudging in the snowy woods one day, Peshke sat down on a log and declared to her brigade: *Leave me here to die.* An elderly man with a gray beard would not stand for it. He held her and counseled: *My dear daughter, even the longest night comes to an end.* The sage words shook Peshke, renewing hope to propel her forward.

That spark was crucial to the survival of other Gulag prisoners as well. "The difference between the German death camps and the Soviet concentration camps lies in one small word, and a whole world of difference lies in it: *hope*," wrote former Israeli Prime Minister Menachem Begin of his World War II imprisonment in the Soviet Union. "The German exterminators gave their victims no prospect of living; the prisoners in the Soviet labour camps have such a chance."

NKVD officers had arrested Begin for "anti-revolutionary" activity. During long nights of interrogation, officers made it clear he had been targeted due to his activities as a leader of Beitar, the youth arm of Jabotinsky's militant Zionist movement. While Begin waited to be sentenced, he secretly celebrated the feast of Passover in his cell. The traditional four glasses of wine were replaced with sips of NKVD coffee. Then the future Israeli prime minister and his cellmate proclaimed the final two sentences of the Passover seder: "This year we are slaves, next year may we be free men. This year we are here, may we next year be in Jerusalem."

Begin would be sent to a forced labor camp in brutal arctic conditions, a harsher Gulag imprisonment than the special settlements. But he, like my grandmother, survived.

* * *

Peshke's will to live reignited, she approached the commandant: *I'm a good dressmaker. Why should I work so hard to cut a little grass?*

The commandant gave her a chance. Peshke was told to report to another barrack, where a pile of torn olive-green uniforms awaited her. From then on, she and her sister-in-law mended Red Army jackets and pants sent east from the front. Sometimes, the NKVD officers demanded extra work, sewing a dress for a wife or daughter. In exchange, Peshke received a cup of milk or some eggs.

For some refugees, additional sustenance came all the way from Poland. The NKVD officers allowed them to write home—but censored their letters, maintaining control while ensuring the outside world knew the deportees were alive. Letters from Peshke's family in Zamość linked her to a world beyond the taiga, to a humanity that had been stripped from her in the cattle cars. She surely found clues in their correspondence of the tightening of the German occupation, with hundreds of men being conscripted for forced labor. Still, despite the hardships, life likely appeared easier back home in Poland.

But then Peshke's parents wrote that they, too, were displaced—forced to move into a ghetto in the poorest part of town. I never saw the letter, having only heard my grandmother's descriptions. So I do not know if they also told her that, like other Zamość Jews, they had been crowded into wooden ramshackle dwellings. Did my great-grandparents share that they were drawing water from dirty open streams since there were no wells in their new location? Was their hunger written in code, like some messages sent out of the ghetto to defy the censors? All my grandmother revealed she learned in a letter was that their relatives left behind in Zamość were forced into a ghetto. Beyond that, nothing.

The fate of the Jews who remained in Poland and those deported to the Gulag would soon irrevocably diverge. Suffering was the road for all, but annihilation would be the destination of Jews who did not escape the reach of the Third Reich. In January 1941, the Nazi leadership authorized preparations for a "complete solution of the Jewish question." Months later, Hitler inadvertently set into motion the liberation of Polish prisoners from Stalin's Gulag, among them our Jewish grandparents.

* * *

Mottel and Peshke were in their barrack on one of those long summer nights in the Ural Mountains when someone rapped on the door and erupted in three unbelievable, ecstatic words: *We are freed!*

On August 12, 1941, the Presidium of the Supreme Soviet had issued an amnesty for Polish prisoners. Stalin had been left with little choice but to do so if he wanted his country to survive the German assault. Two months earlier, after he recovered from his shock over

Hitler's backstabbing attack, he needed to secure new allies. The British, who housed the Polish government in exile, agreed to team up with the Soviet Union on one condition: Polish prisoners must be released and be free to form an army.

The news that Polish prisoners were no longer enemies of the people, but comrades in arms of the Soviets, moved unevenly through the Gulag's prisons, camps, special settlements, and other places of exile. Some were freed within days. For others, it would take months or even years to be released. But Peshke and Mottel, Leon and Pepa, did not need to wait long.

* * *

The commandant instructed the Gerson siblings to pick up papers confirming their release and registering where they wanted to go next. After a year of slave labor, they possessed scant rubles. Some of the deportees considered an offer to remain in the settlements. Despite the misery, they determined at least they'd have a roof against the elements. But most followed this sage advice: *When the Russians let you go, you go. Lose no time because nobody knows whether or when the Soviet authorities might change their decision.*

The band of eight Gerson siblings and spouses assembled their ragged belongings and set out to walk the twenty or so miles to the closest town with a railroad station and a post office. As they trudged, they encountered distant relatives and former neighbors who had been sent to other settlements in the forest, reuniting in joy and trepidation of what they could face next.

In town, my great-uncle Simon secured a treasured job as a tailor for NKVD officers, receiving a pack of cigarettes every day. The others helped out occasionally in the shop and sold some of their remaining belongings from Poland on the black market. For a moment, it appeared they had gained a footing. But by the end of October, the Germans appeared poised to take Moscow, and the siblings decided they had to move again.

How did they, lacking a map or guidebook, determine where to go next? Everyone in my family seemed to tell me a different story. My grandparents said the plan was to get to Iran and then from there on to Palestine. Moishe said they headed south in search of warmth after freezing in Siberia. Simon said that the war was encroaching, and they traveled in the opposite direction of the front.

Whichever rationale dictated their route, the siblings had joined a scattershot departure of the tens of thousands of Polish Jews recently released from the Gulag, all now headed toward the Central Asian Soviet Republics. "Polish Jews who took part in it were probably reminded of the sojourn of their ancestors in Babylon," observed the diplomat Xavier Pruszynski. "It was a migration on a gigantic scale, recalling ancient times."

* * *

To suffer exile is a recurring plight of the Jewish people dating to their origins. Adam and Eve were expelled from the Garden of Eden; Cain was condemned to be a fugitive; Abraham's descendants would be "strangers in a land not their own." And the Exodus from Egypt is a pivotal event in the Torah, reenacted each year in the Passover seder as a paradigm of future redemption. In it, following a rapid release from bondage and crossing the Red Sea, the Israelites entered a new stage: forty years of wandering in the desert.

At their lowest moments, Polish Jewish refugees often found strength from their tradition and the knowledge that others had survived before them. Of more than ten different Hebrew words the Torah uses to distinguish types of displacement, "נוּעַ" or "nua" is often used to describe the Israelites' plight, capturing being in motion without a fixed destination.

Many Polish Jews, after being liberated from the Gulag and arriving in Central Asia, took on a new collective identity as "wanderers." "I wandered through Russia for several months," Menachem Begin, the future Israeli prime minister, wrote of his journey upon liberation from his forced labor camp. "I slept in railway stations, in parks, in yards next to dirty hovels. Hunger and homelessness were the lot of wanderers like myself."

While Russian speakers may still have labeled these Polish Jews "bezhenets," people on the run, they often used the Yiddish word "וואַנדערערס" or "vanderers" to describe themselves. They were not moving fast; they were not fleeing. Rather, after being released from the Gulag, they were stuck wandering for years in the deserts, metaphoric and real, of Central Asia.

* * *

In the fall of 1941, our grandparents, filthy and fatigued, climbed on and off trains. At stops the migrants would congregate in their search for food. Without time for the lines outside the state stores with Stalin's picture hanging on the wall, they raced to the local bazaar for a quick purchase or a barter. They passed fresh posters extolling all who saw them to join the effort to save "Holy Mother Russia." Across the tracks, they surely heard women wail, as sons who had been drafted to the Red Army headed west toward the fighting.

As the Gerson siblings left Russia behind, the air became warmer and drier. They chugged on through the windswept Kazakh Steppe, with its wild horses and antelopes sprinting along golden grasslands that stretched into the horizon. The land transformed to desert, and they must have called out with the thrill of spotting their first camels. Later, as their path traced the ancient Silk Route, where merchants from the Middle East still passed through on their way to China, did they marvel at the towering ancient mosques and madrasas of Uzbekistan? Did they feel the sting of sandstorms that beat around the yurts of nomadic peoples in Turkmenistan?

At last, they approached the Iranian border. But there the Soviet authorities halted their journey, preventing them from leaving the country. Polish refugees, no longer prisoners, but also not free to depart. Peshke and Mottel's train then backtracked to the country where masses of fellow Eastern European Jews had descended: Uzbekistan.

CHAPTER 21

Tashkent Station

My plane touched down with a thud and screeched to a stop. Air reeking of burned rubber seeped into the cabin as the back doors flew open. I descended the stairs, the first person from my family to step on Uzbek ground in more than seven decades. Instead of the elation I had anticipated upon arriving, anxiety rattled through me. Should I have traveled halfway around the world from my wife and children to an authoritarian state?

I was familiar with the risks. I'd studied Uzbekistan's post-Soviet history and longtime dictator, Islam Karimov—infamous for his deadly crackdowns on suspected fervent Muslims, restricting his own daughter to house arrest, and allegedly boiling political dissenters alive. But I also knew that foreigners like me were not often targeted, and, in recent years, the situation had eased. Karimov died in 2016. Civil society had expanded under his successor. Uzbekistan was far from the war in Ukraine, and this was a relatively safe time to visit.

Still, Central Asia felt too far and uncertain for Talia and me to visit together, with or without the kids. She also lacked my long-standing curiosity about this place. Talia's grandparents never spoke about Uzbekistan; we were not even completely certain they had been here. Her uncle Zyg told wild stories of Tashkent, the capital city where I had just landed, but he could not recall whether Talia's grandfather was still with him when he arrived.

While Pepa and Leon revealed nothing of this chapter after liberation from the Gulag, my grandparents, Mottel and Peshke, ensured that we knew their suffering did not end when they left Siberia. Uzbekistan was the far point in their exile, the place where one of their band of eight perished and another sibling came devastatingly close. But this fertile Central Asian country was also a site of rebirth. I had grown up hearing a tapestry of stories and always wanted to experience this place of extremes for myself.

Finally, this was my chance. I had picked my travel dates months earlier based on a break in my teaching schedule. Days before I left Los Angeles, I discovered a coincidence that felt fated. The first memorial paying tribute to Uzbekistan's sheltering hundreds of thousands of Jews from the Nazis would be unveiled the morning of my arrival. The ceremony started at 10:00 a.m. I landed in Tashkent at 7:28 a.m. that morning.

Within a little over an hour, I dropped my bag in a hotel room draped in purple, scrubbed off a night spent lodged in a middle seat, grabbed a blini with rose jam from the breakfast buffet, and climbed into a micro white Chevy taxi. My initial trepidation dissipated as the driver raced along the grand boulevards of Tashkent. Out the window flowed an architectural history of Uzbekistan: Domed exquisite mosques and madrassas, ornate remnants of Russian imperialist buildings, stark Communist-era bloc apartment complexes, and cranes building sleek blue glass structures.

At a central square, I stared up at a giant bronze statue of national hero Amir Timur on horseback, feared as ruthless Tamerlane in the west while heralded here as the courageous founder of a massive medieval empire. Moscow had occupied Tashkent in 1865 and, by the end of the nineteenth century, colonized all of Central Asia. Previously at this site, edifices to Russian conquerors had been erected, then to Lenin, Stalin, Marx. Since Uzbekistan became independent of Moscow in 1991, Timur's bold likeness had reigned.

The taxi pulled up to the sprawling Victory Park complex with minutes to spare. I had arrived at what appeared to be the Disney World of World War II memorials. The scale was massive. Interactive installations stretched over a park the size of twenty football fields, leading to a museum at the bottom of the hill. A series of cement monuments lined the entry path with the dates "1941" to "1945" inscribed in numbers larger than my head—reflecting Moscow's version of how their Great Patriotic War started only when the Nazis turned on them, not two years earlier when they colluded with Germany to invade Poland. Droves of middle schoolers scrambled through trenches and old trains.

I peeked into a giant room filled with a re-creation of Tashkent Station, complete with mannequins of well-fed European newcomers sitting in a spacious waiting room next to soldiers with Red Army wool jackets and green hats. The Uzbek investment in engaging the next generation in this wartime refugee history amazed me, but I was also puzzled. This version of Tashkent Station bore little resemblance to the stories I had heard and read recalling a tumultuous railyard overrun with desperate and sick people.

* * *

"Everyone wanted to go to Tashkent," the poet Aleksander Wat said of the onslaught of refugees. "Why Tashkent? Because Tashkent was a 'city of bread.'" He was referring to a reputation that was conferred by a popular book of that name. *City of Bread,* published in 1923, had rhapsodized about plentiful provisions that many Russians found in the city of Tashkent at a time of famine elsewhere. The next year Moscow had established the Uzbek Soviet Socialist Republic, a new country based on ethnic lines, and soon its food situation shifted drastically. The Kremlin collectivized farms and ordered agricultural producers to focus on cotton for the USSR. By the time of World War II, food that previously could be imported to Tashkent from nearby farms was no longer accessible.

"I was in Tashkent, and people were dying on the streets there," Wat, who also arrived in Uzbekistan after being freed from the Gulag, recounted. But still, all around him he watched as other people came expecting sustenance. "That's the power of a title: *Tashkent, City of*

Bread," Wat reflected. "Magic words." Perhaps that misleading reputation was why the Gerson siblings reversed toward the Uzbek capital, hoping for a respite after being turned away at the Iranian border.

Instead, droves of displaced people, many desperately ill, likely greeted my grandparents' train. There were not just freed Polish deportees packing the platform. Moscow had relocated millions of its citizens in an effort to preserve national prosperity and security against Berlin's attack. Central Asia, a far point in the Soviet Union, was a top destination.

"The plaza before the station was a billowing, raging sea of humanity. Half of Russia had been evacuated to Central Asia and there were also hundreds of thousands from Poland, Lithuania, Latvia, Estonia, Romania," Yitzchok Perlov said, describing the scene in his memoir *The Adventures of One Yitzchok*. "As with refugees all over the world, denizens of the underworld also congregated here, headed by swaggering youngsters from Odessa." Russian actress Tatiana Okunevskaya compared Tashkent to a "leech that has sucked its fill." It is "bursting," she wrote. "There is nowhere left to settle, nothing to eat."

* * *

As I took in the expanse of Victory Park, I was intensely curious as to why a romanticized intake of refugees figured so prominently. But my questions would have to wait.

At the far side of the complex, dignitaries already milled around a covered monument, modest in scale compared with the rest of the park. The Israeli ambassador to Uzbekistan, Zehavit Ben-Hillel, pulled up in a black SUV. Later that morning, she sat with me in the shade and told me how, as the news had gone public that she would be serving in Uzbekistan, people began sending her personal stories. Strangers wrote her about grandparents who fell in love upon being relocated to Tashkent, and fellow dignitaries confided that they'd been born in a communal agricultural village.

The ambassador had previously held diplomatic posts in Germany, Peru, and Canada. Never had she faced this tide of Israelis wanting to share with her a connection to a place. She had anticipated hearing from the hundreds of thousands of Bukharan Jews, whose heritage in Uzbekistan could be traced for more than two thousand years. But these were Ashkenazi Jews whose families had spent only a few—often miserable but lifesaving—years in Central Asia.

As a member of the Israeli foreign service, the ambassador knew well the fabled sagas of Jewish survival beyond the reach of the Third Reich: the Kindertransport, the Shanghai ghetto, the last-minute visas to Latin America. But she had not heard about the Polish Jews who spent World War II in Uzbekistan, even though their numbers were larger than the more famous sagas of refuge.

One reason could be found in the experiences of the writer Julius Margolin. In the immediate aftermath of the war, when he documented his deportation to the Gulag, powerful socialists in Palestine dismissed him for highlighting the crimes of the Soviet Union, which then supported the founding of the Jewish state. Later, a French lawyer instructed Margolin that since Stalin had defeated Hitler, it was "inappropriate for a Jew to oppose the state that saved the Jews." And when the United States and Israel turned on the Soviet Union, saying that it even inadvertently provided a refuge was unacceptable. Survival through imprisonment and forced exile in its territories seemed to be a story no one wanted to hear.

Now, nearly eight decades after the end of the war, one of Ambassador Ben-Hillel's first initiatives in conjunction with the Uzbek government was to publicly memorialize this story of Jewish survival in Muslim Central Asia. And so, on this sweltering day, she stood at the podium and addressed Uzbek men sitting erect in green military uniforms with gold tassels, a couple of observant Jews with long coats and dark hats, and a smattering of foreign dignitaries.

A military band raised their brass instruments as the ambassador revealed a stone monument with a bronze hand outlay on one side and a round loaf of Uzbek bread on the other—along with a proclamation inscribed in gold lettering in four languages, concluding: "Thanks to the hospitality of the Uzbek people, who shared their bread with them, the refugees found shelter here. The Jewish people and the State of Israel remember and cherish this gesture with gratitude."

Was I grateful to Uzbekistan? Were our grandparents? As the ambassador consecrated the monument, I pondered the nature of their relationship with this country. To me, it had always been the most intriguing stop along their five-thousand-mile journey, but also one of intense affliction. I had traveled halfway around the world to see if I could locate the mysterious origins of my father, to tie me closer to his essence now that he was gone, and to probe my connection to this complex place.

* * *

The next morning, I ventured out in the dry heat and chanced upon one of Tashkent's bazaars opening. The market evoked the richness of the souks overflowing with produce and foods I had visited in Arab countries, except more spacious and tranquil; one egg vendor smiled at me as she sang to herself seductively, peaceful in her own world. I inhaled the crimson spices, neatly stacked frisbee-sized loaves of round bread indented in the middle, burgundy cherries, and at last landed on the pyramid stacks of watermelons. This was what I had been looking for.

Bread may have been in short supply, but the fruit of Uzbekistan had been a revelation to my grandmother, reeling from the deprivation of Siberia. "The nicest grapes and watermelons," she would say, "in the whole world." Then she repeated what nobody could comprehend unless they, too, knew Uzbekistan. "The whole world, I'm telling you."

In the next breath my grandmother recalled the devastation that followed the sweetness. Refugees who'd starved in the labor camps sank their teeth eagerly into the luscious flesh. Soon they started to die. Typhoid, which spread through feces in water and grubby fruit, was rampant. Malnourishment hastened the decimation. Each morning revealed more bodies of refugees who had perished. Orphanages filled.

Talia's uncle Zyg recalled vividly the anguish he encountered upon sliding into the Uzbek Republic's capital city as one of an unknown number of illegal refugee residents. "In Tashkent, they sold a hamburger from people," he said. "When they buried the people, they take out the meat." I assumed this was the stuff of legend, as did various scholars, but historian Albert Kaganovitch writes in *Exodus and Its Aftermath* that incidents were documented, and even names the phenomenon: "market cannibalism, when people were killed for the purpose of subsequent sale of their flesh at the market to inexperienced buyers."

* * *

Such desperation was nowhere to be found in the sprawling tribute to World War II at Victory Park. On a second visit, I stared up at a larger-than-life representation of Tashkent Station, a mural at the entrance of the park's Glory Museum, painted as almost bucolic two-way traffic. Robust Uzbek soldiers with dark hair, bronzed skin, and round Turkic faces board a train with a poster of a Russian woman in red, left arm raised in salute and the words "The Motherland Is Calling."

On the arriving side of the tracks, mill families with European features—pale skin, fur caps on the men, scarves wrapped around the women's long hair. "The scene of the arrival of adults and children of different nationalities evacuated from the frontline territories to the station is especially touching," the description reads on the mural. "It is filled with the kindness and cordial warmth inherent in our people."

I noticed an odd absence as I read through the exhibits. The only place I found the word "bezhenets" or "refugees" was in the new monument that the Israeli government had sponsored. Everywhere else, the displaced people were only referred to as "evacuees."

By then I knew that most of the millions of migrants on the move in the USSR during World War II were Soviet citizens whom the Kremlin identified as evacuees. The term was brought into official parlance in 1941 as Moscow endeavored to "manage and control displacement itself," writes historian Rebecca Manley in *To the Tashkent Station*. The scale of the ensuing state-organized population transfer was staggering, and it saved countless lives, including likely tens of thousands, if not hundreds of thousands, of Polish Jews.

But this was not primarily a humanitarian mission. Even though the Kremlin knew of Hitler's targeting of Jews, no specific effort was made to protect them. The Soviet government prioritized protecting national interests—factories, goods, and so-called "human resources"—from falling into the hands of the enemy. In addition to the large-scale evacuations, during and in the lead-up to World War II, Stalin also ethnically cleansed groups of Soviet citizens—among them Germans, Finns, and Crimean Tatars—often due to unfounded allegations of "collaboration" with enemies. Arriving first in Uzbekistan were roughly 175,000 ethnic Koreans violently packed into trains from the Soviet Far East near the Pacific Ocean.

Central Asia during World War II was home to this mix of millions of evacuees, forced migrants, and refugees. Yet my museum guide denied that anyone but evacuees relocated to Uzbekistan during World War II. Why would this cultural institution, so intent on celebrating its history of welcoming the needy, not name the refugees or forced migrants? In this museum, I realized, Stalin was not recalled as a tyrant guilty of deportations or ethnic cleansing. Here he was the hero who defeated fascism.

Over lunch an Uzbek friend from college who lived in Tashkent helped me better understand why these sinister legacies of Soviet history would not be included in the new museum. For years after the end of Communist rule, Tashkent—under its former leader, Karimov—had tried to get rid of any remnants of the colonial and Soviet past, taking Cyrillic out of the Uzbek alphabet, Russian out of official conversations, and even the word "Victory" out of local commemorations of World War II. But the new president was taking a different approach to Russia; this museum was a symbolic gesture of rapprochement.

The renewed relations were particularly sensitive after Putin invaded Ukraine. Uzbekistan did not want to cut off Russia, once again its biggest trading partner, but it also did not want to fall prey to Moscow's renewed imperialism. Officially Tashkent remained neutral. But in this museum, where a video of the Uzbek president sitting next to Putin at

Victory Day celebrations played on repeat, the allegiances to Moscow were laid bare.

* * *

The more complicated historic truth was that the newcomers to Uzbekistan during World War II—regardless of whether they arrived by force, choice, or some combination of the two—were an onslaught of more mouths at a time of widespread debilitating hunger. Not surprisingly, they were not always well received. Still, many courageous Uzbeks did share the little they had with their new Jewish neighbors and went beyond the opening of their homes, which was frequently demanded of them. A teen refugee, whose mother had recently died, recalled being sustained with hot cakes and dried fruit that local Uzbeks placed in her yurt. And one of the most prized Uzbek poets, Gafur Gulom, wrote the poem "I Am a Jew." It presented a powerful statement of solidarity from a Muslim in support of common humanity, ending with "I am a person."

As I walked through the gleaming Soviet-era cement-and-glass Tashkent Station after a few days acclimating to the city, I stirred with gratitude that I was getting to experience Uzbekistan, in all its confounding complexities, for myself—and for my father, who'd dreamed of returning but never did.

But to learn more, I needed to leave the capital.

My grandparents were not allowed to stay in Tashkent. The city was too full. And so, I set out to where their train traveled next, Samarkand, the fabled Silk Road city, prized by Genghis Khan and Alexander the Great, and the place my father believed he was born.

CHAPTER 22

Samarkand Blessings

I settled into my seat on a sleek high-speed train for the two-and-a-half-hour trip to Samarkand. A woman with an emerald dress observed me across the aisle with eyes that flashed below a matching head covering. An older man removed his finely embroidered skullcap and placed it on a hook. A child peeked at me from behind his seat. Just as I took in their unfamiliar clothes, they scoped me out as well.

Samarkand was the place of birth listed on my father's passport. But he was not exactly of this place. He held no memories of it, leaving before he could even walk. He told my mother he feared authorities would apprehend him if he returned, and never let him leave. I thought that was an odd excuse for a global traveler like my father, but then I read of how another refugee mother admonished her daughter who was born in Soviet Central Asia: "Don't ever go there. They'll think you're one of theirs and want to keep you."

Now it was too late for him to ever return. My father was dead, like the older generation of Yiddish-speaking relatives who had once sat around our Passover seder table. And still, it felt right for me to be traveling to Samarkand now, to finally see with my own eyes where he came from, how far my grandparents wandered so we could live. I tingled with an energy that had mounted over the past few days.

The train bell rang. The conductor made an announcement in Russian and Uzbek. I could decipher just one word: "Samarkand."

* * *

"Danyelochka!" The Russian diminutive of my name rang out.

I spotted on the platform a tall and lean Russian couple, my friends Lilia and Oleg. They had recently fled from their native St. Petersburg to Uzbekistan—another reason Talia had encouraged me to make this trip now. Oleg was wearing a T-shirt with "Odious Smell of Truth" scribbled across it in English, shorts, and sandals; Lilia was casual and cool in a knee-length floral cotton skirt. Both opened their arms and took me into a full embrace imbued with the novelty of reuniting in Uzbekistan, as well as the trauma they had endured in recent months.

Our friendship had been sealed sixteen years earlier when we'd been selected as fellows for the German cultural diplomacy fellowship where I'd met my Siberian friend Larisa. I instantly adored Oleg and Lilia, who studied the growth of flea markets in former Communist countries. That winter, I'd traveled from Berlin to spend New Year's with them in St. Petersburg. We sat on Lilia's couch, flipping through old photo albums and laughing at their outfits, which changed as the years passed from the bleak monotones of their childhood to more colorful ones as freedoms and commerce grew. We toasted champagne and sampled caviar, secure in our interconnected future, as Lilia's mother listened to Putin deliver his New Year's address on the television droning in the background.

But that future, now our present, was not what we had imagined.

Even Oleg, an accomplished social scientist, was stunned to wake up on a winter morning to the news that Russia had started bombing innocent people in cities and that troops had crossed the border into Ukraine. "I never imagined this would happen," he wrote to me hours later. His words sounded eerily familiar. My grandmother, reflecting on the days leading up to when Germany invaded Poland, declared, "It didn't come to anybody's mind that there could be a war."

"I feel shocked, and we do not know what to do," Lilia wrote. A week later, an even darker message arrived: "We are lost and depressed, not welcome in our country or outside of it." They were on an unofficial list of foreign agents since they received funding from abroad for their research; they knew their livelihood could dissolve if they remained in St. Petersburg. They also realized within days of the invasion they could not stay in their recently renovated dream home in the city they adored. "Oh, come on, calm down," loved ones chided them. But the couple feared that if they stayed, they would end up in jail like friends of theirs for opposing Putin's war.

"It's getting more and more dangerous here," Lilia wrote.

"Are you leaving the country?"

"Trying to do this tonight. But we do not know if we manage. I have to delete all messengers because they will check my mobile. I'll write to you when we have news."

Thirty-six hours later, in the middle of the night, a message popped up: "We are in Tashkent."

Now, months later, Oleg and Lilia, labeled "enemies of the state" for leaving Russia, had just run a workshop for nonprofit organizations in a far-off part of Uzbekistan. My friends did not intend to remain here. They wanted to get to Berlin where their adult daughter now lived, but they needed to figure out a way to secure visas. For Oleg and Lilia, like my grandparents so many decades before, Uzbekistan was a waystation. We were meeting in Samarkand to research my past and to plan their future.

* * *

The next morning, the call to prayer woke me at 4:30 a.m. Soon the birds were riotous, and bright rays streamed through the yellow curtain. I traded messages with Talia halfway around the world. It was 4:30 p.m. in Los Angeles, and she was trying to complete a report exposing the treatment of asylum-seeking families in US immigration courts—and to get home in time to grab the kids. Gratitude to Talia filled me. So did a tinge of guilt as I tried to fall back to sleep. But I could not drift away. Any jet lag I might have usually suffered had been replaced with adrenaline.

Giving up on sleep, I walked out to the balcony and was greeted with a not-unpleasant mix of the scents of fresh manure from the neighboring animals and blossoms from the fruit trees below. We were in the middle of a city of half a million residents, in the dense, old Bukharan Jewish quarter of winding roads and alleys. And yet within this courtyard, Samarkand felt peaceful, the early twentieth-century former merchant's home now tastefully appointed for international guests with local ceramics and handmade wood furniture.

Lilia emerged from her adjacent room and we walked downstairs to the patio to sip tea in blue and gold enameled porcelain cups. The highly attentive guesthouse manager soon invited us into the breakfast room, once home to the family's private synagogue. "It will make your wishes come true," he boasted of its mystical powers. Lilia, despite her need for a stroke of luck, retreated to write a grant application to facilitate a German visa.

A delectable spread awaited me inside the family prayer room—cottage cheese pancakes, compote made with cherries from the courtyard garden, toasted slices of dense Samarkand bread, fried eggplant. When I finally looked up to take in the kaleidoscope of intricately carved and colorful painted designs covering the walls, I noticed the remnants of the aron kodesh, or holy ark, with a benediction in Hebrew: "May you be blessed when entering and blessed when leaving."

While I was skeptical of any special powers left behind by the long-gone Jewish residents of this house, I welcomed blessings. I needed help to uncover traces of my father's origins in Uzbekistan. Trying to nail down the details of my family's time here back before the trip, I returned to family testimonies and found that despite what it said on my father's passport and obituary, his parents did not live in Samarkand. They landed in the region, but not in the big city. Instead, his first home was in a nearby rural village called Juma.

I then found another clue. My grandfather's name and an address in Juma—5 Kaganovich—was listed amid files from the Joint Distribution Committee. The American Jewish organization sent 250,000 aid packages of emergency supplies to Jews in Central Asia, via Tehran, during and in the aftermath of World War II. The Soviets would not allow them to distribute, labeling the distribution committee a prohibited "sectarian" organization, so instead they had to locate the refugees via other outlets, such as the International Committee of the Red Cross, Polish organizations, and synagogues that were still allowed to function. Somehow my grandfather had made it onto one of the committee's lists. With his address in hand, I left home confident I would be able to find my father's first home.

Upon arriving in Uzbekistan, I immediately discovered it would not be so simple. A professor in Tashkent told me that the street name would have been changed in the intervening years. So did every other Uzbek I asked. My grandparents' street had been named for Lazar Kaganovich—a Ukrainian Jew who had been one of Stalin's henchmen. He was one of many Jews who believed Communism was a way out of being a permanent stranger, a way to be fully equal members of a new type of society. Symbolizing his commitment to the cause, Kaganovich received the nickname Iron Lazar for his role as head of the Ministry of Railways.

Even when Stalin turned on the Jewish members of the party and expelled all the others, Kaganovich remained, conspiring to murder millions of innocent people and ensuring many more were sent to the Gulag. After Khrushchev, Stalin's successor, took over in 1953, he booted Kaganovich from the party, reportedly shouting: "Your hands are stained with the blood of our party leaders and of innumerable innocent Bolsheviks!" Throughout the Soviet Union, tributes to Kaganovich were erased, including Kaganovich Street in a small town in Uzbekistan, and with it the clue that could lead me to where my father entered this world.

* * *

I was finishing my breakfast in the prayer room when in strode Anait Garaeva, the Samarkand guide I had hired to help me find records of my family.

"So how can I help you?" she asked. Anait was dressed in black with bold silver earrings. I was immediately drawn to her direct style.

I told her that I wanted to see the house where my father had lived his first months, that the address was Kaganovich 5.

"That street would have been changed twice," she told me with complete confidence. After Stalin and Kaganovich fell out of favor, the new name would still have been Communist and in Russian. But upon Uzbekistan's independence, she was convinced it would have been changed again as the country tried to reverse the Soviet influence.

I dipped into the doubts that had been gnawing at me. "Maybe it will be impossible to find."

"Why do you doubt?" Anait stopped me. "I have found so many."

Anait, part of a dwindling Armenian minority in Samarkand, told me how she had spent years guiding Israelis who'd come on group tours to see the local sites: the magnificent azure-tiled Registan Square; the necropolis of the Living King where, according to legend, Muhammad's beheaded cousin was interred. Every time a member of the group would take her aside and ask to see a different type of history: Could she help connect a memory to a place? They wanted to find a mother's watery grave, a place where their parents fell in love in the refugee years.

I told Anait that my father had often spoken of returning to his birthplace. But then his mind faded, and his body froze—at warp speed. "He got sick, and he was dead two months later."

Sitting across the table in this old prayer room, Anait shared her own story of loss. "My father also died, at age sixty-five, so very fast. That was a stroke. You never get ready for that." She kept going. "My father-in-law died last night."

Last night? I was not sure I had heard correctly. What was she doing working with me on this day? I insisted I could find a way to do this research on my own.

"Everything is done. He was eighty-two years old." She reassured me that she had helped her husband prepare for the funeral in Russia, but had chosen not to go herself, having seen her father-in-law very recently. "Still, it was very painful."

I wanted to tell Anait about losing my father-in-law, but I hesitated. She did not know I was married to a woman. A source who worked in the region had told me it would be better not to share. The country had a conservative culture. My guidebook stated that in Uzbekistan, "homosexuality is illegal." But how could Anait help me with this intimate quest without my telling her about Talia?

"My father-in-law also died..." I struggled to explain, then just let the truth fly. "Actually, I'm married to a woman."

Anait nodded. Encouraged, I kept going. "He died at sixty-eight. And he wasn't my father, but it was devastating."

"Do you have kids?" Anait seemed, thankfully, fine with my reveal, steering the conversation from our dead fathers-in-law to our lives as two women in love. "Have you adopted children?"

"We have..." My words trailed off. I was stuck on thoughts of being a child, not a parent. I felt the soul-wringing pain of losing a father, the instinctual desire to be taken care of, to hold on to something from the people you loved. I thought of a woman Anait had just told me about whose mother had drowned here when she was a child refugee and who had returned in her elderly years to pay tribute. I was surprised to find tears sliding from my eyes.

Since the day we had buried my father, more than two years earlier, I had scarcely been able to cry. The emotion stayed boxed up inside of me. The moment I got on the plane to Uzbekistan, I was hit hard with longing to share this journey with him. In Samarkand, as I squeezed through a hidden door that opened upon the magical city's central complex of magnificent azure mosques and mausoleums, I could almost see my father pausing to photograph and marvel at these structures that were part of his origins and yet also completely new.

"I don't usually get so emotional," I told Anait, embarrassed by my outburst.

"You came here with your mission. You are fulfilling his wish." She paused a moment. "It's time to get to work."

CHAPTER 23

Kaganovich Street

I had arrived in Uzbekistan alone, but now a team had joined my quest to find my father's first home. Anait, Lilia, Oleg, and I packed into a small taxi for the thirty-minute drive out of town to Juma.

Oleg, in the front seat, chatted with the driver, who could not understand why my friends had left behind their home in St. Petersburg. He saw Russia, where millions of Uzbeks moved every year to work, as a land of opportunity. Next to me in the back, Anait and Lilia talked in Russian. I let their words float by as I stared out the window, cramped and hot, sweat trickling down my legs.

In the early winter of 1941, my grandparents, aboard a train out of Samarkand, also would have passed cotton fields, donkeys hauling carriages. Perhaps foreboding filled them as they spotted other refugees, even worse off than themselves, trudging and pushing wagons, desperate with hunger and ill with typhoid.

After the brief twenty-mile trip west along the Trans-Caspian line, the Gerson siblings' train slowed into the Juma station. By then they were accustomed to rejection. In the big cities of Tashkent and Samarkand, they were told to keep going, to find somewhere else that had fewer refugees. But in Juma, officials at last permitted them to disembark.

Were they more relieved or terrified? The town of a few thousand was built around the railroad stop, with straw-and-mud homes and mostly cotton fields stretching around it. There were no beds available for the Gersons and it was getting dark. They gathered their satchels and walked through the dirt roads until they found a field where they could try to rest on the frigid earth.

The men, grabbing a hatchet, left to scavenge roots to make a fire. While summers in Uzbekistan are scorching, winters freeze at night. This was not the snow-packed negative double digits of the Ural Mountains, but it was still cold enough to make teeth chatter. And they failed to find anything to burn and provide some comfort. "The earth at that time was frozen and there was nothing," my great-aunt Chuma said. "I was never a big eater. But there were days it was too painful. Absolutely starving in hunger."

The next day officials must have cajoled or forced a local Juma family into allowing the Gerson siblings a room to cram in with them. Under Soviet rules, the authorities could demand a family make space in their home or even kick residents out in the name of the revolution. Polish citizens, being at the bottom of the social hierarchy, were often squeezed into the most basic of accommodations. With time, however, my grandparents made some improvements. Somehow, they were eventually able to move out of the shared space with all the siblings into their own room in a home owned by a Tatar family, a Muslim minority. This, I determined, must have been their address at Kaganovich Street #5.

* * *

At an intersection in Juma, we flagged down local taxi drivers and asked if they knew where Kaganovich Street was. Not one had ever even heard of it. Our driver parked at what we assumed was the center of town, dusty buildings clustered near a pedestrian bridge over train tracks. Juma was no Samarkand, no Lviv, and definitely no Zamość—those architectural gems and UNESCO World Heritage towns where my family had previously resided. Flat and dry, now boasting a cotton gin and mechanical repair factory, this town of about twenty-five thousand must have felt starker and more foreboding when my grandparents arrived.

We walked into a restaurant to inquire about Kaganovich Street. None of the people mulling there had heard of it. If the street's name had changed twice in the years after Stalin died in 1953, a resident would need to be over seventy to hold memories of it. So far, not one person in this town looked that old.

My grandmother had said they lived near the station. The train no longer stopped for passengers in Juma, the restaurant manager told us, but the old depot with the tracks heading away from Samarkand to the Caspian Sea was over the bridge. Anait then recalled a detail I'd recounted to her.

"Is there a Tatar neighborhood in Juma?" she asked people in the restaurant.

The conversation took off, too rapid for my companions to translate for me. An Uzbek man with warm eyes and a loose gait led us over the pedestrian bridge toward the old train depot. That's when I learned that he had offered to drive us to the sole Tatar family in Juma.

Awaiting us on the other side of the bridge was his car, an aged Soviet Lada with broken windows. "This was once the coolest car around," Anait reminisced about the model. The driver steered us across cobblestone roads, honking and waving at each passing car, until about five minutes later, the houses began to spread out.

In a courtyard on the outskirts of town, we found the four remaining members of Juma's once numerous Tatar community taking a break from their morning labor. A woman with a floral head scarf confirmed that once many people from their minority group had lived around the train station. But everyone else had moved on from Juma, and she had not heard of Kaganovich Street.

I was about to concede that we would never find the house, when an animated conversation erupted between the Tatar farmers. My interpreters caught me up: "There is a Russian woman left who is very old. Perhaps she might know?"

* * *

A petite and sprightly Slavic woman wearing a velour jacket adorned with rhinestones invited us inside when we showed up at her turquoise house. The interior walls were painted the same brilliant hue, the worn floor covered with carpets, and a bowl of raspberries she'd picked from her garden rested on the counter, soaking with sugar. Inside, it was cool and earthy.

The woman, named Zoya, chatted easily in Russian as my translators told her of my inquiries. "Wow, wow!" they exclaimed in unison. Lilia told me we did not need to search any longer for my grandparents' street. Miraculously, we were on it. Zoya had lived almost her whole life at what was once #6 Kaganovich. The address we were searching for, #5, was directly across the street. She even knew the Tatar family who'd once lived there, from whom my grandparents presumably rented. Without even realizing it, we had driven right up to Kaganovich Street. And Zoya, who lived on it, was perhaps the only person alive who remembered its old name.

She told us that Kaganovich Street had, indeed, been renamed twice. First "Communist Street" when Stalin and his murderous regime fell out of favor in the 1950s. After the dissolution of the Soviet Union, it received its third name in half a century: "Do'Stlik" or "Friendship Street" in Uzbek.

She believed the descendants of the people my grandparents rented from had left Juma when the borders opened. In 1989, Tatars, more than 150,000 of whom Stalin had forcibly brought to Uzbekistan during a rapid and brutal World War II relocation, began to leave en masse. Other minorities also departed as the Soviet Union collapsed, looking for opportunities and fearing that the renewal of Uzbek leadership could push out the rights of other peoples. Zoya said almost all Russians left, including her children, but she did not want to give up the place she had lived her entire life.

I was eager to see my father's first home but also reluctant to leave Zoya's cozy kitchen. I sensed she had more to teach me about my family's life in Juma. Zoya offered us black tea, raspberry compote, and chocolates, and then launched into recounting her own childhood of hardship. Her father had been a mechanic at the railroad and was thrown in the Samarkand jail after an accident. He died there before she was born. I homed in on this tragic detail and excitedly asked my Russian companions to translate a question.

"When her father died, where had he been buried?"

I had only recently discovered that one of the eight in my grandparents' group had perished in that same jail. He was someone I had never known existed until I began this search, and I was hoping to ensure he was not completely forgotten.

* * *

After my father died, I found in his photo collection a yellowing black-and-white photo of him hoisting four-year-old me on his knee in front of a Bronx apartment building. To our left stands Ruksha, my grandfather's sister, in a warm coat with a fur collar turned up, chunky big-framed glasses, and pumps—flashing a smile that looked more like a grimace. On our right is my great-uncle Henik looking straight at the camera under a broad-brimmed hat, cigar dangling from his lips. I always assumed Ruksha's only husband was the charismatic man in this photo with the numbers from Auschwitz burned on his arm, who would laugh and twirl me around as a kid. Only when I started listening to the family recordings did I discover that Henik was Ruksha's second husband. Her first husband was named Moishe (not to be confused with my grandfather's strong and stubborn youngest brother). Of the eight who entered Uzbekistan, he was the only one who never left.

Moishe's final day in Juma began smoothly enough. He caught a train to Samarkand with Mottel and Chuma. The three would have left the station and navigated the winding roads toward the bazaar, likely passing Uzbeks in colorful sashes with camels. Did they pause to take in the offerings—dark wheat flour, grapes as big as walnuts, and fermented milk in goat skins—at a market selling food they could not afford? Their few rubles were reserved for black market purchases.

A foundational tenet in the Soviet Union, which the atheist Lenin ironically adopted from the New Testament, followed the refugees everywhere: *He who does not work, does not eat.* But for many, particularly Polish Jews at the bottom of the social hierarchy, there was little work to be found. To survive in Central Asia, many refugees relied on the black market. Two weeks after arriving, my grandfather sold the suit he wore at his wedding as he began to unload all his treasured belongings. My grandmother later sold her wedding ring. For what, she could not recall, guessing she received in exchange something as basic as milk at a particularly desperate time.

"Every one of them was involved in some form of illegal trade," recalled Roma Talasiewicz-Eibuszyc of fellow Polish Jewish refugees. "But we still had to look behind our backs at all times, living in constant fear of arrest and jail and the knowledge that at any moment the Russian authorities could send our men to the front lines. There was no relaxing."

Talia's uncle Zyg learned this lesson. As a daring entrepreneurial teenager in Tashkent, he purchased yards of fabric at the black market. Then he cut them into smaller swatches and rode the trains to towns to sell at a profit. "I was sliding onto the wheels where the train was; I was jumping from one wagon to the other one," he recalled breathlessly. "My friend didn't notice that there was a bridge and his head got cut off. It was unbelievable." Zyg survived, but he was arrested and dumped in a Kazakh jail where, starving on a diet of thin soup, he caught and ate a rat: "It was delicious. I cooked it."

* * *

On that fateful trip to Samarkand, my grandfather, Moishe, and Chuma found the black market gathering spot where people stretched down their arms swatches of fabrics, likely stolen from government stores or factories, that they were selling. My grandfather, deft in buying, took the lead in negotiations. A rate was established, and they illegally purchased reams of fabric to resell later at a profit.

Work completed, my grandfather Mottel took leave of his siblings to mail a letter to an address he kept close on his journey, that of Peshke's brothers in Buenos Aires: *I'll meet you at the train station.*

As soon as he left, Chuma and Moishe heard dreaded words in Russian: *What are you carrying? Are you smugglers?* Two policemen arrested them. At the jail, guards shaved the heads of Chuma and Moishe, stripped them of all belongings, and tossed them in cells filled with killers and petty thieves alike. Chuma, who never even got to sell a piece of fabric, received a sentence of seven years; Moishe eight.

* * *

Mottel visited the Samarkand jail daily, week after week, crippled with guilt. One afternoon in the cafeteria, he spotted a military man.

Maybe you can do something? Mottel was ready to offer a bribe to save his brother-in-law, who he had heard was very sick.

What do you want? To get him released for eight years? And I will go to jail for ten to fifteen years! The military man, who oversaw the medical services in jail, was not interested.

You know what? My Russian is not so good, Mottel said, quickly backtracking. *You didn't understand me. I don't want to give you money.* Then he let slip in Yiddish, *Oy Gottenyu helf mir! Oh dear God help me!*

The man's demeanor softened. He took my grandfather in and asked quietly, *Redstu Yiddish?* He, too, was a Jew. My grandfather felt like he had been given new life.

The military man secured, months later, a release for Moishe. But it arrived a day too late. The strong young man perished alone in the jail. Of what, I'm not completely certain. One relative said he died of diarrhea and diphtheria. Another that an infection attacked his heart. Whatever the sickness, it slayed him, helped along by the beatings, the malnutrition, and the desperation of jail. Ruksha's Moishe was not yet thirty.

"I envied him," Chuma said in the recording her children made of her as an old woman. Her brother-in-law had died, while she remained in jail, sleeping on the dirt floor. "Sometimes you imagine death coming in the dark in a white sheet to relieve you. This wouldn't be death.

This would be a relief." But the siblings refused to let their youngest sister perish.

Chuma had gotten word to them that the jail doctor could be a good target for a bribe: He was so poor that his shoes were kept together by strings tied around rags. Mottel visited the doctor. An NKVD agent sat down next to him just as he planned to make an offer. My grandfather knew he was being watched, but he kept his cool.

My heart. I have pains. Maybe you can help me? The doctor, knowing this was a front, provided a prescription and a return appointment.

The next time Mottel met the doctor, the secret police officer was gone, and my grandfather spoke freely: *Look, I need your help getting my sister out, and I will pay.*

The doctor wrote a huge sum on a piece of paper and then ripped it up.

Back home the six remaining Gerson siblings and spouses huddled together. *How much could they come up with?* They were only barely surviving. But my grandmother would not tolerate wavering.

Everything! she said decisively. *We give everything! Family is everything!*

Months later, a guard came to Chuma: *Tomorrow you will be released.*

Seven decades later on the blustery New England day when we buried my father, Chuma's firstborn son, Sol, voice raw with emotion, repeated the words that secured his mother's freedom: *Family is everything.*

In Juma, that familial dedication had saved his mother, but the Gerson siblings were forced to leave one of their group in Uzbekistan. Ruksha's first husband, Moishe, remained with the unknown thousands of Polish Jews who perished there during World War II.

I had hoped to visit his grave in Samarkand and place a stone to demonstrate that my great-uncle hadn't been completely forgotten. But now in Juma, Zoya explained that the plot of her father, who died in the same jail, was marked with an anonymous number, not a name. She'd never been able to pay tribute to him, and she was certain there would be no way to locate my great-uncle's burial site.

* * *

Eager to find any remnants of my family that did remain, I asked Zoya if we could go over to the house where my father spent his first months. She jumped up and led us across the street. Two young girls in sundresses lounged in the broad arched turquoise entryway. A balding Uzbek man with a copious stomach came out to greet us. When Zoya introduced me, he smiled broadly, showcasing a mouth of gold, evidently tickled by the American visitor.

As I entered the threshold to the home's inner courtyard, the structure revealed itself not to be as grand as it appeared from the stucco exterior, with walls of exposed cinder blocks. This house, Zoya told us, had like all in the area once been mud and straw. Just one wall remained with the original composition. The rest was rebuilt, the owner was proudly telling me.

When my grandparents lived here, there had been no running water, heat, or coolant. On sweltering nights, they would sometimes sleep on the roofs, likely among braided strips of cantaloupe, grapes, and figs that had been set out to dry. I looked toward the windows, trying to imagine my family huddled in a room covered with textiles, perhaps gathered around a coal fire.

Here, my grandparents would have debated the rumors, shared by another landsman who passed through town spreading heart-stopping news: *Zamość is Judenrein—cleansed of Jews*.

The family could not believe this wild claim. How could there be a Zamość without Jews? Who would run the shops? And what devil murdered innocent old women and babies? Their parents and sisters, cousins and nephews?

Months later, in July 1944, the loudspeaker by the post office in Juma trumpeted thrilling news: *The Red Army has liberated Zamość*. Nearly five years after the Nazis occupied Zamość, three years since communication had been cut off with family, the German soldiers had hastily retreated from the beautiful town they had once planned to rename Himmlerstadt. Mottel and Peshke and the siblings and their spouses embraced and giddily spun each other around, breaking into dance.

Soon after, leaders from the Union of Polish Patriots, a Soviet-directed organization that was formed by Poles in exile, arrived in Juma on a tour of hamlets across Central Asia to ready citizens for an eventual return. They also brought a devastating directive for the Jews: *You need to say the Kaddish for your families.* The Gerson siblings could not even imagine that saying the mourner's prayer could be needed. "We took it like nothing," my great-uncle Simon recalled so many decades later, transposed to that moment when he was not able to let the dehumanizing truth penetrate. "It's impossible that they killed, innocent people, killed?"

When mail service renewed to Poland, Peshke penned a letter to the mayor of Zamość, determined to find out the truth. It must have taken many weeks for the sparsely worded response to arrive: *The fate of your family is the fate of all of the Jews in our town, Zamość.* This newly appointed mayor did not write that Peshke's family had been murdered, nor that Zamość was *Judenrein*. Without details, he affirmed the rumors of extermination that any Jew from Zamość in Uzbekistan had likely heard whispered by now. In a room in this house, my grandmother must have held that letter and read it again and again, slowly beginning to take in the unimaginable: All they had endured paled in comparison with those who'd remained in Zamość.

They had, in the end, been the lucky ones.

* * *

A ferocious urge to tear apart Germans overcame my surviving great-uncle Moishe. Strong as a mule, he was determined to fight. Already, he had missed out on joining the army affiliated with the Polish government in exile. Named for General Władysław Anders, its soldiers had years earlier moved through Uzbekistan. Among the Jews to depart with them on a route back to Europe via Iran and Palestine was Menachem Begin, the former Gulag prisoner and future Israeli prime minister. But most Jews never received that chance to fight, rejected even when they were highly qualified to do so. The tensions and distrust that long colored Polish Jewish relations had followed the refugees to Central Asia.

Then Soviet relations with Poland's government in exile collapsed after Moscow's massacre of twenty-two thousand Polish officers was revealed. Stalin was now supporting the formation of a second Polish army, this time with a Communist foundation. It welcomed Jews. And Moishe was determined to fight with them. *I must go*, he declared to Mottel.

My grandfather erupted in fury: *And what shall we do? You want that we should survive the war?* He knew his younger brother Moishe was a genius for finding work, protecting them from thieves and anti-Semites. Together as a family, seven out of eight of them, out of nine if you counted baby Arik, had survived, barely, five years on the run. What would happen if Moishe went his own way? How many more would perish?

But Moishe was convinced that fighting back was the only way to live with the failure to protect his parents. At the outset of the war, he had ventured back into Nazi territory from Lviv determined to bring their mother to them, only to be arrested. When he escaped from the jail, he almost perished fleeing across the River Bug. Never mind his heroic efforts; he could see only his failure to protect their parents. *How could I not have saved our father, our mother?*

Mottel, the stalwart family leader whom his younger brother had never seen shed a tear, could stand it no more. He collapsed and matched Moishe's weeping with his own tears.

It's better to be a living dog than to die as a hero, to be a dead lion. Mottel, when he regained his composure, counseled his younger brother, adapting a biblical saying. *We are alive; let's save the lives.* Moishe agreed to remain with his family.

* * *

As I stood where my grandparents once had in Juma, I did not share with the owner of the house the overpowering loss my family had confronted at his address. I had just shown up, unannounced, and this felt too complicated to explain across languages and cultures. I needed a moment to myself and asked the owner if I could use the bathroom.

Above: At our wedding; Talia's father shields us from the sun. *Below:* Dancing with my father at our backyard reception. *(Photos by Laura Layera)*

Above: My grandfather, far right, at the 1964 unveiling of a monument to the Zamość martyrs at the Beth El Cemetery in Paramus, New Jersey. *Center:* Among the murdered, I found Talia's last name, Inlender, imprinted. *Below:* My father, in the 1980s, at the memorial.

Above: Talia and I sit in front of her grandfather's home in Zamość. Across the square is my grandmother's first home, the blue one to the right of the town hall. *Center:* Talia and Alma look back across the square at her grandfather's home, the one to the left of the flagpole. *Below:* Historic photo of the square, courtesy of Marek Kolçon.

Above: Peshke stands behind her father's left shoulder in a photo taken around 1927, shortly before her two brothers and older sister (to the right of her father) left for Argentina. The Nazis murdered her two sisters (far left and right in the picture) and her parents. *Below left:* Mottel as a young man. *Below center:* He is the blond boy in the bottom left. *Below right:* Peshke always loved the latest fashions.

Peshke and Mottel in their courtship and with their baby son, Arik, shortly before Germany attacked Poland.

Above: Leon (far right) stands with his first wife, Manya, his brother-in-law, Khaim Sherf, and the Sherf parents. Khaim survived and kept this photo and others of the family. *Center:* Manya holds baby Kolonimus. *Below:* Pepa, Leon's second wife, is the woman on the left. She was much younger than him and only a teenager when she left Poland behind. *(Sherf/Shavit family collection)*

Above: Our children appreciate Zamość vistas from Hotel 77, built over the mikveh. *Center:* Talia's father, Nachum, squats next to the family chickens in Israel. *Below:* His half-brother, Kolonimus, stands in a tailored suit in Poland.

Above: Mottel is the little blond boy holding the sign in a fund-raiser for HeChalutz, "The Pioneer." The photo is from the memorial book.
Below: Manya's father, Shlomo Sherf (far left), at a meeting of Revisionist Zionists.

Above and below: We received two photos from the NKVD archives of Mottel and Leon in the labor camps. *Center:* Pepa kept an autograph book throughout the journey, which made it possible to confirm her whereabouts.

Above: A re-creation of wartime Tashkent Station at Victory Park. *Center:* A Tashkent Jewish cemetery's graves from the wartime years reveal the large refugee death toll. *Below*: Reconnecting with Lilia and Oleg in Uzbekistan.

Above: Visiting Samarkand's Ulug'bek Madrasah. *Center:* The interior courtyard of 5 Kaganovich Street. *Below:* In Juma, finding Zoya, who lives across the street from the house where my father spent his first months.

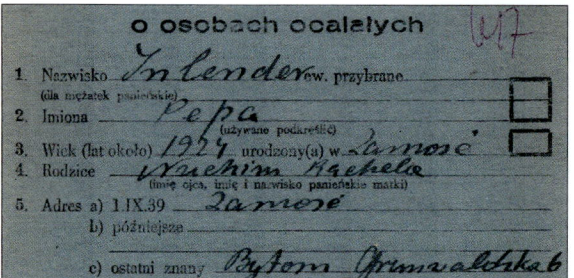

Above: Leon and Pepa from 1945 in Dzhambul, Kazakhstan. *Center:* The registration form upon arriving in Bytom, Poland, is the first record I located of Pepa using the last name Inlender. *Below left:* She sits in front of what we believe is the building in Bytom where she and Leon landed briefly. *Below right:* The Bytom courthouse, where Leon attempted to claim his murdered cousin Wigdor's property.

Above: The Admont DP camp. Pepa is the woman near the center in the striped shirt with a vest. *Center*: An Inlender family portrait from Austria, likely shortly before leaving for Israel. *Below:* The view from the refugee camp, now a residential development in the small town of Admont.

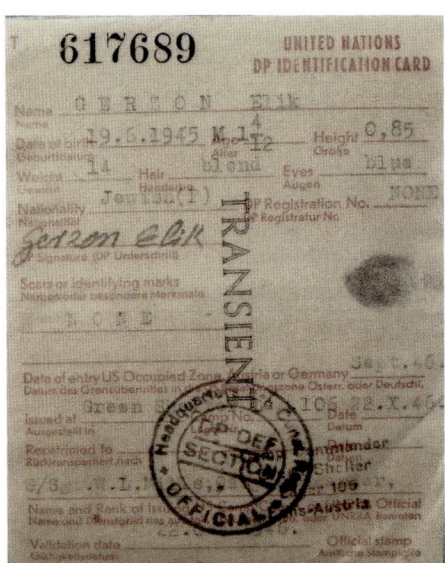

Above left: My father received this ID card upon entering Austria as a displaced person in October 1946. *Above right:* Mottel works in the Föhrenwald DP camp office helping fellow refugees. *Center:* My father's kindergarten class at Föhrenwald in 1949/50. *Below:* Family photo at Foehrenwald; my father is the larger boy in lederhosen on the left.

Above: My father's family after their train journey north to Bremen to take a military ship to New York. *Below:* Under the identity of "Blumstein," the Gersons left Germany on November 14, 1950.

INDEX CARD	A. J. D. C.	EMIGRATION SERVICE MUNICH	
Last Name	Blumstein	File No.	USA 1045
First Name	Abraham Sex M	Opening Date	29.6.1949
Address	Camp Foehrenwald	In transit from:	
Birthdate 31.VII.1944	Birthplace Suma	Accompanied by	Moszek, Rachela, Samuel
Nationality: Present Former			
Occupation: Present Former		Closing Date	*Australien port closed* 27 Jan. 1951
Country of destination	USA		

Left for USA 14. Nov. 1950

Above: Leon holds Nachum shortly after arriving in Israel. *Center left:* My great-aunt Ruksha, her husband, Henik, and my father, holding me, in the Bronx. *Center right:* Talia and her brother, Daniel, and their grandparents Pepa and Leon. *Below:* My grandfather Mottel watching me as a baby.

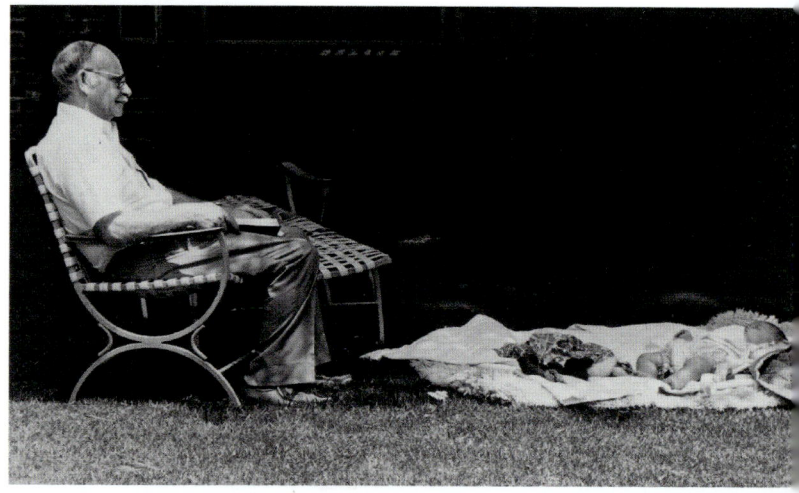

He pointed to a shack in the back of the property. The basic hole in the ground lacked even the ceramic footprints customary in standing toilets in Uzbekistan. This was one part of the house that I imagined could not be that different from when my grandparents lived here.

I lingered in the garden, washing my hands in a cistern offered by a woman I assumed to be the owner's wife. As my eyes traced her loose pink dress that fell to her ankles and the purple scarf wrapped around her head, she took me in with a grimace. She was not unwelcoming but possessed none of her husband's joviality. The wind blew through the laundry she had just placed on the line. Magenta zinnias and fruit trees grew up against the rough-hewn cement block exterior walls.

I had come to Uzbekistan determined to find this address. But this home was now another family's story. Zoya held the memory of my family's shared past that I had hoped to discover. She had made our history tangible amid all the changes and erasure—and demonstrated how the human spirit finds a way to endure. Surprising myself, I did not ask to enter past the courtyard and into Kaganovich #5, the structure this family had proudly rebuilt. Instead, I thanked them with the Uzbek gesture of gratitude, putting my right hand to my heart in a fist.

* * *

There was one last place I wanted to see in Juma. We walked a few blocks to the shuttered train station, with its boarded-up ticket office and five mint-green chairs.

No matter how destitute the years in Uzbekistan, in the hot and dry summer evenings or the windy winter ones, my grandmother recalled the women would change into slightly less ragged dresses and stroll along the train tracks, a nightly ritual to relax and socialize. They were all young people in prime childbearing years. Not one had birthed a child since they fled Poland. My grandmother told my mother and aunt how in Siberia she had developed a technique of falling off a table onto her stomach to ensure no baby endured the hellscape of the Gulag. But now her stomach began to stretch. One day on the walk she noticed that many of her friends' waists also bulged.

"We knew already the war was ending," my grandmother recalled. After the Soviet victory at Stalingrad, soldiers had begun to return from the front with exuberant news. The Nazi army was in retreat. On May 8, 1945, nearing midnight, Jews across Central Asia gathered to hear radio broadcasts over loudspeakers. Our grandparents surely rejoiced when the announcer proclaimed: *The Germans have capitulated. There is peace now. Tomorrow, May 9, we will have a holiday. Nobody is going to work.* From Leningrad to Samarkand to Vladivostok people kissed and hugged in the streets, celebrating the blessed success of the Red Army and its allies over the Nazis.

My grandmother felt ready to bring new life into the world once more. Just over a month later, on June 19, her water broke. Of three cousins, born in rapid succession in Uzbekistan, my father arrived first: a very large, and slightly orange baby.

I had no photos of my infant father in the former Soviet Union. The sole image from my family's six-year exile in the Soviet Union was the one I had unearthed of my grandfather as a prisoner in Siberia. Our family's recorded stories and an address had been the only evidence that they had once been in Uzbekistan. But in the Samarkand archives, I had that morning received official proof: my father's birth certificate.

I now carried with me, stamped with an elaborate blue seal, Cyrillic letters that read: "It is realized that the Department of Registration Office of Pastdargom Region, of Samarkand Province, there is information about the fact of birth of Gerson, Ilya Martkovitch. Jewish."

I knew that in Yiddish my father was known as Elik, but this Russian name, Ilya, was new to me; nobody among my living family members had ever heard it. Did my dad ever know his original, official name?

As we walked back toward the pedestrian bridge, I summoned once more my father's presence. I wanted to linger in his exuberance, to uncover more layers, and to marvel with him in awe at how unbelievably far he had traveled. But the others were ready to leave, and my time in Uzbekistan was almost complete.

On our drive back to Samarkand, the cool evening air blowing through the windows, I felt renewed. Mysteries remained, but what was once only a vague outline of these years of limbo, released from slave labor but not yet free, was now a place that smelled of plov cooked over an open fire, freshly baked bread, and cherry blossoms. I had been touched by the generosity of a people that had once opened their homes so that our family could survive and bring new life into this world.

CHAPTER 24

Repatriates

I returned from Uzbekistan aglow with discoveries and lugging a suitcase stuffed with Bukharan puppets, ceramic dishes, and pomegranate-embroidered pillow covers. But even as I doled out gifts and recounted what I had learned, a disconnect yawned.

For the past two weeks, I'd enjoyed the farthest trip Talia or I had taken since our children were born. I adored when the kids squealed and hugged me upon coming home after twenty-four hours of travel, but return was hard. I missed taking uninterrupted showers where nobody ran in to use our shared bathroom or to ask me where I had left the keys. Battling intense jet lag but with no time to readjust, I was irritable, even though I knew I was the one who needed to be grateful.

Meanwhile, Talia was justifiably frustrated with my mood, and I suspected that something else was bothering her. I had gone to do research on our families' shared history and come back with stories only of my own.

I, too, was frustrated. The question rankled: Where were her grandparents for the five long years between the amnesty from the Gulag and the end of the war? When had Leon turned to Pepa, nineteen years younger, strong-willed and full of life?

As I had come to expect with Talia's grandparents, tracing their past led to a house of mirrors. The few records I located provided conflicting places and times. On one document, Pepa and Leon stated they married in 1946, but the Austrian birth certificate of Talia's father stated they were married in 1943. If this was true, they likely wed before Leon knew that his first wife and child had been murdered, since little information came out of Zamość before the Red Army arrived a year later.

On the birth certificate, the place of marriage written appeared to be Schimbu, Russia. I read, and reread, the handwriting in a looping script, enlisting the help of various native German speakers. But they saw the same words I did and no Schimbu existed in the former Soviet Union.

* * *

Then, not long after I returned from Uzbekistan, a clue arrived from an unexpected place: the Central Zionist Archives in Jerusalem. Adi, the granddaughter of Leon's brother-in-law, had recommended we submit a request to their immigration archives. She had done so for her grandfather Khaim and the archives had yielded some interesting details. Months before I traveled to Central Asia, Talia and I had filled out forms, requesting a search for documents related to her grandparents' arrival to Israel in 1949. The file we now received in response included ship registries, but also fifteen pages of correspondence from the Search Bureau for Missing Relatives.

As the war came to an end, the remaining Jews of Europe, those who had survived in Third Reich territory and those now scattered around the globe, engaged in an urgent quest to locate loved ones. With no phone numbers or addresses remaining in many cases, and of course no internet, they relied on a constellation of agencies, news outlets, and word of mouth.

In Leon's file, I read a familiar name: Khaim Sherf. Three days before Germany surrendered to the Allies on May 4, 1945, Leon Inlender had sent a letter to Palestine trying to locate his brother-in-law, "Sherf, Khaim ben Shlomo."

Leon's message to the Search Bureau for Missing Relatives stated that he was writing from a place called Dzhambul. With the help of my Uzbek friend, I found this was the name of a city that had existed in the

Kazakh Soviet Socialist Republic and after the war been renamed as Taraz. I realized that Schimbu, written on Nachum's birth certificate, must have been an Austrian midwife's misunderstanding of her Polish Jewish patient's former Kazakh residence: Dzhambul.

Located roughly 180 miles north of Tashkent, the city was a hub for refugees. I didn't find more details of Leon's and Pepa's lives there, but I could imagine from other testimonies left behind. Did Talia's grandparents work in the surrounding collective farms, walking ten kilometers to get to the bathhouse? Or did they fill rooms left vacant in a city apartment by Kazakh boys sent to fight in the war, and mix dough in a bakery where they needed to steal wheat to survive?

Among the recollections of Dzhambul, I also found one with a potential hint to their union. Hanche Waintraub, now an elderly woman living in La Paz, Bolivia, recalled how when she was moored in the city during the war, Soviet authorities started taking single men away to work in often deadly mines. There was a mad rush to wed: "So six at once people would get married. They would get a little bread, and they were labeled married, and it saved the men." Could that explain a decision to wed again before Leon knew for certain that his wife was dead?

* * *

As Talia and I puzzled over Pepa and Leon's life and union, we reconnected and resumed our family routines. One morning our son, newly five, received an award at school. We were early arriving at the auditorium with its big American flag. Only two other proud parents waited in the multipurpose room. The mother wore a headscarf; the father was tall with Turkic eyes.

"Are you from Kazakhstan?" I asked, knowing a group of young professionals from the Central Asian country north of Uzbekistan had also selected this Los Angeles public school for their kids. The couple nodded.

"Have you ever been to Taraz?" I asked, using the contemporary name for Dzhambul, eager to find someone who might know about this faraway place.

"That is where we lived," they said. We were stunned. These were the first Kazakhs we'd encountered since discovering that Talia's grandparents had found refuge there, and they were from the same place.

Timur, the father, had been born in the city, and seemed as surprised as we were that we had a connection to it. Though he had grown up in the area and lived most of his life there, he said he'd never heard about Polish Jews taking refuge in what was then Dzhambul during World War II. Then Timur described his hometown to us, which, like Samarkand, had once been an ancient trading city and a stop on the Silk Route.

Enraptured in a vision of this far-off place suddenly linked to Talia's family, I barely noticed as the room filled with other parents, kids, and their teachers. Here, in the shadow of Dodger Stadium, on the other side of the world from a city we had never heard of until weeks before, we'd found another connection. This distant past, so removed from our own lives, but so integral to understanding how we came together, kept revealing new layers.

* * *

On a Saturday in July 1945, Leon and Pepa in Dzhambul, and Mottel and Peshke with their new baby in Juma, surely celebrated another revelatory radio broadcast: Most Polish citizens could soon return, including Jews.

It could easily have gone a different way. Other minorities who had been Polish citizens before the war—notably ethnic Ukrainians and Belarusians who constituted nearly 20 percent of those deported to the Gulag—were not granted the right to repatriate and leave the Soviet Union.

Why, then, allow the Polish Jews to return? Stalin, a shrewd strategist, surely weighed the political benefits. He saw a role for Jewish Communists in establishing a Polish satellite state. At the same time, Stalin knew that many Polish Jews would want to move on to Palestine, and that offered another advantage. He supported the establishment of a Jewish state with Soviet sympathies. And he was eager to destabilize the British and their interests in Palestine. Perhaps these refugees could tip the balance.

Whatever Stalin's determining political calculus, for our grandparents the announcement that they could leave felt like a liberation. Repatriation meant a chance to escape the Soviet Union. "Our intention was to get out of Russia. Any place but Russia," my great-uncle Simon said.

The vast majority of the Polish Jews also signed up to depart, overcoming any initial apprehensions that this could be another secret loyalty test that would land them in the Gulag. The novelist Perlov explained the rationale: "One thing *was* certain: This was the only, the final opportunity and one was determined to take the risk."

* * *

In the warming days of 1946, the season of renewal, our grandparents clutched tickets written in Russian on one side and Polish on the other. "The scene at the freight station already resembled the one on the shores of the Red Sea before its waters parted," Perlov wrote of the scene that likely greeted them, invoking once more the biblical Exodus. "Here and there fires had been lighted and already people were boiling milk, brewing tea and cooking porridge for little children."

Freight trains with bunks installed, previously used by exiles, prisoners, and soldiers, awaited them. This was no luxury trip, though it lacked the terror of the deportation cattle car. They were free to stop at stations as they moved west, traveling thousands of miles back to where their forced journey had begun.

After a more than six-year exile from Zamość, my grandparents focused on preserving a new life. Peshke scrubbed along the way a singular cloth diaper she used to dress her baby, and I imagine Mottel furtively traded for milk at station stops. On a parallel train route, Pepa and Leon must have sat next to each other, both anxiously imagining what it would be like to return to Poland, where his first wife and child had been left behind.

As Mottel and Peshke, Pepa and Leon traversed once more the steppes of Kazakhstan, the endless forests of Russia, and the bloodied earth of Ukraine, they each arrived at the same conclusion. Leon would not linger again in the wooded parks where he once strolled with his wife, Manya, and son, Kolonimus; nor would Pepa visit where her father had been buried before the war. Mottel and Peshke would not peek through the windows on the Rainbow Square to see what happened to his family's candy shop or her father's butchery, nor would they walk up the stairs to the apartment on the Salt Square where they had welcomed their first baby boy. To choose life, they decided never to return to Zamość.

CHAPTER 25

Alive and Free

"They went back?" Both of my siblings asked the same question when I told them Talia and I were traveling to Warsaw again, this time to visit the place where our grandparents landed after the war.

We all recalled being told that our family had vowed never to return to Poland. But that was not the full story. After Siberia and Central Asia came a long-sought return. Only not to Zamość. Peshke and Mottel, and Talia's grandparents Leon and Pepa, moved to the other side of Poland. They landed in a new western borderland, one that contained a vision for a Jewish future that could have created different endings for us all.

When Talia and I met up in Warsaw for her migration conference after my solo trip to Ukraine, we embarked on a journey to fill in this overlooked chapter. Clouds hung low, skies signaling a summer storm as we boarded our morning train at the Central Station. We eased into cozy seats in a café car with white tablecloths. Soon a waiter presented us with a steaming plate of apple pancakes. Far from home and the stress of life with small children, we savored a European train adventure.

Our grandparents' journey across Poland, seventy-seven years earlier, bore little resemblance. By the time they chugged past these same thick pine forests, they'd been confined for weeks to a dirty train car, sleeping on shelves. They had already hurtled past an increasingly ravaged Russia and Ukraine. And the long-awaited return across the border back into Poland had been no homecoming.

Jewish refugees reported Poles pelted rocks at their trains and jeered at them to keep going. One woman who gave birth to her son on the journey—lacking clothing, food, or diapers for him—asked a Polish stationmaster for milk. Instead, he threatened their lives. Yiddish writer Dovid Sfard described a new dimension to the "old hatred and contempt," that Poles often felt toward Jews. "A sort of bitterness and schadenfreude that shocked the heart." Poles killed more than one thousand Jews in the year after the war.

Even as our grandparents felt the rush of spotting fields resplendent with the wild strawberries of their youth and the comfort of conversing with native fluency at station stops, anguished stories passed like wildfire. Zamość, unlike many demolished towns, remained. "The houses, the streets, the city square with the municipal building in the middle—everything stands as it was before, but it is ossified," wrote Helena Schaffner, one of the first to return in 1945. "The deathly silence that I encountered, was so disassembling, so suffocating, that one thought that the air had been expelled from here." She left the following morning.

Months later, those who returned to Zamość from the Soviet Union in the spring of 1946 still perceived a stench of burned flesh, smoking bones. "It is not the song of birds that reaches our ears—we hear the plaintive cry of the ones who were tortured," Akiva Eierweiss wrote of his return. Others described looking to the windows where Jewish mothers once lit candles for Sabbath. The lights were on, but Polish Catholic families now lived there.

Former neighbors again and again greeted Jews who knocked on doors with the same piercing words: *Pan żyje? You're still alive?*

* * *

"I didn't want to go back to Zamość," my grandmother said definitively, with a "feh" and the shake of white hair. She feared the void or the ghosts of her murdered father who predicted her baby would die and her younger sister she had refused to bring with her. "I knew if I would go there, I'd be dead."

Instead, our grandparents entered a new stage of displacement. They traveled to a region of Poland where, back in Uzbekistan, they had been told they would receive the most help. This was a place where a radical role reversal had taken hold and Jewish life was rekindling in a repudiation of the Nazi destruction.

The so-called "New Zion" had been seeded in 1945, about a year before our grandparents began their repatriation journeys. After the Red Army liberated the concentration camps at Gross-Rosen, survivors sent a telegram—*We are alive and free!*—to Warsaw's fledgling Central Committee of Jews in Poland. The organization dispatched Jacob Egit, a Communist activist, and Yitzhak Zuckerman, a hero of the Warsaw ghetto uprising, to survey the situation. On a summer day, their plane touched down in a mineral-rich territory of coal mines, textile mills, and recently liberated concentration camps.

Emaciated survivors recounted how they had moved into vacated German homes, adopted their former persecutors' clothes, and appropriated their factories, farms, and businesses. The ambitious Egit resolved then that his people's future was not in Palestine or in America. No, it was at this very site in Lower Silesia, an area just east of the prewar Polish-German border. "I was haunted by the thought that here, in this land which the Germans had cultivated for so many years, the Jews could exact their retribution and justice and repudiate Hitler's 'final solution.'" Europe would not be Judenrein after all.

Egit's epiphany arrived at an opportune moment. With Soviet control over Eastern Europe established as the Allies carved up spheres of influence, Stalin now planned to claim this land for Poland. The shift westward became official weeks later after the Potsdam Conference. Warsaw needed bodies to inhabit land vacated by the millions of Germans being forcibly displaced in these newly "reclaimed territories," so-called because they had been Polish hundreds of years before. Homes were plentiful; towns were relatively intact.

Jewish revival, in stark contrast to the utter devastation elsewhere in Europe, emerged. "Everywhere you turn you see Jews going about their business or standing in small clusters on street corners," reported the secretary of the American Jewish Labor Committee, Jacob Pat. "If an occasional German passes by, you know him by a white armband—just as the yellow badge with the Star of David had once marked the Jew."

More than 3.3 million Jews, the largest community in the world at the time, had called Poland home before the war. Only about 4 percent of those who had remained in the country had survived—hidden in forests and even graves, protected by courageous gentiles, passing as Aryans, or enduring concentration camps. In stark contrast, an estimated 90 percent of those who had fled to the Soviet Union lived to see the end of the war. They had suffered deportation to the Gulag, forced labor in communal farms, or conscription into the Red Army. But they were alive. They now constituted an estimated three-quarters of Polish Jews who had survived.

Egit, actualizing the plans of Warsaw policymakers, invited Polish Jewish refugees in the Soviet Union to join their community in formerly German territory. He called it a new "Yishev," a Yiddishized take on the Hebrew word "Yishuv," used for the Jewish settlement in Palestine. The response from the Committee of Polish Jews in Russia was ecstatic: "As we read your letter, we saw before our eyes not only the shattered, tragic picture of the martyrdom and pain of our people, but also your faces, your eyes burning with creative fire, the resolve to build a destroyed life anew."

"The Russian nation rescued us from annihilation," organizers of the Community of Polish Jews said in explaining their situation to Egit. "Now we are on the verge of achieving repatriation to our liberated homeland."

Most of the Jews who returned to Poland would be directed toward these "reclaimed territories." The refugees from the Soviet Union would provide bodies to work, and unlike the Nazi camp survivors who were almost all adults and too emaciated to reproduce right away, as many as twenty-five thousand children. "It was they who were to decide the future of the Jewish nation in Poland," writes the historian Kamil Kijek. Among that renewing generation, my father.

* * *

When my grandparents stepped off their train onto Polish soil, the town where they landed was not the promised "New Zion." Legnica, until recently known as Liegnitz in German, teemed with occupying Red Army soldiers and Polish citizens returned from the hinterlands of the Soviet Union. The once beautiful town felt like "Sodom and Gomorrah," in the words of one refugee. "This was the home that our new-old homeland provided for its citizens, returning from Siberian imprisonment," she bemoaned.

Four of the Gerson siblings, two spouses, and two babies perched on the side of the road, disoriented. Moishe, with his strength and knack for work, was not with them, having ventured back to Poland separately with the wife he had met in Uzbekistan and their infant son. As Mottel, perhaps questioning how he let the youngest brother leave them at this dire moment, tried to determine a plan, a passerby from Zamość chanced upon them. What were they doing in Legnica?

We just arrived from Russia, and we have nowhere to go. Is there a shelter where we can spend the night?

The man had other ideas. He revealed a gun.

We can just kick out the Germans. Let's go!

They approached a home. At the sight of the weapon, a distraught family scrambled to gather their belongings. "Even a German family, even I knew what they did to our parents, I couldn't do that," Simon realized as he watched his landsman drive them out. But that did not stop the Gerson siblings from moving in.

* * *

About 150 miles south from where my family was settling in Legnica, Talia's grandparents had arrived in the Upper Silesian town of Bytom. It was there that Pepa and Leon would sign registration cards with the

Central Committee of Jews in Poland as Mr. and Mrs. Inlender, leaving behind the first record I'd found of them as a couple.

Talia and I had traveled a few hours by train west from Warsaw to Katowice and then on by car to Bytom, where we were staying. It did not take long for the town's history to become palpable. Upon entering Aparthotel Centrum, we were immediately greeted by a retro map of Bytom circa 1945 featuring its prominent central "Adolf Hitler Platz." We dropped our bags and headed to explore the town center steps from our hotel. Rain gushed as we entered the dreary former Hitler Square, which had been renamed Market Square immediately following the war.

Talia and I approached a café on the enormous square just as rays of sun broke through to glisten on the soaked bricks. A woman in her early seventies with short reddish hair and hot pink lipstick, awaited us, smiling. With no remaining organized Jewish community, a rabbi friend in Warsaw had connected us with Izabella Kuehnel, a Polish woman who had curated an exhibit on the town's Jews.

Izabella's warmth eased us into Bytom, even as she told us its diabolic history. "These were all Jewish houses here." She pointed across the sprawling central square of a town that was once home to about thirty-five hundred Jews. Known before and during the war as German Beuthen, Bytom held a macabre distinction: Its residents constituted the first documented transport among the nearly 1.1 million European Jews deported to Auschwitz for extermination. By the time the Jews of Beuthen understood there was no escaping, Zyklon B filled their lungs. Gasping for air, trampling each other, bodies convulsed in agony until hearts seized and stopped beating.

After the war, by the time Stalin claimed Beuthen for Poland in the summer of 1945, most German residents had already fled, fearful of reprisals from Poles and their Soviet-backed government. Very few Jewish residents had survived, and those who did mostly moved elsewhere. For a brief period, homes stood eerily vacant. But when Pepa and Leon landed here in the early spring of 1946, the city buzzed again as repatriated Polish citizens arrived by the trainload.

* * *

Izabella led us to a large, once-stately apartment building, one of two addresses where Talia's grandparents resided in Bytom. This, she told us, would have been Pepa and Leon's first stop: Here they signed their names as they registered and were provided a place to sleep in a shelter. Could this serene vacant plaza once have pulsed with the displaced—among them Talia's grandparents? Leon's voice, always so reserved in Talia's memories, may have resounded loud and raw in Yiddish as he reunited with his nephew Zyg. The young man, who had found his way out of the Kazakh jail and back from Uzbekistan with his father and siblings, had arrived first in Bytom.

Pepa and Leon soon left the shelter for a building nearby. As we walked around Bytom searching for their second address, we carried a photo of Pepa that I had found stashed in my mother-in-law's closet. From her age and the surrounding architecture, it appeared to be taken after the war in Poland. Just twenty-two to Leon's forty-one, she wears a light summer dress, her hair perfectly coiffed, a flirtatious glint in her eye.

We paused where Izabella suspected the photo had been taken. Though the Communist-style cement building had been redone, by the slope in front we spotted a banister similar to the one Pepa grasps in the photo. Knowing the ghastly truths that must have greeted her in Poland, I considered her enticing smile. How had she found a way to look with pleasure at her partner? How could she not? Upon facing the depths of humanity, she appeared to have found love.

* * *

After Izabella said goodbye, Talia and I wandered through Bytom on our own. The initially foreboding site of the former Adolf Hitler Platz had transformed into a festive square with young people lounging in open-air cafés. We sampled savory waffles and a local sour cherry rhubarb ale, but didn't indulge for long. In Bytom, we had one more place to visit.

I would never have considered submitting an inquiry to the Polish state security archives if not for Polish historian Dariusz Stola. He urged me on, speaking from personal and professional experience as he told me that I might be surprised by what the Communists collected on our families. My initial request to the Polish Institute of National Remembrance for our grandparents' files had come back as I expected—no records. But months later, I received an email with Leon's name detailing a lawsuit that he had filed in the spring of 1946, the day after he arrived in Bytom.

Talia and I made our way across the square toward the courthouse in the waning summer light. The hulking neo-Renaissance building was topped with the scales of justice. Talia's grandfather had once also climbed these stairs, determined to claim the property of his wealthy cousin Wigdor.

When had it dawned on Wigdor that he would be forced to abandon his home, the grandest in Zamość? That perhaps he should have fled to the Soviet side with his ailing wife? At first, he appeared protected. Wigdor was among a group of eight prominent local Jews the gestapo called to a meeting upon occupying Zamość in October 1939. The new mayor had instructed the gathered men to compose a Council of Elders to represent their community's interests to authorities. A few months later, the group expanded to a twenty-four-member Judenrat, or Jewish Council.

"At that moment, no one knew what sort of character the Judenrat would assume; what its functions would consist of," Jekuthiel Zwillich, a Zamość survivor, wrote in the memorial book. "Otherwise, many of these Jews would have fled to Russia." By the time they understood their heinous responsibilities, it would be too late.

The Nazis designated Judenrat members a class above. Initially, they seemed immune from the leather whips with lead balls that Germans and their Ukrainian guards used to beat Jewish men. Then, in the spring of 1941, the SS officers placed the order: All Jews must immediately move to the poorest part of Zamość, where a ghetto was being established.

Even as Wigdor was forced to abandon his beloved home, he still preserved privileges as part of the Judenrat. His new house was better than most of the dilapidated structures in the packed ghetto of seven thousand Jewish residents—about a third of whom had been forcibly relocated from Austria, Czech Moravia, and Germany. As many began to starve, Wigdor and the other members of the Judenrat could eat at a restaurant serving fried and roasted meat, fish, and a variety of drinks.

But with advantages came responsibilities to the German overlords: The Judenrat was charged with creating a list of all Jews relegated to the ghetto, one that would later be weaponized for mass murder.

This ghetto census counted Wigdor's relatives who had remained in town—among them Inlenders who had long been a mystery to us. I had searched since the first day Talia and I made our Zamość connection for signs of three people memorialized on the wall of martyrs that my grandfather had helped create in the New Jersey cemetery: Tuvia, Leah, and Chaya Inlender. But for years nobody seemed to know who they were, least of all Talia. Then Marek, the Zamość high school teacher, found a Polish version of their names on the Judenrat census. With that, he searched in the archives for a marriage certificate, deducing it would likely be from the year before their child was born.

What he unearthed next shocked us all. On Tuvia Inlender's marriage certificate, the parents listed had the same names as those of Leon. The two men, Tuvia and Leon, must have been brothers. That meant the man enshrined on the New Jersey monument was Talia's great-uncle. Three more murdered Inlenders that Leon kept contained inside himself, never revealing them to his surviving son. What did he know of the fate of his brother's family?

Surely the powerful Wigdor Inlender did everything he could to protect himself and his one daughter who remained in Zamość from the encroaching Nazi death machine. But what about the family of Tuvia, who would have been his cousin? What did he do?

* * *

When the gestapo blocked exits to the ghetto one day during Passover in 1942 and then proceeded toward the Judenrat headquarters, its members must have sensed the terror they were about to engage in. A couple of weeks earlier, Lublin's Jewish council had reported to them a bizarre and chilling phenomenon: Polish railway workers had seen thousands of Jews disembark trains in Bełżec every day; no one ever left.

What options did the Zamość Judenrat have when the gestapo officers, armed with whips, gnashing dogs, and rifles, next ordered them to round up twenty-five hundred fellow Jews for deportation? Wigdor most likely joined the other members in dividing the streets and going house-to-house, instructing horror-struck families to pack up for a trip "to the east." Soon grandparents and small children alike gathered in the square, many dressed in their Sabbath finery, hoisting satchels for their journey.

It was already dark when the gestapo forced with trudgens and bullets the assembled thousands of Jews—among them hundreds of children—into train cars. Likely in their ranks were Mottel's parents, Chaim and Esther, and Peshke's parents, Shmuel-Josef and Chaya, as well as her sisters, Dora and Feiga.

Was Wigdor able to protect his Inlender cousins and their families from this Aktion? Or was Leon's brother Tuvia also forced into trains then, with his wife, Chaya, and daughter, Leah? Was Leon's first wife, Manya, along with her parents, and son, Kolonimus, selected? Is this when the young boy stepped out of line and was shot with his grandfather? Or did he suffocate to death from the exhaust of a Soviet tank in the airtight chamber at Bełżec? We will never know.

Remaining ghetto residents demanded letters from family who they were told had been sent to labor camps in the east. But no messages arrived. Until, one night, a few days after the deportation, the teenage son of a council functionary, Lejb Wolsztejn, showed up at the apartment of the head of the Judenrat in the early hours of the morning. He told a story too revolting and devastating to believe.

The train had departed Zamość packed so tightly with human cargo that people were trampled and smothered to death. When the surviving passengers piled out at Bełżec, they were told to line up in rows of four, men separated from women, and go through a shower and disinfectant before they were transferred to the east. Lejb lowered his body into the excrement of a latrine pit that SS officers allowed them to use. He escaped notice while the others were packed into barracks, poking his head up later to see doors open to reveal bodies, collapsed and devoid of life, dumped into carts. Eventually, the teen stealthily pulled his soiled self out of the pit, crawled under the barbed wire, and with the help of nearby Roma, miraculously made his way the thirty miles back to Zamość.

Upon hearing his story, "The last spark of hope, which flickered among a part of the hapless, was then fully extinguished," the head of the Judenrat, Miesczyslaw Garfinkel, recalled after the war. "There were then no illusions about what Bełżec was." But the boy's revelations could not stop the deportations, nor the Judenrat from supporting the SS in selections. Wolsztejn was apprehended in another Aktion. That time he did not survive.

* * *

By August 1942, the Zamość Judenrat was no longer untouchable. Wigdor had no choice but to welcome the gestapo officer who liked to visit his ghetto home. Adolf Bohlmann, a native of turn-of-the-century Berlin, liked to linger, conversing about art and literature with the business magnate. When the Nazi departed, he would tuck under his arm a treasured piece of the Inlender family's rapidly diminishing art collection. After a long chat one day, Bohlmann ordered Wigdor onto the street. Then he shot him. Wigdor Inlender, the richest Jew in town, was ultimately powerless to save anyone in Zamość, including himself.

In the predawn hours of October 16, 1942, the German military police ordered all remaining Jews out of their homes. When the order was made to march to Izbica, some twelve miles away, one teenager took action in the only way she could. It was Wigdor's granddaughter Roma Inlender, whose photo Talia had discovered the day after we made our Zamość connection, the one that revealed to us a glimpse of the lost extended family Leon hid. The adolescent refused to move, stopping to take off a pair of boots that were rubbing her legs as she walked. A Nazi officer shot Roma, and then her mother. Soon, signs went up in the ghetto declaring it Judenrein.

* * *

Talia's grandfather went to court in the spring of 1946 to avenge, in one small way, the decimation of his family. He filed a case for the return of Wigdor Inlender's "abandoned and deserted" property. The first step: Prove the death of the owner. This for many victims was an impossible task since no records or witnesses existed of millions murdered. But the wealthy Wigdor's death had been observed—just not by the people Leon called as witnesses in court.

The first, a baker, stated on the record, "I recognized his corpse and took it to the cemetery on a cart to bury him." The second, a photographer, also claimed to see Wigdor's body. But neither man's name appeared in the census of the highly regulated ghetto. One of the men provided a conflicting, highly detailed account of how he survived the war by escaping a concentration camp and living undercover not far from Bytom, the other side of the country from Zamość. To get a chance at justice, Leon must have lied, convincing these men to provide false witness. That part worked. The court accepted their testimony, and Wigdor's death certificate was promptly issued. But this alone was not sufficient to get Leon the deed to his former home.

The next court decision, on the property rights, found that Talia's grandfather, being "the first cousin of the owners, and therefore, a distant relative... does not have an active right to demand possession." No matter that all Wigdor's direct descendants were now dead. Of those who remained in Zamość, three had been shot and one, his daughter Sala, deported to a death camp. And Wigdor's family members who fled to the Soviet Union also perished. His wife, Rywka, succumbed to cancer. One son, Salek, died of typhus in a Kazakh prison. Another son, Moniek, remained in Lviv when the Nazis invaded and was executed, as was his other daughter, Rozia.

But even though nobody from Wigdor's immediate family had survived, Leon had no recourse. Such was the Communist justice in the wake of Nazi atrocities. Outside the circuit court in Zamość, graves of Jews formed the sidewalk. Inside, the attorney general of the Republic of Poland "discontinued" Leon's court proceedings on April 30, 1946. Wigdor's property now belonged to the government, and the Zamość chief administrator and his appointees would remain in the house.

Did Leon, upon discovering no justice or vengeance was available to him, determine to hold his anger and sadness inside? Was this when he and Pepa decided they could no longer stay in Poland? Or was it another deadly attack on Jews, after the Nazis had been defeated, that pushed them to flee once more?

* * *

"Do you know what is a pogrom?" My grandmother sits stiffly on the black leather sofa in my father's office, a classical CD softly plays in the background, red and yellow tulips in glass vases line the windowsill behind her. My sister, Merissa, then a teenager, interviews her for a school project: "Can you tell me?"

"They killed forty-two people, women and children, in a terrible, terrible attack." My grandmother does not detail for my sister how on July 4, 1946, Poles mauled, beat, and stabbed concentration camp survivors and returned refugees from the Soviet Union in a town called Kielce. Nor does she explain how the virulent fallacy dating back to the Middle Ages, of Jews killing a Christian baby to use the blood for Passover matzah, fueled the ruthless attack.

What my grandmother shared was that the pogrom coincided with her return to Poland and haunted the move into their newly appropriated home. In other recordings, she and her brothers-in-law told more. How one evening weeks after the Kielce Pogrom, the siblings let their guard down during a joyous reunion. Moishe had arrived for a visit from the nearby town where he had landed upon repatriating. They laughed at the antics of the baby boys, caught up on gossip, and prepared a Shabbat dinner—when a harsh rap at the door silenced their gathering.

Polish fascists barked in piercing tones to open the door. A pitched scream ricocheted across the dark streets. More shrieks ensued, voices bleeding fear. Like in Kielce weeks before, a rumor had permeated that local Jews kidnapped a Christian child. The insidious blood libel again unleashed, leaflets circulated calling for a pogrom. Chuma grasped baby Sol tight; Peshke held my father to her pounding heart. They dove together into a closet. The men grabbed knives and barricaded the door.

But here is where their stories diverge. Moishe recalled they next heard a signal for the Haganah, a militia of Jews with ammunition and grenades who battled the Polish fascists. In the early dawn hours, he opened the door to see Jews patrolling the street and realized they were safe.

Simon remembered the night differently. The men had run to a Soviet property nearby where a guard always stood watch and begged him to come help. *They're going to kill us, and we have three small children.*

The guard responded that he could not leave his post. But then he opened the window and stuck out his gun. *If they're going to break the door, help me God, I'm going to shoot.*

These opposing memories of what saved their lives that night—one of nascent Jewish power, the other of dependence—perhaps explains what came next. Moishe soon moved to Legnica and joined the Jewish cobblers' cooperative. He had faith that this could be a place to settle down and grow his family, to use his two strong hands to build a Jewish future in a new Communist Poland. But Simon, along with my grandparents and the other three siblings, lost all hope in the country of their birth.

* * *

Within months of the Kielce Pogrom, most Jews who had returned in the spring and summer of 1946 prepared to depart. Within a decade, the Moscow-controlled Polish government would crush Jacob Egit's dream of building up a Jewish zone within the Communist state, blasting it as a traitorous, "Zionist" initiative. Authorities threw him into a Warsaw prison. They soon purged most Jews in prominent positions. Never mind that, like Egit, they tended to be among the most committed Communists. In 1968, a virulent anti-Semitic campaign would denounce the remaining Jews as disloyal Zionists. In months, more than thirteen thousand Jews left Poland. This was the death knell of organized Jewish life in Poland until the end of Communist rule.

In retrospect, the departure of our grandparents and those who followed from Poland felt inevitable—due to the growing anti-Semitic violence and resurgent Polish nationalism. But did it have to be that way? I could now imagine a time when a different ending still seemed possible, when our families claimed a formerly German home in the country of their birth.

As Talia and I boarded a train headed for the Czech border, I felt heavy with the finality of leaving behind the generations of Yiddish culture woven through our families. Days before my family decided to leave, my grandfather had petitioned the Legnica health service, pleading that it "save my young life and help me to regain my health." Unable to work due to back pain, he requested balneotherapy, a mineral springs treatment that doctors recommended. But by the time a response arrived from the health ministry months later in September 1946, my grandfather was gone. He had packed up again, lugging my toddler father to an unknown place, undertaking a grueling journey with a damaged back. My grandmother's bitter, disappointed words rang in my head: "We decided, me and Grandpa, we can't stay here." They were done with Poland, and, after seven years running, a spark had been struck that they could move to another place to help build a home where their Jewish child could thrive.

CHAPTER 26

Flight

Our train picked up speed, passing freight cars loaded with coal. Soon emerald fields, pristine lakes, and oak forests took over the industrialized landscape. We only realized we had crossed out of Poland into the Czech Republic when our cell phones dinged an alert, switching carriers. There were no metal detectors, no identity checks between countries in this common Europe. Soon our phones dinged again. We had seamlessly entered Slovakia. Along a riverside trail, a woman biked leisurely with her young child sitting behind her. The trees grew higher and we cut through ancient beech forests of the Carpathian Mountains.

Our grandparents must have been terrified as they traversed these same lovely places, mine with a baby in their arms. For them, on foot, in lorries and cargo trains, this ground Talia and I sped past in less than two hours was a multiday journey of defiance and desperation.

My grandparents' recollections of the illegal crossing out of Poland were hazy, as if a mythical force propelled them. The Kielce Pogrom, and the one that followed in Legnica, shoved them toward the border. I knew why they feared for their lives in Poland, but what lured them forward? While some refugees, like my grandfather, were ardent Zionists, many more had only wanted to return to Poland. Now tens of thousands of people departed on this exodus, many determined to travel on to Palestine. What had convinced them they could find a refuge in a Middle Eastern country—one whose British occupiers and majority Arab population remained equally determined to keep them out?

* * *

Toward the end of the war, representatives of the remnants of Poland's varied Zionist movements had gathered about fifty miles northwest of Zamość, in Lublin, as the Red Army secured its control of Warsaw. They took in each other's faces, creased from years of separation and catastrophic loss. Those at the table surely recounted their survival stories: hiding and fighting in Poland's capital, as partisans deep in the forests outside Vilna, and as "Asiatics" who had followed Hashomer Hatzair's call that they flee illegally to Uzbekistan. Then, together, they plotted a path forward.

A fiery voice at the symposium was one of the two men the Central Committee of Jews in Poland months later deployed to scope out Holocaust survivors. Whereas Communist organizer Jacob Egit, upon seeing concentration camp victims taking over Germans' homes, would envision a new Jewish home in Europe, Yitzhak Zuckerman interpreted the tumult differently.

The tall, mustachioed man, who had attacked SS officers as a leader of the Warsaw ghetto uprising, saw yet more evidence of what motivated him to join the Zionist leaders in Lublin. He believed Jews were a "cursed people" because they lacked what others had: "The bond with a little piece of earth he calls his own." Zuckerman had noticed the majority of the Jewish ghetto fighters were affiliated with the left-wing Zionist movements and found that connection to a land invigorated them. If Jews were to survive, he was convinced they could not remain a Diaspora people.

In Lublin, Zuckerman and his wife, Zivia Lubetkin, a founder of the Anti-Fascist Bloc and a fellow Warsaw ghetto uprising hero, had eagerly joined the leadership of the new Zionist effort. Like them, most of the organizers came out of the worker youth movements such as HeHalutz, Hashomer Hatzair, and Dror, but it also included representatives of

Jabotinsky's Revisionist Party. Though their Zionist politics differed, they all agreed on one thing: The surviving Jews desperately needed an exodus, a parting of the Red Soviet Sea that was rapidly encroaching on Poland. Together, they created a new organization, Brichah, Hebrew for "Flight," a movement to get the remnants of Europe's Jews to Palestine.

Brichah volunteers began to smuggle out of Poland tens of thousands of former Nazi camp inmates, partisans, and forest fighters. They implemented skills cultivated during the war—drafting false documents and identifying hidden routes. The organizers knew how to slide a few hundred refugees onto a train, whom to bribe with American cigarettes and whom with Russian vodka. Smugglers handed off migrants at stash houses and even the remnants of concentration camps; each individual member only knew what they needed to move people from one point to the next so they would not endanger the others if caught.

Then, in the winter of 1946, the focus of the Brichah leadership shifted from west to east, to prepare for a larger group of arriving Jewish survivors. "We realized that 180,000 Jews were returning to Poland from the Soviet Union," Zuckerman recalled, estimating the number of refugees who had survived as deportees, evacuees, serving in the military, and other ways in the Soviet Union. "We had to organize."

Their interest was twofold: to provide these repatriates a more secure future, and to get as many Jews as possible to support the Zionist cause. By 1939, the Jewish presence in Palestine had grown to about one-third of its total population, numbering more than half a million people. An influx of the refugees who survived in the Soviet Union could push the Jewish community closer to majority status, seen as a crucial threshold for asserting a right to sovereignty. But the British maintained the same strict immigration limitations established in 1939, when they had responded to Arab protests that Jewish immigration was undermining their political rights and national aspirations in Palestine. Warsaw, under pressure from London, which had supported the Polish government-in-exile during the war, refused to authorize departures. And so the question the Brichah leadership focused on was how to break these refugees across the border.

* * *

An opportunity emerged out of the darkest days for Polish Jews since Germany's surrender. Yitzhak Zuckerman had been pleading the Brichah's case to the Polish prime minister on July 4, 1946. A telephone call interrupted the discussion. The prime minister held the phone to his ear and grew pale. *Gentlemen, there is a pogrom at Kielce!*

Zuckerman raced to his apartment, grabbed his gun and a few grenades, and pocketed his fake documents with the Polish identity he'd used to survive under the Nazis. Soon a car with an Aryan-looking Jewish driver picked him up and drove him at breakneck speed a hundred miles to Kielce.

"I saw dozens of bodies; and meanwhile, more bodies of Jews killed on the roads were brought in. I saw pregnant women whose stomachs were ripped open," Zuckerman recalled. "And that wasn't in 1942, that was in 1946!" Body bags lined up next to each other testified to what he already believed: Poland without Nazis was still not safe for Jews.

After attending to the dead and their families, Zuckerman boarded a military plane. He berated the officer next to him: *Our lives can't be protected... They are killed on the trains and everywhere else, and there's a pogrom in Kielce! And there will surely be other places. Open the door for the Jews to leave!* Forty-eight hours later, he received a call from a senior member of the Polish government's security office.

Officially, Polish citizens, Jews included, were still not permitted to emigrate without special permission. But Warsaw offered Zuckerman a loophole: a clandestine stamp that would signify permission for Jews to exit Poland with the Brichah.

It's doubtful this decision was made solely out of concern for Jewish safety in Poland. Moscow was consolidating its control of Warsaw, in defiance of London's promises that the country would regain its independence after Germany and the Soviet Union tore it up at the beginning of the war. Reflecting years later, Zuckerman concluded that Stalin, who was eager to implant Communism in Palestine, supported the agreement to let Jews out in defiance of British desires:

"It's absolutely impossible to think that the mass exodus of Jews, after Kielce, was allowed without the knowledge of Moscow."

But at the time, the fear of deportation back to Poland ran high and necessitated a carefully orchestrated, secret operation. The first step was often trekking through farmlands dotted with daisies, buttercups, and Queen Anne's lace—which at night became refugee thoroughfares. On the Czechoslovak side, our grandparents likely boarded a freight train to Prague or Bratislava. But there was no chance to relax.

Before my grandparents entered Soviet-occupied Austria, the Haganah officers, the members of the Jewish Agency militia that had arrived to help spirit them to Palestine, informed refugees that their journey would become harder. Warsaw had turned a blind eye to their exit, and Prague was sympathetic to their plight, but there was no similar official order from Moscow. They had no travel permissions, and they now needed to reenter Soviet territory in Austria to arrive at the American sector.

To do so, the Brichah employed a time-tested way to get their Polish Jewish charges through to the American and British zones. "They told us not to speak Yiddish," my great-uncle Simon recalled. "We have to say we are Greeks."

* * *

Greeks? My grandparents? Mystified, I turned to the USC Shoah Foundation's massive archive of about sixty thousand Holocaust survivor testimonies and typed in "Greek." The words "Greek bluff" immediately popped up, linked to 288 entries.

Rapt, I listened to aging Jews perched in living rooms from Melbourne to Montevideo tell their stories of escape with the "Greek bluff." Recorded mostly in the 1990s and captured on VHS, Polish Jews spoke in the languages they'd adopted over the ensuing decades—Spanish, Hebrew, English—all with a familiar, nostalgic Yiddish inflection, even a man in Georgia who meshed it with a strong southern drawl and said "US of A." They shared, with a glint in their eyes, how once they'd crossed a border disguised as Greeks.

The "Greek bluff" went on for more than a year, beginning with concentration camp survivors pretending to be Greek Jews returning from Auschwitz. By the time our grandparents made their illegal departure, Soviets allowed Greeks to travel freely in hopes they would join the Communist forces fighting in a civil war in their country.

Their accounts were remarkably consistent, sharing the same instructions Simon said he had received as a cover: *Only speak in Hebrew prayers.* Not only did they not speak Greek, many could not converse in Hebrew. But they all knew certain prayers. They were instructed to recite holy words like "Baruch atah Adonai," "Blessed are you our God," while gesturing as if talking about lunch. Somehow the ruse worked, tricking countless soldiers who understood neither Greek nor Hebrew.

* * *

If Moscow had given the nod to let Jews travel to Palestine, the Brichah leadership did not yet know of it. What they did know was that Poles and others were being deported back to Iron Curtain countries. How else to explain the second harsher, even cruel, measure demanded of many refugees? To ensure their identity as Polish citizens would not be revealed, they were told: *Leave behind all documentation, including photos.* Gasps must have rung out among the refugees. For some, parting with a last likeness of a slaughtered mother or a memento of one's prewar accomplishments was too much. *We're not going to go.*

My grandmother surely found a rare solace in the photos she had carried of her parents and sisters. That family portrait from a time before her brothers left for Argentina. Another of the bright-eyed days when Mottel courted her in Zamość's verdant parks. Embracing her firstborn son, with a smile innocent of what was to come. Now her baby Arik, beloved parents, and her sisters were all dead, and she was being told she needed to wrench herself away from these precious few mementos.

The members of the Brichah were firm. If refugees wanted to continue with the group, they needed to follow their precautions. One slip could endanger the entire operation.

My grandmother summoned her steely courage. She parted with the photos of her past for a chance that her second son—my father—might grow safely. Their bags lighter, the Gerson siblings trudged together out of Czechoslovakia. They joined an exodus of people hauling belongings in satchels, wearing multiple layers of clothes despite the summer heat. Mottel must have struggled to suppress his groans as pain shot from his back with each step. Simon helped him walk, hauling Mottel's body weight on his own back, while my father, a baby, was carried on the broad shoulders of a young man from the Jewish underground militia of Palestine.

* * *

Days later, my aunt Raya, who had survived elsewhere in the Soviet Union—she never wanted to speak of where exactly—stopped in at a transit site. She spotted a pile of discarded photos on the ground. Could that be her cousin Mottel? She locked onto the likeness of her earnest cousin, and then traced other loved ones from her childhood cut short.

How Raya, the elderly relative I took Talia to visit many decades later in New York, spotted the family heirlooms was a miraculous mystery, an aberration in the family horror story. That she was able to return the photos to my grandparents when they reunited in Germany, another miracle. The rules and permeability of the borders were in flux. Raya found a different passageway and carried the documents and photos with her, eventually presenting them to my grandparents.

"There's something you say, it has to be, b'shert," Raya told me. "It was meant to be. This must have been b'shert."

* * *

Surely nothing felt meant to be for Peshke in the summer of 1946, once more on the run with a baby. The Gersons would have joined thousands at the reception center of a huge dark brick building in Vienna, the Rothschild Hospital shelter. The Brichah had swiftly gotten them out of Soviet territory, but now there was a crush of people with nowhere to go. The way to Palestine required secretly ascending the Alps to Italian or French stash houses and hiding out while awaiting rickety boats to cross the Mediterranean. But the Brichah deemed my father too young for that journey.

Instead, my grandmother and Chuma must have held their baby boys tight in another line to be deloused, to be sprayed with DDT. Safely arrived in the city's American zone, they joined the mass of humanity packed into cots everywhere in the formerly renowned hospital, clothing and diapers hanging from a nail or a pipe. The air was surely foul and heavy with human perspiration and the filth of thousands of people. Did my grandmother tirelessly scan the notes left by refugees searching for lost loved ones that lined the walls to the ceiling, hoping to chance upon a sign of her sisters or parents? Or was all they could think: Where were they to go from here?

When it was all done, the United Nations issued my one-year-old father his own displaced-person identification card. Stamped across it in big letters in English was the word "Transient."

CHAPTER 27

Displaced Persons

Evening light glistened on the swift Enns River as Talia and I strode over a two-lane bridge toward a street lined with spacious country cottages. We had left Poland behind that morning, moving quickly via train to Vienna's gleaming station. There we'd rented a car, racing into tunnels dynamited through breathtaking mountains, to arrive in Admont, population 5,010, just in time for dinner. Now signs enticed with offers of white-water rafting, trekking, and mountain biking, and though that was not what we were here to do, an unexpected glee bounced between us.

This precious town was one of the two former sites of Austrian displaced persons camps where our families had landed in 1946. Talia's grandparents had lived here; the next day we would drive about sixty miles north to the place where mine lasted just one miserable winter. We had anticipated visits to bleak sites at the outskirts of society. Instead, we now found ourselves in a pristine vacation destination, encircled by towering mountains and emerald-green fields that evoked *The Sound of Music*.

If only we could have shared this discovery with Talia's father. I could envision Nachum donning his spandex bike shorts and riding into the Alpine foothills, making friends with even the crotchety lady at the bakery, enfolding everyone in his exuberant return.

Though my father-in-law had come very close, he never returned to the site where he spent his first months. In 1995, Nachum invited Talia's older brother to join him on a work trip to Vienna and an excursion to his presumed initial home. They drove to a town called Rottenmann, where the mayor welcomed Nachum with a firm handshake and helped dig up his birth certificate. But we were to discover that Rottenmann was only the site where he was born. With great urgency, a pregnant Pepa had been driven the thirty minutes to its hospital, where she labored in a birth so terrifying that she never risked another child. The displaced persons camp where she returned, cradling infant Nachum, was in Admont. Now we hurried down its charming main street, eager to uncover what remained of this site of limbo and new beginnings.

* * *

The displaced persons camps were intended to serve as brief, temporary housing sites. Years before our grandparents moved in, as the end of World War II drew near, President Franklin Roosevelt had welcomed men representing forty-four allied nations to the White House. They signed onto a global social services agency: the United Nations Relief and Rehabilitation Administration, or UNRRA. Among its chief charges was repatriating war-ravaged Europe's millions of displaced persons, or DPs.

A relatively small group among the displaced were the Jewish survivors of Nazi camps, skeletal beings who upon liberation had been too ill and destitute to depart on their own. Nearly half perished within weeks of the Allied arrival. Three months after the Nazi surrender, many of the remaining sixty thousand or so camp survivors still languished behind barbed wire, filthy, hungry, and sickly.

"As matters stand now, we appear to be treating the Jews as the Nazis treated them except that we do not exterminate them," Earl Harrison, the Quaker dean of the University of Pennsylvania Law School, wrote in a commissioned report to President Truman. "They are in concentration camps in large numbers under our military guard instead of SS troops." Harrison may have engaged in some hyperbole, but he was also genuinely appalled at the conditions. US Army General George S. Patton, who oversaw the DP Camps, did not share his concerns. "Harrison and his ilk believe that the Displaced Person is a human being, which he is not," he wrote in his journal, "and this applies particularly to the Jews who are lower than animals."

Harrison recommended the DP camps provide Jewish victims with additional care and house them separately from ethnic Poles, Ukrainians, and others—among whom were former Nazi collaborators and virulent anti-Semites. Truman, in turn, ordered Patton to change US policy, with the general officially complying but in his journal revealing his plan to put Jews "in sort of improvised ghettos." Then the US president endeavored to convince the British that Jews needed separate camps.

A fierce diplomatic battle ensued, exposing fundamental differences in approach stretching from the DP camps to Palestine. The British made the case that to separate Jews would implicitly endorse the racist policies of the Germans. "We do not of course admit that Jews constitute a separate nationality," assessed the British Foreign Office. What's more, to say Jews could not return to their countries of origin would in effect support that "Nazis were right in holding that there was no place for Jews in Europe."

Beneath the humanitarian argument lay a means to promote London's political aims. The British—who had moved away from supporting Jewish statehood in Palestine—knew that recognizing Jews as a distinct nation would also strengthen Zionist arguments for sovereignty.

Washington, in contrast, began to advocate opening immigration to Palestine for Jewish refugees. Harrison reported that it would be impossible for most DPs to return to their birthplaces. Since Palestine was the overwhelming choice of the survivors, it was owed them by the "civilized world," particularly since "their opportunity to be admitted into the United States or into other countries in the Western hemisphere is limited, if not impossible."

Responding to British fears that Jewish migration would enrage the Arab nations, Truman, in his communication with London, rationalized that threat was now tempered: "The number of such persons who wish immigration to Palestine or who would qualify for admission there, is, unfortunately, no longer as large as it was before the Nazis began their extermination program."

The British government eventually acquiesced on one point and created Jewish-specific DP camps. In Austria, they set up a few in resorts that Nazis had once frequented, but such comfort was extremely rare. Some were linked to former concentration camps and most, like Admont, were converted from former barracks built for Wehrmacht soldiers. But the British, as the powerful occupying force in Palestine, refused to budge on Zionist demands for broader Jewish immigration.

That did not stop the rapid influx more than a year after the war ended of Jews who survived in the Soviet Union arriving in Austria and Germany with dreams of making it to the Holy Land. "Jews were getting off with bundles and children on their backs," wrote Alexander Squadrilli of the US Army in Frankfurt. "They had a hard glitter in their eyes, that told me they had reached the end of their tolerance—they would cut my throat if I did anything against them."

The Americans and British alike labeled them "infiltrees," who had suspiciously arrived from the Communist east. Even the British conceded these latecomers could not be returned to a Poland where Jews were being killed in pogroms, but what to do with them? Despite the refugees' steely determination to get to Palestine, these journeying survivors were soon stuck in a liminal state.

* * *

Before our trip, through a call placed by an Austrian friend to the Admont Town Hall, I'd connected with another high school teacher who'd excavated his town's little-told Jewish history. We planned to meet Josef Hasitschka for dinner, and were now running late, delayed by our long day of travel from Poland. When we at last ducked into a guesthouse with a backyard beer garden, every table was taken, the scene redolent with summer evening joy. Talia spotted first the muscular man in his seventies with a bushy white mustache setting off his rosy cheeks. Josef waved, inviting us to take a seat at the large rough-hewn wood table and introducing his warmly smiling wife and adult son. A waiter in lederhosen brought us beer steins. Nearby, a monk in a frock drank with friends at the loudest, most boisterous table.

We soon learned we were not the first North Americans to show up in Admont on a search for refugee roots. Nearly three decades before us, a Canadian had inquired at the town hall, claiming he had been born in a Jewish displaced persons camp. *Did anyone know about what had happened?* Since Josef researched local history, the town clerk pointed the visitor his way.

But at that time Josef knew nothing about Jewish refugees in Admont. The older generation did not talk much about World War II. This was a widespread phenomenon throughout Austria. Witnesses shared about the last weeks of the war, the Allied bombings, and the terrible years of foreign occupation. But not their role. Austrians primarily saw themselves as victims of Hitler's Germany, rather than as perpetrators.

As a result, the presence of Jewish refugees was largely forgotten over the generations. Josef was determined to find out more. He discovered then that his charming mountainside development had been constructed upon the site of demolished barracks where Jewish displaced persons once lived. Josef realized many townspeople who had witnessed the DP camps did not want to recall that time, during which they also suffered. But he, as a historian born in the next generation, was persistent in seeking the full story of his town.

After we made plans to meet up in the morning for a tour of what he had uncovered, Talia and I made our way back over the bridge, invigorated by Josef's welcome and stomachs full of beer and rich mushroom risotto. We were not ready to return to our room, and instead followed a side path, tracing a stream over narrow footbridges until the trail widened into a resplendent field of wildflowers, the wind rustling through the grass.

The last whispers of sun illuminated the bald face of the Alps. As we breathed in the crisp Admont night, I felt as if we'd chanced upon a wonderland. What was it like to arrive here for Pepa and Leon? Did they sigh with contentment, finally, at a place to rest in a mountain paradise? Or was this a bewildering, remote town with a ferocious winter approaching?

* * *

In the brilliant morning light of the following day, Josef drove us up a hill shaded by a canopy of green. To our right, he pointed out a tidy residential community with spectacular views of the town and mountains beyond. Josef told us the last building that had been a barrack was demolished some years before. The only sign he could point to of the historic presence here of Jewish displaced persons was the concrete remnants of a foundation.

As we walked around, Talia lingered behind, initially seeing more than I did. "It feels a bit like a kibbutz," she said, referring to Israel's communal agricultural settlements. There had, indeed, been an active kibbutz structure at the camp, and I tried to imagine where there had been a shared dining room. I recalled an American newsreel about the camp that Josef had shared, where young men in shorts and button-up shirts, women in light linen dresses, rolled up their sleeves, some surely to reveal concentration camp numbers. They walked purposefully into the camp under a welcome sign with "Blessed is the one who enters," spelled out in large Hebrew letters, "ברוך הבא." Here, they had put their still-young bodies to work growing rutabagas and cauliflower, milking cows, and performing calisthenics; they had learned trades and found new loves, or at least the comfort of another lonely warm body.

Josef had also gifted me a book on the Admont DP camp, which I'd stayed up late reading the night before. It detailed how tensions erupted when two thousand Jews who had emerged from death camps and Gulags descended on the quiet town, then home to fourteen hundred Austrians, at a time when everyone suffered hunger. The self-administered camps were not always able to contain their traumatized residents, who were blamed for everything from petty thefts to breaking into a nearby castle, smashing its windows and tearing oil paintings. A visiting British officer concluded that the Jews at Admont were the most troublesome DPs in

Austria and that "these people were poor specimens of their race." The UNRRA authorities that oversaw the camp saw it differently, decrying "the open hostility of most Austrians to Displaced Persons not only in the Admont area, but throughout the British zone."

Inside the camp, trauma hung heavy. That first summer, bars of soap arrived with the imprint RIF. Residents protested, convinced that the acronym stood for "Reich Industry Fat" and that the bars had been cooked with the bodies of the slaughtered. Not until decades later would Holocaust scholars conclude that despite persistent rumors, no evidence existed that Nazis had manufactured soap from human fat. The imprint meant "Reichsstelle für Industrielle Fettversorgung," which translates to "National Center for Industrial Fat Provisioning." At the time, camp authorities, unable to decipher if some bars contained human elements, handed them over to the Jewish administrative body for their disposal with the guidance, "No publicity should be given to this matter." Presumably, the bars were buried somewhere under the Austrian earth.

* * *

Seven decades later, with not much to see of the DP camp beyond its magnificent vistas, our tour was soon over. We retired to Josef's home, where he led us to outdoor seats and presented a tray laden with warm walnut croissants and coffee. Then he retrieved a giant folder. Together, we examined his collection of dozens of brittle, yellowing camp newspapers, *Admonter Hajnt,* where residents had documented their plight.

Josef had thoroughly explored the documents on his own and highlighted for us poems among its pages. The words of writer Blic Majer captured the sentiment of a pervasive longing for a place to settle:

> *We are here in Admont waiting. Not imprisoned, but also not free...*
> *How much longer must we wait before we can leave?*
> *How much longer will they stop us from going?*

After we'd examined the newspapers, Josef walked us across the greenest field I'd ever seen, past a pristine herb garden and toward a massive baroque monastery that adjoined the school where he taught. DP camp residents had been taken to see its magnificent hall with terrifying murals of death and judgment, heaven and hell, and tens of thousands of books. In archived editions of the library's guest book, Josef had found that the displaced persons repeatedly left variations of the same message: "We want to go to Palestine."

A collision course between British opposition to Jewish immigration to Palestine and Zionist aspirations was ramping up in this quiet Austrian mountain town.

* * *

Despite repatriating nearly seven million migrants back to their former countries within a year after the conclusion of the war, UNRRA had failed to complete its mission. More than a million displaced persons, among them our grandparents, refused to or could not return to their prewar homes. The agency began to disband in 1946.

In its place, the United Nations created the International Refugee Organization (IRO). The new effort had a smaller budget and a different goal: to resettle displaced persons in safe third countries. Its charter would forge the foundation of future international protections for refugees who could not return home due to "persecution because of race, religion, nationality, or political opinion."

The British administered the refugee camps in accordance with IRO regulations but used their own military staff. They refused to concede that Jews were unable to return to Poland, Germany, or other countries where they lived before the war. And they also did not trust IRO to prevent illegal emigration out of the camp toward Palestine.

Meanwhile, at Admont, tensions escalated. Residents had revived the varied prewar Jewish political groups. But there was a shift. In February 1947, five hundred Admont camp residents attended a meeting where the disparate factions announced support for a common approach to Zionism, focused on getting as many Jews as possible to Palestine despite British opposition.

Each morning, camp police officers performed a roll call to see how many residents had stolen away in the night. Despite the British having selected Admont precisely because it was farther than other camps from a border leading to the Mediterranean, a steady flow of its DPs set out on the treacherous journey toward Palestine.

Were Pepa and Leon tempted to venture over the mountain? Perhaps they rationalized it was not worth the risk since the British would likely block their entry to Palestine. Those caught making the illegal sea voyage were increasingly being forced into a place much worse than Admont: internment camps on British-controlled Cyprus that reporter Ruth Gruber described as "a hellhole of desert sand and wind" where tens of thousands slept in tent cities behind barbed wire.

In the summer of 1947, Admont residents likely crowded around the radio, breathlessly listening for details about the *Exodus* boat packed with fellow DPs. British destroyers had blocked it from entering Palestine, with officers hurling smoke grenades and tear gas bombs onto the ship and killing three Jewish passengers. The attention of the world was focused on its plight as bereft survivors on board launched a hunger strike. It failed, and this time the British authorities, instead of sending the *Exodus* passengers to Cyprus, forced Holocaust survivors to disembark in Germany.

Then Zionists began retaliatory attacks against the British in Austria. The Irgun—an underground militia that former Soviet prisoner Menachem Begin now headed in Palestine—boasted of committing two such strikes: a suitcase bomb that exploded in the basement of Vienna's stately Hotel Sacher, the regional British army headquarters, and bombs placed on tracks that, according to a *New York Times* dispatch, "nearly sent a British military train with 175 aboard rolling down a mountainside in the high Austrian Alps."

In Admont, DPs affiliated with the Irgun staged their own action, exploding a "propaganda bomb," a cardboard cylinder releasing the likeness of a British soldier with "Nazi England" written in Hebrew, Yiddish, Hungarian, and Romanian. Weeks later, 138 British soldiers surrounded and raided the Admont camp. For hours, the DPs were ordered to stay in their rooms and not allowed to use the toilet as authorities searched for militants. Some reported being strip-searched and that their children were denied sustenance. They said it evoked being reduced to the Nazis' dehumanizing control.

Pepa and Leon must have asked, "What is to be our future?" How much longer would they be relegated to the mountains of Austria, under the thumb of the British, dependent on aid from groups in America? They were free, but remained in a place of confinement nonetheless.

* * *

Then the British, fed up with the intractable divide in Palestine, declared themselves done. Moving away from colonial pursuits, His Majesty's government began the process of handing its mandate over to the United Nations. This would be the first major test of the UN Charter to serve as a global peacebuilding force and to "save future generations from the scourge of war."

The United Nations charged eleven men—delegates representing an eclectic group of nations around the globe, including Guatemala, Peru, Yugoslavia, Iran, and Sweden—to find a solution to the Palestine problem. With the beginning of the Cold War icing relations, the United States had suggested neither its government nor that of the USSR should be on the commission, nor a Zionist or Arab interest. Instead, most of the eleven delegates to the United Nations Special Committee on Palestine, known as UNSCOP, knew little about the subject before being selected. The UN representative accompanying them, African American diplomat Ralph Bunche, was unimpressed with the group and surprised by how many members expressed anti-Semitism.

One of the first and most charged issues considered by UNSCOP was whether to consider the plight of the roughly 250,000 Jewish DPs in Europe. The two Muslim members of the committee echoed the Arab Higher Committee's position, in determining it would be "improper to connect the displaced persons, and the Jewish problem as a whole, with the problem of Palestine." This was Europe's problem, not theirs, no matter how much the Jewish refugees wanted to go to Palestine. Still, after weeks spent assessing the situation in Palestine and two neighboring Arab countries, UNSCOP sent a subcommittee to the refugee camps.

In Germany and Austria, the DPs' message to the UN delegates was unified. "One hundred percent" wanted to go to Palestine, reported the Australian delegate, John Hood. "In whatever language—German, Russian, Polish, Rumanian, Hungarian, Yiddish—the desire was one: to go to Palestine and only to Palestine," the Guatemalan delegate, Jorge García Granados, wrote in a memoir.

In truth, not all Jewish refugees wanted to move to Palestine. Holocaust historian Lucy S. Dawidowicz would later write how "Zionist organizations exercised discipline and pressure to keep many liberated Jews in line with Zionist political demands." But a multitude desperately and passionately wanted to go, and authentic to the full plurality or not, those were the voices the UNSCOP heard.

Of all the Jewish refugees the committee met, only one group showed joy, according to García Granados. They were near Bergen-Belsen's former death camp. At this train station stood euphoric survivors, their suitcases and crates marked with addresses in Jerusalem and Tel Aviv. "That picture—of the sheer ecstasy which transfigured the faces of the Displaced Persons knowing they were going at last to Palestine," García Granados wrote, "was the picture we took back with us to Geneva." There, the eleven delegates of the UN committee would reunite to debate a future for Palestine and, by extension, our grandparents.

* * *

After Talia and I left Admont and parted from Josef, we felt drained, despite his gracious welcome, from trying to take in so much history that was new to us. It did not help that we had indulged in a heavy alpine hut lunch of cheese dumplings fried in butter. Nor that while Admont was breezy and pleasant, the weather turned clammy and warm as we descended the mountains and approached Enns, the town where my grandparents landed in Austria as DPs. We rallied our energy to enter a Billa und Bipa grocery store with vaulted ceilings that hinted at its past as a horse stable.

"Do you know what this building was before?" I asked the checkout girl about its pre–grocery store history.

"It was a riding hall," she said as she swiped products.

Then a middle-aged man who was in line to buy beer chimed in about his memories. "As a child I played with the horses here," he told me. "An ideal place."

* * *

"Terrible." My grandmother and great-uncle used the same word to describe this location. When they arrived here in the fall of 1946, the Green Shelter DP camp was overrun. Refugees believed, rightfully, they had a better chance of getting to Palestine through the American zone and so ten times as many had opted for it over the British. But camps were not equipped for the influx. At Green Shelter, Jewish survivors had slept in former cavalry barracks about six miles from the Mauthausen Concentration Camp.

After making it through a freezing winter plagued by constant food and soap shortages, Simon determined they needed to leave. He and the three Gerson sisters packed their belongings, threw away their UN-issued IDs, and took a chance on registering as new arrivals from the east in the American zone of Germany to gain entry to a camp with better conditions.

My grandparents, for the first time in eight years living as refugees, were alone. Mottel was still determined to realize his Zionist dreams. But he quickly regretted the decision to separate from family after the Brichah informed him again that the only way he could join the illegal, increasingly difficult journey to Palestine was to leave behind his wife and son. I cannot imagine my grandmother would have stood for that. Instead, months later, Mottel and Peshke also left Green Shelter and set out to reunite with their relatives in the German DP camp.

In Enns there was even less to see of our family history than in Admont, and I was ready to go by the time we pulled out of the supermarket parking lot and drove on to a final night out in Salzburg. I felt no desire to ever return to the site of the DP camp in Austria where my father may have said his first words. But I hoped one day to take our children to see the spectacular surroundings of the demolished first home of their saba, whose love and joy they never knew. As we approached the setting of *The Sound of Music*'s film version of the Von Trapp family's iconic escape, I thought of how I wanted to hike with our kids up the Admont mountains, where Josef had led us on our last day, and show them the routes where Jewish refugees had once stolen across the border with the diminishing promise of reaching Palestine. For them to grasp the tensions of the uncertainty that shaped our fathers' lives as young children, so mercifully different from their own, and how easily we could have landed in another place.

CHAPTER 28
Lies

Did I ever tell you about when I was Abe Blumstein? My father, known to me and the world as Allan Gerson, would often launch into a favorite story, enthralling guests at our Shabbat dinner table. He tended to start the same way: *I kept having this sense that my father was delaying my bar mitzvah, and I could not understand why.*

Then, the story took a turn. Sometimes, the reveal came in the 1950s, when my dad and his younger brother, Sam, were collecting stamps. As they peeled one off a letter from their uncle Moishe in Israel, they noticed that his last name was Gerson. But they were the Blumstein family. *Aren't brothers supposed to have the same last name?* They cornered their parents at dinner, squished around the Formica table.

My grandparents' faces drained paler than usual. Then they revealed the truth they'd kept from their boys for a decade: *Our name is not Blumstein; we are Gersons.*

Other times, my dad told a different version. It was 1973 in Jerusalem, days heavy with mounting tensions. My parents, still dating, were visiting a hotel popular with journalists and academics in East Jerusalem when they bumped into an acquaintance. She was dining with her father.

Don't you remember me? the older man asked my dad upon being introduced. *I was your immigration lawyer. Your father was too scared to tell you the truth. So, he had me tell you.*

Which story was true? Did my father find out his real identity at the dinner table in the Bronx, or in the Manhattan lawyer's office? I don't think he knew. Trauma appeared to block his recollections. One version he had heard his younger brother recount, the other the attorney. So, a fan of a good story, my father would alternate between the two.

Either way, he gave the same reason for why his parents adopted another family's identity. The Gersons and Blumsteins were refugees at the DP camp and desperate to leave. The real Blumstein family gained sought-after entry to the United States but then, at the last minute, changed their minds, going to Israel instead. My grandparents snagged their visas—my dad often said they bought them on the black market—and sailed to New York under their names.

The Blumstein family had a little boy, who was about a year older than me. I was big for my age, so it was not a problem. Guests believed the incredible story. For years, so did I.

* * *

Dressed in Bavarian lederhosen, hair parted to the right, the young boy looks straight at the camera. Four years old, my father was among the children who made refugee camp life pulse as Jews were born at record rates—an at once redemptive and vengeful act proving that Hitler had not won. This photo was taken at the displaced persons camp my family always spoke about. Not the terrible converted horse stalls at Green Shelter in Austria, but the one where they eventually landed in Germany—Föhrenwald.

In the foothills of the Alps, thirty minutes outside of the Third Reich's blown-up headquarters, refugees packed into neat brick two-story homes previously occupied by forced munitions laborers. The village's Adolf Hitler Platz was renamed Roosevelt Square; my grandparents moved into part of a house on New York Strasse where six adults and two babies shared a room.

It was in Föhrenwald, after a decade-long gap in the photographic record, that my grandparents captured their story again. They'd survived the cataclysm and were growing their families. In fine hand-tailored suits and dresses, they'd seized moments to remember with their siblings. Everyone was there except for Moishe, who'd remained in Poland. Peshke and her three sisters-in-law hold up four small boys, their promise for a future.

When the older children—my father and Sol, along with Moishe's son Calman—were born in Uzbekistan in 1945, the Gerson siblings could not yet believe their parents had been murdered. But by the time their younger children were born back in Europe, there was no disputing the truth, and each was named for a grandfather. Chuma gave birth to Chaim, named for her father, in 1947. My grandmother named my uncle Sam for her father, Shmuel-Josef, in 1948. And a year later, Moishe gave his daughter Esther, born in Poland, the name of his slaughtered mother.

I knew my father's family lived for years in Föhrenwald, had seen photos and heard countless stories about Dad's first memories of his adopted little dog, Blackie, that ran around with him. But in my twenties when I searched microfilm at a DP archive in Berlin, I failed to locate a single record of a Mottel or Peshke Gerson living in Föhrenwald. What I did find repeatedly was my family's fake name: Blumstein.

Many of the references were connected to a man working in the office of the Joint Distribution Committee, which helped administer the camp. I knew my grandfather held that job. Could my family have already been presenting as the Blumsteins by the time they arrived at Föhrenwald? When I raised this question with my father, he pondered it for a moment and then went back to telling the familiar story that my grandparents purchased the Blumstein family's name shortly before they left the camp, to get a visa to the United States.

While this did not seem quite right to me, I did not pry further, feeling this was my father's mystery to unravel. But when Talia and I embarked on our search after he died, I found a second clue that drove a hole further into the story he'd told me. My source at the US Holocaust Memorial Museum sent over a trove of documents linked to my grandparents' alias, the Blumsteins. Among them, two ship registries.

The first listed Abraham Blumstein, age six, departing Germany for New York Harbor on December 10, 1950. I was familiar with this record—my father under his fake identity. But the second was new: Abram Blumstzein, exact same birth date, on a boat headed to Sydney, Australia, on August 18, 1951.

This thrilling, long-sought trace with Abe Blumstein's Yiddish spelling confirmed my father's story could not be correct. This boy left Europe a year after my father, and not for Israel, which by then was the most popular choice of refugees and open to Jewish immigration, but for Australia. The story I'd been told that my family snagged the Blumstein visas to enter the United States was not adding up.

I returned to the family videos to see if my dead relatives left more clues. My grandparents gave away nothing. In more than ten hours of testimony, they never once mentioned living for a decade under a false identity. Oddly, in all these interviews, my siblings and I failed to ask our grandparents about the Blumsteins. Each of us seemed to sense an unspoken rule not to probe too deeply into this leg of their journey.

But after my grandmother passed, we did ask other relatives. My great-uncle Simon, in the video my brother shot of him shortly before he died, was most revealing.

Simon recalled that my grandfather Mottel, in 1947, after deciding he was going to stay behind in Austria and follow his dream of making it to Palestine, surprised him at the German displaced persons camp. He was desperate.

Simon, you have to help me!

By the time Mottel realized his Zionist aspirations were not possible—with still no resolution as to what the United Nations would decide on the fate of a Jewish homeland in Palestine—the United States was no longer permitting new admissions to DP camps in Germany. Officials worried about more infiltrees flooding the American zone, particularly as another group began to arrive from the east—Romanian survivors facing anti-Semitism and a Communist takeover. Mottel could still enter Germany, but he and his family were now barred from the DP camps, which were safer and provided more provisions.

Simon said he turned to a Zionist committee in the camp that dealt with illegal crossings. They had an idea. A family with a young son had left recently without notifying authorities. They "gave me the name, the papers, Blumstein."

At last, I had my answer: My grandparents had not adopted the Blumstein identity to enter the United States; they'd done so to enter a displaced persons camp in Germany. My family slid into the Blumstein spot, becoming the other family for more than a decade and across countries.

Then Simon added another startling detail about the real Blumsteins: "They went to Paris." This was not Australia, and certainly not Israel.

As I listened to this tape, I expected my father to jump in to ask pointed questions of his uncle as he did at other times in the recording. But he failed to so much as ask why this story did not match up with his version of how the Blumsteins sold their visas to move to Israel, the one he had presumably heard all his life and continued to tell after this recording.

Why had my father, whose life's work was based on gathering evidence to prove a case, not challenged the narrative? Perhaps his parents had told him the simpler story. And when you grow up in a lie, you hold tight to whatever part of your story you believe.

* * *

I had always assumed that my family's bending of truths to enter the United States was unique among Holocaust survivors. But as I started to dig, I found that fabricating identities and wartime experiences on visa applications was common for Polish Jews like them who survived in the Soviet Union. Desperation had already propelled them to dispose of beloved photos, pretend to be Greek, and traverse borders illegally. As the months bled into years in the displaced persons camps, the need for subterfuge only grew—whatever it took to enter the United States, Palestine, or beyond.

Jewish displaced persons had scant immigration options after the war, similar to before and during the Holocaust. Though the International Refugee Organization, which oversaw camps in the US-occupied zone, banned religious discrimination, a clear preference toward resettling Christians prevailed. Displaced persons from Baltic countries and Ukraine tended to be unambiguously white, possessed needed labor skills, and were physically stronger.

Meanwhile, Polish Jews who survived in the USSR were intentionally barred from the United States. Congressmen accused them of being "the least desirable people of the whole of Europe" and "a gang of well-trained Communists...who will spread out over this country for the purpose of plotting the overthrow of this Government." While a few spies may have been planted among the DPs, the accusations were ludicrous. These were Jews whom Stalin had deported to the Gulag after falsely accusing them of spying for the Nazis. Now they were being accused of plotting to infiltrate the United States as spies for the Soviets who'd imprisoned them.

The Displaced Persons Act of 1948 sent to the president's desk included a cutoff date for entering Germany, Austria, or Italy of December 22, 1945. That effectively banned almost all Polish Jews who survived in the Soviet Union, since repatriation trains did not begin until 1946. Truman reluctantly signed the legislation, not wanting to cut off the support it offered to Christian refugees, but deploring that it "discriminates in callous fashion against displaced persons of the Jewish faith...more than ninety percent of the remaining Jewish displaced persons are definitely excluded."

For those determined to enter North America, fraudulent papers were often the only way in. So, they lied. "It is impossible even to estimate the number of refugees who obscured their past in order to enter the United States," historian Eliyana Adler writes in *Survival on the Margins*.

In our family, I unearthed various tactics. Some relatives falsified dates, indicating they arrived earlier in Germany so they could qualify for the DP Act. Mordechai Gerson, my grandfather's cousin, bought a visa and entered as Isaac Tager in 1948. In the mid-1950s the forgery caught up with him. Isaac Tager's identity, apparently, had been sold multiple times. This cousin was called into the Immigration and Naturalization Service and narrowly avoided being returned to Poland. He hired a lawyer who cost more money than he possessed; he'd already married an American-born woman, and his wife was pregnant. Something in the combination worked and he was ultimately allowed to stay, but he spent the rest of his life as a Tager, as did his descendants.

The lies opened doors but came at a price. A very distant relative, the last Zamość survivor I interviewed, refused to let me publish her name. She was ninety-six at the time I spoke with her and had spent more than seven decades on US soil. But she still feared the consequences of exposing the fact that her father had falsified his tuberculosis X-ray results to pass the health entry exam. The anxiety of deportation never ceased.

Like immigrants everywhere who cross a border illegally or remain after their visa expires, they broke laws not out of malice, but desperation. This is what was required for these Polish Jews whom Hitler tried to exterminate, Stalin deported to the Gulag, and Poles threatened to murder upon their return, to find a refuge in the United States. So, the story that my father told and retold—his parents buying an identity for a chance at a visa—made perfect sense. But I was discovering that the truth, as it often does, took a more circuitous route.

* * *

My father often ruminated, "Who is Abe Blumstein?" In the question was an assumption he might feel a special connection to the real man behind his alias, but it was also always a humorous theoretical. He never actually sought out the man. Was my father simply too enmeshed in his present? Or was this another example of how he did not want to scratch the surface of the story he had internalized?

While I researched our family's story in fits and spurts over the years, I had always felt the alter ego was my father's to pursue. But now I delved into the search with a focused energy. I had new clues to track down Abe Blumstein, or Abram Blumsztein, according to the last record I had of him: his 1951 voyage to Australia as a seven-year-old boy. He would be a man in his late seventies, assuming he was still alive. Into the night I searched Australian records. In the back files of the internet, a singular law school graduation record emerged. It was for an Albert, not an Abraham, Blumsztein. But the age seemed right.

If this was the right man, despite their both having studied law, my father and his alter ego seemed very different. While my dad had an outsized personality and lived in an international sphere of high-stakes legal actions, his alter ego appeared to retreat. After weeks of searching, I identified him via Max Wald, vice president of the Australian Jewish Genealogical Society. The most recent information he could find on Albert was from nearly fifty years ago: A 1977 census listing an address in Melbourne's Jewish neighborhood. Finding himself in the area one afternoon, Max decided to try ringing the buzzer.

"Excuse me for interrupting you," Max said when a man's voice answered. "I'm looking for a former resident of this flat, an Albert Blumsztein."

"Well, you're talking to him," came the matter-of-fact response.

Albert had been reserved but pleasant with Max, agreeing to meet him later for coffee and sharing that after the DP camp his family had, indeed, been in Paris, where classmates had trouble pronouncing Abraham. That's why he'd become Albert. He expressed interest in how my family had taken his name, but did not appear particularly surprised or moved by it. After their coffee meeting, I heard nothing back when I sent an email to the address Max had supplied. Unsure it went through, I sent another. Still nothing. Was Albert angry that someone had lived under his identity? Indifferent?

Then, six months after I sent him my message, a reply popped up.

"G'day," Albert wrote. "You must have been disappointed at my failure to reply to your emails—for which I must apologize." He explained that he had wanted to first figure out how to video chat with me, but had been unable to do so. "I feel that I cannot procrastinate any longer in writing to you, and have felt all the more impelled to do so by the palpable excitement of a niece."

I immediately replied, realizing the date was my father's former fake birthday, which he celebrated until he turned 12, Albert's actual birthday. I did not hear back. I would have been more disappointed if Albert had not revealed that he had a niece who did want to connect. From the Holocaust Memorial Museum archives, in addition to discovering that the Blumszteins moved to Australia, I had also learned they had an older daughter, Malvina. I dug up records indicating that in her twenties she had moved to Israel, falling in love with a South African immigrant.

On a trip to Israel to visit family a few months after receiving Albert's message, I tracked down the number of one of Malvina's two daughters and called. A woman picked up and my words rushed out: "I think my father took on the identity of your family; he lived under the name Abe Blumstein. Do you know what I'm talking about?"

Full of warmth with a jumbled mix of multinational accented English, she replied: "Oh yes, of course. It's like a Steven Spielberg story."

My tension evaporated.

After all these years wondering where the Blumsteins were, it turned out that one of the sisters lived in the very same town as my brother-in-law. A couple of days later, I dropped Talia and the kids at a park in Ra'anana, then drove six minutes through the Tel Aviv suburb to a café adjoining a soccer field. A woman in a jean jacket strolled toward me, neatly put together, with fine features and a bursting smile.

I hugged tight this niece of Albert Blumsztein. Although the background to our connection was a heavy one, we could not help but erupt in laughter as we tried to make sense of who we were and how we'd ended up sitting across a table together. A few minutes later her sister, the one I had spoken with on the phone, joined us.

I felt bound to these women in ways I didn't anticipate, connected by our desire to unwind the memories we'd inherited from lost parents. Like my father, their mother's mind had left ahead of her body, as she'd suffered from severe dementia for more than a decade. But they, too, had heard stories. The Blumszteins, Communist Polish Jews, had fled to the Soviet Union. Despite extreme hardship, they had two children during the war: Malvina and Albert, who was born in a city in the southern Ural Mountains.

What happened after the war, like in my family, was the subject of sometimes conflicting stories. I found most convincing what Malvina's husband later told me. As the Blumszteins made their way to a German DP camp, a cousin named Bernard, who had survived Auschwitz, was working out of France for the Irgun. He purchased ammunition across Europe, transporting it to the Zionist militant group's headquarters in Paris. As he trafficked guns and grenades, he'd stop in refugee camps to study the Red Cross lists for relatives. When he discovered the Blumszteins, Bernard convinced them to surreptitiously leave Germany with him in the middle of the night. They hid among the weapons in his truck, crossing illegally over the border to France to reunite with other relatives who had survived.

Could they have sold their identities before jumping in his truck? Perhaps, but I'm inclined to believe that the Blumszteins never knew that another family had taken their name. I even wondered if we Gersons had taken an opportunity from them. By 1951, when the French would no longer allow them to remain, and not wanting to face more war in Israel, the Blumszteins put in applications for Canada, the United States, and Australia. They never received permission to enter the United States. Could it be because my family had already entered under their names? Instead, Australia came through and they sailed to Sydney. Such were the odds between courage, luck, and timing that rolled the die, propelling these Polish Jewish refugees to at last board ships sailing away from Europe. My family, the Gersons, would become Americans; the real Blumszteins, Australians; and the Inlenders, Israelis.

CHAPTER 29

Promised Lands

The Inlenders departed Europe first. Leon proposed moving to Canada, where Uncle Zyg had slipped through the year before on a special youth refugee visa, shaving his face and presenting a false birth date. But how would Leon and Pepa, with baby Nachum, gain admittance when Canada's doors remained mostly closed to Jewish refugees? And besides, Pepa was determined that they should immigrate to the newly established State of Israel. Her desire was as practical as it was idealistic. She had received miraculous news: Her mother was alive, along with three of her siblings who had survived elsewhere in the Soviet Union. They would reunite in a Jewish state, whose new government enthusiastically welcomed them.

Nearly two years earlier, when the Inlenders were still marooned in Admont, it had not been clear which way the United Nations would move on Palestine. According to the diplomat Ralph Bunche, the eleven UNSCOP delegates had departed Palestine undecided. It was the visit to the DP camps that "proved decisive" in its majority backing a partition plan, which would open parts of Palestine to Jewish immigration and self-determination. Confronting the plight of Jews who had been subject to systematic mass extermination still languishing in German and Austrian camps had swayed them.

On August 30, the UNSCOP's majority proposal to the United Nations declared Jewish immigration to be "the central issue in

Palestine today...the one factor, above all others, that rules out the necessary cooperation between the Arab and Jewish communities in a single State." It outlined a plan for splitting British Mandate Palestine—which was a little larger than the state of Vermont—into two countries, with connected commercial zones and an international sector in Jerusalem.

The United Nations General Assembly member states, still without a building to call their own, met in a former Queens ice-skating rink to discuss and then vote on the committee's partition proposal. On November 29, 1947, the United States and the USSR, in one of their increasingly rare acts of diplomatic alignment, joined thirty-one other countries in ratifying the partition plan.

The condemnation from Arab leaders, the majority of the thirteen nations who rejected the plan, was immediate. They condemned it as unfair to Palestine's Arab majority in giving 55 percent of the country to a minority that was largely immigrants. "My country will never recognize such a decision," the Syrian delegate said. "Let the consequences be on the heads of others, not on ours." The British, who abstained with nine other countries, refused to support the transition.

Even with UN majority backing, it was not certain whether this new Jewish state would be realized. While evidence exists that Washington had pushed for the pro-partition vote, President Truman soon appeared skittish. And much of the US government was against the plan: the CIA, the Pentagon, and nearly all State Department officials opposed partition, warning it would trigger a broader war, provoke retaliation against the United States, and fail in the absence of British enforcement.

That winter in the Austrian alps, the blue-and-white flag of the Zionist movement—designed to resemble an unfurled prayer shawl with the six-pointed star, a Shield of David—was hoisted against snowy Mount Admont. The camp newspaper wrote that residents sang the Zionist anthem "Hatikvah," "The Hope," dreaming of soon seeing Mount Hermon instead. But nobody knew if this would become a reality.

* * *

As Pepa's stomach bulged round, the British Mandate was set to expire. On May 14, 1948, the Inlenders surely hovered near the camp radio as Zionist leader David Ben-Gurion's voice rang over the speakers, declaring "the establishment of a Jewish state in Eretz-Israel, to be known as the State of Israel." Eleven minutes after the clock turned midnight in Jerusalem, Truman officially recognized the world's newest country, planting American allegiance. The president's decision to support the new Jewish state was personal and moral, but it was also strategic. If Israel was going to exist, he believed the United States should support it, and he surely wanted to thwart Soviet efforts to claim it as an allied state.

What mattered to most of the DPs at that moment was probably not the relentless political wrangling that once again directed their fate, nor the protests of the Arab leaders, but that a modern Land of Israel had been created. After generations of persecution in the Diaspora, these refugees had a place they dreamed of claiming as their own, one officially "open for Jewish immigration and for the Ingathering of the Exiles." I imagine a very pregnant Pepa and Leon dancing at last with frenzied joy, perhaps exalting in prayers of Shehecheyanu, thanking God for being alive to see this day.

The Inlenders waited a year, perhaps to ensure after Nachum's difficult birth that he was healthy enough for the journey. But they could delay no longer. Days after Admont, the last of the Jewish camps in Austria, shuttered in 1949, they left Europe. It had been nearly eight years since their liberation from Stalin's Gulag. Cradling their nine-month-old baby, they traveled through Italy and boarded a 217-foot former US Coast Guard gunboat moored in Venice's harbor. The nascent Israeli Navy had recently purchased the ship and renamed it *Eilat,* after a biblical city that was a waystation in the Israelites' exodus from Egypt.

Despite the nausea, claustrophobia, and pungent odors aboard, the mood on refugee ships headed to Israel tended to be boisterous. I imagine Pepa bouncing a giggly Nachum as they spotted Mount Carmel above the port city of Haifa. Around them prayers surely erupted as hopes soared for a new beginning in an ancient land. Perhaps this was the moment Leon broke his reserve: At once weeping for all he had lost and overcome with relief? Or was he terrified of a new unknown, in a country still negotiating the end of its first war, with the promise of more to come? With Leon, it is impossible to know.

* * *

In the months after the Inlenders departed Europe, the Gerson siblings began to board former military transport ships that had taken on the postwar mission of ferrying refugees to new homes. Simon and Chuma received a visa to the United States first, sailing in September 1949 from Bremen, West Germany. Two months later Moishe left behind his shoemakers' collective in Poland, along with any dreams of rekindling Jewish life there under the Communists, setting out instead for Israel with his wife and two children. The remaining Gerson sisters, Feiga and Ruksha, had both partnered with men who had survived Nazi death camps but whose first families had not, and would eventually move with them to the United States.

Mottel and Peshke must have felt left behind in Germany, five years after the end of World War II, as the decade turned to the 1950s. At Föhrenwald, refugees departed daily. Most traversed the Mediterranean for Israel. Some soon sent letters back indicating that the Holy Land was not what they had expected. They were stuck living once more in war-torn refugee camps, often in even worse conditions than the ones they'd left behind in Germany, relegated to hastily hoisted tents where snakes and scorpions crawled, caring for sick children struck with typhus and malaria. Some refugees even began to return to Germany and the DP camp, hoping for a chance to immigrate to another country where life was easier.

My grandmother made up her mind. She would not move to Israel. No matter how ardently my Zionist grandfather advocated, he could not sway her fierce determination to avoid a region where their boys would face more war. *I have given enough.*

Where else could they go? They did not immigrate to Argentina where Peshke's brothers moved before the war. Perhaps, after surviving together for so many years with their Gerson siblings, they wanted to follow Chuma and Simon's lead. So in 1950, when Truman signed an amended DP Act that now allowed US entry to more Polish Jews who had survived in the Soviet Union, they took their chance.

* * *

In the most iconic family portrait from my father's youth, his parents stare out a train car window with their two small boys at their sides; box springs from raised sleeping cots hover above them. On a journey north through the bombed-out towns of Germany, this appears to be a happy family setting off to a destination of their choosing. Peshke, hair neatly coiffed, kerchief wrapped halfway around her head, breaks into a rare full smile with painted lips. Mottel is even debonaire, a fedora just off-kilter, large dark-rimmed glasses. My dad is officially six, having gained a year according to his false documents. "Abe Blumstein" offers a hopeful smile. Only my uncle Sam, a tender two-year-old with big eyes staring below a hat, reveals trepidation.

Bundled up at Bremen's port on a December day, they grasped their satchels and ascended a gangplank to the USS *General C. C. Ballou*. Previously, the army ship had transported more than three thousand returning US troops on a voyage around the world, with far-flung ports of call like Calcutta and Manila. Now the passengers were refugees—among them a Hungarian pastor, a Yugoslav meatpacker, a Polish farmer—and my father. The destination: New York Harbor.

As the ship lurched through the English Channel in the last week of 1950 and emerged into the gray and churning wintertime Atlantic, nausea set in for many on board. My grandparents had left behind a Jewish island in postwar Germany. And now, who knew? Did Peshke and Mottel overhear on board, as others reported, Ukrainian passengers whispering of how they'd worked as prison guards for the Nazis? Fear must have clawed at their minds. They would be beginning their lives again in their forties, under a false identity in a country where they did not speak the language.

Their ship at last eased into New York Harbor as seagulls swooped in its wake. My father held his hand up and was able to completely obscure the skyscrapers from his view. *Tata,* he said to Mottel in Yiddish, his only language at the time. *New York is not so big. I can cover it with my small hand.* They had arrived.

* * *

Not long after my grandparents departed Germany, the International Refugee Organization began to shut down its work in the US-occupied zone. Föhrenwald would remain open for seven more years, the final of more than seven hundred DP camps to shutter. Still, by 1951 almost all its residents except for the most sickly and forlorn had already departed. And the United Nations had shifted its focus to a new refugee crisis: Palestinians.

On November 29, 1947, the United Nations General Assembly voted to partition the tiny territory into two states—one Arab, one Jewish. While Zionists celebrated the decision, Palestine's Arabs rejected the plan and organized to prevent the partition. Attacks and counterattacks quickly led to an ugly war between the two communities, with massacres and terrorism perpetrated by both sides.

Arabs began to flee their homes in anticipation of the end of the Mandate. Hoping they would soon be able to return with their side victorious, few likely imagined they would be locking their doors for the last time. Then the Haganah, soon to be the Israeli army, in March 1948, issued a policy permitting expulsions of Arab communities that mounted resistance. A month later, the Irgun, working with another underground right-wing militia, the Stern Gang, attacked the Arab village of Deir Yassin; the ensuing massacre left more than one hundred residents dead. After that, the stream of Palestinians fleeing and forcibly expelled from their homes became a flood.

In May, following the battle for control of Haifa, Golda Meir, then the head of the Jewish Agency's political department, expressed dismay at the scale of Arab displacement. "It is a dreadful thing to see the dead city. Next to the port I found children, women, the old, waiting for a way to leave," said Meir, who two decades later would become Israel's prime minister. "I entered the houses, there were houses where the coffee and pita bread were left on the table, and I could not avoid that this, indeed, had been the picture in many Jewish towns," the Kyiv-born Meir recalled.

The following month, on May 14, 1948, Israel declared its independence. Within a day, Lebanon, Syria, Iraq, Transjordan, and Egypt invaded. Saudi Arabia sent support for the Arab League effort, and Palestinian Arab militias continued attacking as they had for months. Many Zionists feared the eradication of the short-lived rebirth of the Jewish state. But by the time the war formally ended fourteen months later with United Nations mediated armistices, Israel had succeeded not only in defending itself but also in gaining land beyond that envisioned in the partition. Two Arab countries had also claimed territory in what had been Mandate Palestine. Egypt occupied the Gaza Strip. Transjordan took the West Bank and the eastern half of Jerusalem, expelling Jewish residents from the Old City and blocking access to their most precious site for prayer, the Western Wall of the ancient temple complex. The Arabs of Palestine were left with no state to call their own. What for Israel was its War of Independence, Palestinians would come to remember as their *Nakba*, Arabic for "catastrophe." .

Neither Ben-Gurion, Meir, nor almost anyone else in Israel's leadership was willing to accept the return of the more than 700,000 Palestinians displaced from their homes, whom they feared would be a fifth column that would endanger the existence of the newborn state. Jews should treat the remaining Arabs "with civil and human equality," Ben-Gurion said, referring to the 150,000 Arabs who remained within Israel's borders after its War of Independence. But he concluded, "It is not our job to worry about the return" of those who had fled. Instead, more than 100,000 Jewish refugees would move into what the Israeli government labeled "abandoned" homes.

* * *

No record exists of Pepa, Leon, and baby Nachum's first days in the land of milk and honey, but there was likely little milk or honey, nor was there much butter, eggs, or meat. Upon landing in the summer of 1949 at Haifa's port, the first stop for all was a former British army camp, renamed the Shaar Ha'aliyah or Gate of Immigration. In Israel's version of Ellis Island, Pepa and Leon would have once more been checked for lice and covered with DDT powder, then X-rayed for TB, before being instructed to claim an empty army cot in yet another shelter. Many of their fellow refugees wore unfamiliar clothes—turbans, long white robes, embroidered floral head coverings. They spoke Arabic, Farsi, Ladino, and dozens more languages and dialects.

In 1949, immigrants entered Israel at a rate of more than four times what the government, in its commitment to welcoming every Jew, had planned to absorb. The biggest group from a single country were those, like Pepa and Leon, born in Poland. But more than twice as many Jews arrived from the combined Arab nations—expelled or forced to flee amid the often deadly backlashes that accompanied the establishment of Israel.

This rapid influx of humanity stretched beyond the resources available in a new country scrambling to defend itself. Among the most immediate crises was how to feed and house everyone. In the four years after the establishment of the State of Israel, more than seven hundred thousand Jewish immigrants would arrive, doubling the country's population. While Israelis would take over about a hundred thousand Palestinian homes, there were not enough for everyone. Many vacated simple peasant structures were uninhabitable. They lacked electricity or running water, and what their owners had left behind, Israelis had often looted and vandalized. In other cases, the government bulldozed homes to create more agricultural land needed for kibbutzim, the growing socialist communities.

* * *

Pepa and Leon were relatively fortunate. After a year in temporary housing, they joined a new neighborhood of basic homes built for immigrants in the northern outskirts of Herzliya. The town just north of Tel Aviv was named for Theodor Herzl, the founder of the modern Zionist movement. Today, its seaside development features some of the most valuable property in Israel, but back when American Jews began to develop it in the 1920s—after a Zionist organization purchased the land from the Syrian Omri family based in Beirut who had decades earlier purchased it from the Turkish government—they described a noxious swamp.

In what would be Pepa, Leon, and Nachum's neighborhood of Gan Rashal, the early settlers, inspired by the "California Model" of agricultural practices, planted oranges, bananas, and other fruit trees, along with a small pine forest. But by 1946, the orchard business had failed, and the land was turned over to the de facto Zionist government, the Jewish Agency, which had a more urgent use for it—new homes for immigrants. The fruit trees were dug up, and simple structures were built as fast as possible. Pepa and Leon moved into a stucco, one-bedroom house, settling for the first time into a home to call their own as a family.

Nobody that I could identify was directly displaced to build Pepa and Leon's house. The census taken in 1945 counted 4,650 Jews living in the area and no Muslims or Christians. But in nearby El Haram, 520 Muslims lived with 360 Jews. In this village, now considered part of Herzliya, the British began to expel Arab peasants and tenant farmers back in the 1920s.

More than two decades later, as war erupted, most of El Haram's remaining Palestinian Arab residents fled. In a few cases, Jews stood by Muslim residents, like a man named Naftali who told his neighbor Abed: *Stay and don't leave, you have a gun and I have a gun, and the two of us will protect your house.* But this type of connection was not common. When the El Haram region fell to Israeli control, Abed, along with the few remaining Arab neighbors, also fled. One courageous neighbor was not enough to ensure his safety. El Haram would be one of four hundred Arab villages emptied of its Palestinian population. Above the beach stands the stunning fifteenth-century Sidna 'Ali Shrine, its cemetery now a parking lot.

As a child, Talia loved taking the bus to the nearby beach, frolicking there without ever being told who else had once enjoyed it. How had her grandparents, Leon and Pepa, confronted the legacy of the Palestinian families who had been forced to flee their homes? Not surprisingly, they said little. In this instance, they were not the only ones. The displacement that accompanied their new country's founding was not discussed often in its early days. And I imagine that for the Inlenders, as for so many of the refugees who landed in Israel, taking in another people's pain—especially a people threatening to expel, or even to kill them—may have been beyond reach.

Pepa and Leon instead focused on building a future for their own son, who was displaced no longer. Nachum grew up in a country as old as he was, with a sense of total belonging. "I felt connected, loved everything," he told Talia when she interviewed him in 2006. "I'm growing up in a place that belongs to me and my friends and to my family." With other young people in his scouts group he traveled across Israel, hiking the verdant hills of the Galilee and sleeping under the stars in its desert wadis. His group of childhood friends, all born around the country's founding, forged a bond so close that they would go on to meet weekly, into their seventies.

But Nachum also knew that another people did not believe he belonged in Israel. In school, he learned to hide in the bomb shelters as soon as the air sirens would ring. When he was eight, many of his friends' fathers marched off to fight against the Egyptians. Some did not return. This cycle of violence, with two wars within a decade and countless skirmishes, was not what any of the Zamość Zionists had envisioned—whether they were convinced an Iron Wall of fear or partnership with the Arab working class was the path to a Jewish homeland. Perhaps this is why, years later, when Nachum said he wanted to go to America to study, Leon and Pepa let their only son move across the world.

* * *

Compared with the hardships of Israel, my grandparents appeared to have it easy in the United States, arriving at a time with unprecedented opportunities for Jews. As kids, my siblings and I asked them variations of the same question: *After you immigrated, did you at last find a good life?* We assumed that this was a story with a neat and happy ending, where they tasted a version of the American Dream that shaped our lives.

They scoffed. Landing in New York as Polish Jewish refugees in the 1950s was no golden ticket; it was where new struggles began, in yet another country that did not want them.

In the last week of 1950, Peshke and Mottel Gerson, living under the aliases of Rachel and Morris Blumstein, awoke in a stately four-story brick former mansion with arched windows. Later it would become the East Village's famed Public Theater, but at that moment its gracious rooms were subdivided into a cramped shelter. Babies howled, and kids hacked with bronchitis. My grandparents had two young sons to feed and $30 to their names. Their possessions consisted of a baby bathtub, my grandmother's beloved sewing machine, and two old flannel blankets.

Within a few months, Mottel found a job as a factory floor boy, and they moved on to a walk-up apartment for $39 a month at 84 Beaver Street in Brooklyn. But they never had enough, particularly when Mottel's debilitating back pain flared. My grandfather returned to Manhattan to plead with the Hebrew Immigrant Aid Society. He claimed they had no relatives in the United States to help them. This was not true. In addition to Chuma and Simon, there was also a cousin, Morris Gerson, who had immigrated before the war, helped sponsor them, and provided a job. The social worker uncovered this secret and confronted my grandfather: Why was he hiding the truth?

That was the last time my grandfather visited the HIAS office, even though they needed its help. I assume the fear that their identity could be revealed drove them to try to disappear into New York. For the next six years they would live as Blumsteins, even as they eventually gained a better financial foothold and moved to the Bronx.

What reassured my grandparents in 1957 that they could reveal to authorities their true identities? My father never knew the answer. This was the last secret I uncovered in my search, more challenging than Leon's hidden first family, photos buried in the Soviet secret police archives, or the real Abe Blumstein in Australia. Various legal experts I consulted did not know how the government would have resolved their perjury. Talia helped me search private bills in Congress, often introduced to aid sympathetic cases, but we came up empty. Then, more than a year and a half after I submitted a request with a special US Citizenship and Immigration Services genealogy program, a thick package arrived in the mail.

I flipped through dozens of typewritten pages until I found the answer that I had been searching for all these years. "Gentlemen," began the letter from the lawyer sent on my grandparents' behalf to Immigration and Naturalization Service in Manhattan, making the case that their trespasses should be overlooked due to the "recently promulgated Section 7 of the Immigration Act of 1957."

What was that? Neither Talia nor any of the legal scholars I consulted were familiar with this historical intricacy in the patchwork of American immigration laws. But the one-paragraph section, easily overlooked in its limited scope, shines a light on how legislation can sometimes cross political boundaries to conform to the complexities of migrants' lives.

As the Cold War deepened, President Eisenhower urged Congress to increase protections for Eastern Europeans fleeing Communism. Among the measures was a rare waiver of the strict penalties for committing perjury to enter the United States. The Republican president wrote that "a large number of refugees, possibly thousands, misrepresented their identities when obtaining visas some years ago in order to avoid forcible repatriation behind the Iron Curtain." Fear of being sent back to Communist countries was indeed a rationale for many to lie about their identities. But it was not the direct reason for my family's misrepresentations.

Among lawmakers, Eisenhower may have been one of the few Americans who knew that Eastern Europe did not want its Jewish refugees back. As supreme commander of the Allied Expeditionary Force in Europe, he oversaw the development of DP camps. He may have known, as historian Tony Judt writes in *Postwar*, that "there had never been any question of returning Jews to the east—no one in the Soviet Union, Poland or anywhere else evinced the slightest interest in having them back." Still, even if not intended for Jews, in September 1957 this immigration act designed for refugees fleeing Communist regimes would become law, and within it a window for my grandparents to come clean.

Two months later Mottel and Peske submitted a form to the INS admitting that they had "given false testimony to obtain benefits under the immigration or naturalization law." For them to make such a wide leap of faith, my grandparents' lawyer must have convinced them that he was certain this new law could protect them. "We gained absolutely nothing under the Immigration laws by assuming the identity of Blumsteins," their typed petition reads. "They like us were Polish born Jewish refugees. We did gain however ration cards and shelter in a refugee camp in Germany and felt ourselves safe while in camp from being forced to return to Poland." Not satisfied this sufficiently made their point, my grandfather in his neat cursive later added: "We are unable to return to Poland because we would be persecuted there because we are anti-Communists. And are Jews."

The Gerson family became naturalized citizens of the United States on April 7, 1958. Two months later my father turned thirteen and was called to the Torah on his real birthday. Mottel and Peshke adopted new American names: Morton and Paula. They let my father choose his own. His younger brother Sam, who was stuck with his name since he was born after the family had adopted the Blumstein guise, urged him to choose Fabian, Tony, or one of the cooler Italian names popular with their Bronx neighbors.

My dad could've used a boost. He was a misfit at the Orthodox school where his parents had sent him, choosing it since the teachers spoke Yiddish. This helped ease the transition for them, but not for my father. The other kids tended to be American-born and from more religious backgrounds than his own God-questioning family, which did not keep kosher. When they found out he was born in the Soviet Union, someone scribbled on the bathroom walls "Abie is a commie." Now he told them not only was he not a commie, he wasn't even Abie.

Disregarding his brother's suggestions, my father chose the name Allan, closer to his Yiddish name, Elik. Half of his eighth-grade yearbook messages were inscribed to Abe. The other half to Al. When his barber asked, *How's it going, Abie?* He responded simply: *I'm no longer Abie. I'm Al now.*

Allan Gerson raced to become the first in his family to graduate high school, finishing early as a midyear valedictorian, and then enrolled at City College of New York. He was a sixteen-year-old freshman living with his parents in the Bronx. They had opened a small dry-cleaning and dressmaking shop near their apartment. When my father decided to move on and leave their watchful eyes, enrolling in faraway SUNY Buffalo on a state scholarship, his mother took ill.

What's the matter? inquired a gentile customer at the dry-cleaning shop. When my grandmother shared that her son had left for college, the woman was confused: *But that's wonderful!*

That night, relaying the story to my grandfather, she concluded: *You see, the goyim do not love their children like we do.* The statement could be seen as reflecting a sense that she saw herself as better than her non-Jewish neighbors, but I find it more telling of my grandparents' feelings of alienation in a country whose customs still felt foreign to them. Morton and Paula, despite their new American names and official status as US citizens, would always be outsiders. Even though they crossed the border, they were not fully of the country.

* * *

Our grandparents had been called bezhenets, repatrianci, infiltrees, and displaced persons. Now, they took on new labels and identities in new languages. Sometimes the most painful names came from fellow Jews. My father never forgot his cousin, who had arrived a year earlier in New York, calling him griner, or greenhorn, introducing him to the Yiddish term in an immigrant rite of passage used to deride those who followed them. In Israel, Pepa and Leon, now called olim, the Hebrew term for Jews who have immigrated—or literally ascended—to Israel, faced other challenges. Israelis often urged the newcomers to hide their Polish past of subjugation, to stop speaking Yiddish. Pepa and Leon changed their baby's name from what they had initially called him, Nunik, to the Hebrew name he would stick with, Nachum.

But even if Morton and Paula in the Bronx, and Pepa and Leon in Herzliya, would remain on some level outsiders, their refugee children arrived young enough to pass as natives and hungrily pursue the promise of the lands where they came of age. To us, their descendants, they gifted a legacy of belonging.

CHAPTER 30

Home

Our backyard spills over with friends gathered around firepits and a spectacular spread of couscous tagines, pyramids of crispy potato latkes, and whole roasted cauliflower heads. The late evening sun graces our palm trees and bird-of-paradise flowers with a glint of pink. Aviv and Alma race around gleefully with a crew of kids hoarding chocolate coins.

As darkness descends, strings of lights twinkle over our cascading garden. We hung the bulbs nearly ten years earlier to fête our wedding. I can still see our parents on the deck over our garden, toasting with glasses of sparkling rosé. Where the kids now chomp on jelly donuts under the arch of the lower terrace's pepper tree, I glimpse our fathers spinning and dipping us in our long white dresses.

Our home pulses with vivid images of my dad and Talia's abba, yet our children have no memories of their grandfathers. They will never again shriek as my father tosses them from his strong shoulders in the air or learn from Nachum how to use the tools in the large metal box that was always at the ready in his trunk. This wrenching disconnect still sometimes catches me by surprise, even though my father died four years ago, and Nachum seven.

In their absence, I find some solace in the way that probing our families' journeys has revealed to me dimensions of our deceased relatives' personalities. My grandmother, whom I knew as an old woman riddled with anxiety, I now see in her youth, fiery and fierce. I catch glimpses of Talia's grandparents, whom I never met in life. Pepa, so brusque with Talia, I see as the determined force who kept Leon out of despair. And I understand better how both of our grandfathers confronted the crippling pain of their experience: Mine could not stop commemorating, while Leon guarded the devastating loss of his first son, the older brother Nachum never met.

As our ancestors come alive as complex individuals, I also better see their commonalities. They were products of a time when radical social movements captivated young people, when borders opened and closed. Their propelling impulse, as it was for the displaced since biblical times, was shared: to secure a home, where they could be free to live with those they loved, to protect and grow this spark of life from one generation to the next.

* * *

By the 1970s, our fathers—born stateless sons of Zamość—had adopted their own identities and paths. My dad an American, Talia's an Israeli, began to pursue careers and life partners. The two men did not meet until we introduced them, but they did overlap for a few months in an Israel reckoning with a new phase of its brief existence, that of occupying state.

Three years earlier, in the summer of 1967, Nachum was months into his mandatory service as a soldier in the Israeli army. Arab threats loomed—particularly from Egypt, which had moved troops into the adjacent Sinai Peninsula—to invade the Jewish state. When the nineteen-year-old returned from his military base to his parents' simple home, he must have seen the terror in their eyes. They had sought a safer place for their son. Now he was in the army, about to fight in a war in which they feared Israel could be obliterated.

But then, as dawn broke on the fifth of June, Israel attacked Egyptian airstrips, destroying their warplanes before they even had a chance to take off. Faces around Nachum radically lightened. Two days later, on the seventh of June, Israel captured the Old City of Jerusalem from

Jordan. He joined his fellow soldiers in rejoicing as they touched the cool ancient limestone blocks of the Western Wall, the sacred remnant of the ancient temple complex from which Jews had been cut off for almost two decades since Israel's founding war. A people who had existed primarily in a diaspora, praying toward this place, now had claimed it.

Within a week, Israel had broadened its borders in a lightning-fast conquest of territory that would be known as the Six-Day War to Israel and often as the *Naksa*, meaning the "setback," to the Arab world. At its conclusion, Israel had captured from Egypt the Sinai Peninsula and Gaza Strip, from Jordan the West Bank and the eastern half of Jerusalem, and from Syria the Golan Heights.

The conquests raised moral and legal questions that would shape my father's future scholarly pursuits: Was there a just path for Israel to occupy territories sacred to the three Abrahamic religions, which one million Palestinians inhabited? If they should be returned, who should govern, given that Egypt and Jordan had occupied Gaza and the West Bank since 1948? These were among the questions my father pursued a few years after the war when he arrived in Israel to pursue graduate studies at Hebrew University Law School.

My father was also on a personal quest in Israel. Nachum, who had not yet begun his higher education, possessed something my father lacked: a deep-rooted sense of belonging. My dad wanted to experience this country where he had heard the legacy of the Holocaust was not only about building memorials, but about building a country that proved Jews, reunited after millennia, could create a society tied to the land and never be victims again.

He relished living in this new state, so different from being a minority in the Bronx or Buffalo, imbued with Jewish pride and dense layers of history. But he was also troubled over Israel's land acquisition and recurrent violence with the Arabs. In studying international law, my father hoped to find "signposts to justice, fair and universal standards for the equitable resolution of conflict," he later wrote in a memoir. "I looked to international law for a way out of the impasse of the Arab-Israeli conflict."

He knew a shift was critical if Israel was to have a peaceful future, one that he might want to be part of. Perhaps he would have stayed longer were it not for an invitation to pursue a doctorate of law at Yale University. This was an opportunity he could not resist as a refugee who was the first in his family to graduate high school.

One evening in New Haven, he attended a lecture featuring a charismatic former deputy mayor of Jerusalem. Accompanying the speaker, he spotted a familiar woman with short black hair and slim ankles. He recognized her as an American he had met at the Western Wall; the one he blamed for spoiling his reconnaissance assignment. According to my father, Israel's Justice Ministry had tapped him to seduce a Russian dissident to decipher if she was an undercover KGB agent. The dissident was going to be at a protest in Jerusalem where he could meet her. But at the event, this Joan—then working as Jerusalem Mayor Teddy Kollek's press attaché—did not give him a chance to chat up the Russian woman, connecting her instead to interviewers from the press.

Now, two years after that initial encounter, my father was more successful at a different act of seduction. He set his sights on my mother, who said yes to his offer of a date. Soon, she began to imagine a quiet, scholarly life with this tall, charismatic blond man who was either a bit arrogant or adept at covering up insecurity about his immigrant roots.

* * *

Months later, on the other side of the country, chance or fate directed two other young people to cross paths. With his military service plus an extra voluntary year completed, Nachum had gotten the idea to study in America. He penned a letter to a distant relative he had met just once, an Uncle Zyg, who years earlier had left Canada for California. Leon's younger cousin from Zamość responded enthusiastically, offering to sponsor Nachum so he could secure a visa and provide a couch to sleep on in his suburban Los Angeles home.

To support himself, Nachum worked at a car wash and used his army connections to get a job with the Israeli consulate. One night he went to a party to celebrate the twenty-fifth birthday of his country, which shared his age. There, he chatted up a pretty Californian in a sundress with very small white polka dots.

A week later they met for a date. Tobi, a second-generation Angeleno, told him in fluent Hebrew how she had recently moved back to LA after living for a few transformative years in Jerusalem. As soon as she had arrived in Israel, she knew it was where she wanted to be. Growing up, she enjoyed singing Christmas carols along with her schoolmates, but she also wanted to share with them about Chanukah. Her father told her not to, worried it might not be well received. In Jerusalem, she loved living by a Jewish calendar and finding shared connections with residents who had moved there from around the world to build a new country. She was determined that the return to the United States be temporary. A few months later, when she traveled to Tel Aviv on her own to plan her next move, Nachum made sure she visited his parents.

Pepa and Leon welcomed Tobi as if she were already their son's bride. From their warm response she could only surmise that this handsome, hardworking Israeli who made her laugh must be serious about the relationship. She slept on Nachum's childhood bed—a sofa couch in a small room that doubled as a den and an office. Pepa introduced Tobi to her younger siblings and even took her to visit the grave of their mother, who had died in Israel. By the time Tobi flew back to Los Angeles, where Nachum picked her up at the airport, she knew she would marry him.

* * *

Our parents wed within months of each other, in 1974, at synagogues on opposite coasts of the United States. Neither of our mothers would land in the lives they'd imagined when they married our fathers.

The regimented pace of academic life did not suit my dad. He instead joined the Justice Department in Washington and became the first trial attorney in an office charged with uncovering the lies of Nazi collaborators who had immigrated to the United States. It would be an initial stop in a colorful and peripatetic career journey leading him into global halls of power. Meanwhile, my mother cultivated a reputation as a food writer specializing in Jewish cooking that would take her all over the world.

Although Tobi had agreed to marry Nachum on the condition that they would move back to Israel, it was not to be. First, he wanted to finish university, then earn enough money to return with a solid foundation. The right moment never arrived. Instead of buying at the housing development next to the Mediterranean that Tobi had selected for them, they eventually purchased a ranch house in the San Fernando Valley. She developed a career in Jewish communal service, and he followed Zyg into the real estate business.

Ultimately, it was likely Leon and Pepa who were responsible for them not returning to Israel. "Don't come back," they had urged Nachum, even though Leon had gone into a major depression after his son left. Every time his grandchildren got on the phone, he would cry. But ensuring they remained in the United States, as painful as it was, must have felt like one way Leon could provide his surviving son and his descendants with a more secure future.

* * *

Even as neither Nachum and Tobi, nor my parents, would ever live permanently in Israel again, they bestowed on us an indelible connection, exemplified through the choice of our names, Daniela and Talia, which were popular Hebrew ones at the time. I also received a middle name, Hope, upon which my parents placed dual significance. For the past, I was named after my grandmother Peshke's murdered mother, Chaya. For the future, they saw a second meaning tied to Israel, one that would later come to feel like an unfulfilled promise.

I was born in 1977, days after Egyptian President Anwar Sadat visited Jerusalem for the first time to meet with Menachem Begin, who was now Israel's prime minister. Neither man was a likely peacemaker. Only four years before, Sadat had attacked Israel on the holiest day of the Jewish calendar, and Begin's Irgun had ruthlessly killed Arabs in pursuit of a Jewish state. Watching the one-time enemies shake hands on television as I came into the world, my parents chose Hope for my middle name, as a wish for peace between Israel and its Arab neighbors, a hope that reconciliation and courage could win out against hate.

A year later, the two countries, along with the United States, would sign the Camp David Accords, leading to a treaty that included mutual recognition and provided for Israel's withdrawal from the Sinai Peninsula. But this period of hope was brief. In 1981, Egyptian Islamic Jihad members assassinated Sadat during a military parade in Cairo, a warning to other Arab leaders of the consequences of making peace with Israel.

That same year my father received a call that the new US ambassador to the United Nations needed a legal adviser with Middle East expertise. Soon my father, who as a stateless baby received his first identification from the United Nations, proudly took a seat at its headquarters on the East Side of Manhattan.

He entered a very different global body than the one that, thirty-four years earlier, had backed a partition of Palestine. In an expanded United Nations, which included many newly independent countries from Asia and Africa, criticism toward Israel had escalated dramatically since the 1967 war. As counsel to the US ambassador, my father relentlessly fought against efforts to delegitimize the Jewish state and equate Zionism with racism.

But he also held critiques of Israeli government actions, believing that it needed to stop Jewish settlement in the Occupied Territories and to support Palestinian autonomy if peace was to be achieved. When my father's first book, *Israel, the West Bank and International Law*, was published in 1978, he had warned: "The danger that the Arab-Israeli conflict will engulf the world in its web of tragedy has not ebbed."

* * *

Nearly five decades after my father's warning, we are deep into a season of soul-scraping bloodshed in the Middle East. I struggle more than ever before to maintain hope for a peaceful resolution. Still, the night of our Chanukah party, I find sparks of joy. Talia and I belt songs with our children and friends about stomping out darkness, light candles, and chant prayers using the same Hebrew words our ancestors once spoke in Zamość.

After the guests leave, I peek into our children's room. At six, they are now older than Leon's firstborn son, Kolonimus, was when his father was forced to flee. Aviv, our constant climber, lies prone, legs spread and relaxed. Alma rests her tousled hair and flushed face on a small, royal blue velvet pillow my grandmother Peshke embroidered for me when I was a young girl. On one side white needlepoint letters spell out *Shalom*, on the other *Love, Grandma*.

Talia joins me in an awestruck study of our children's lightly breathing bodies. "We are so lucky," she utters quietly. Her words mirror my thoughts, but I hold back. I don't want to tempt the evil eye; I am all too aware of how quickly good luck can become Jewish Luck. How new this life of comfort and freedom is for our family, and how capricious fortune can be.

Instead of speaking, I take Talia's hand in mine. With the charge of her touch, I cocoon myself in the miracle of our union, and marvel at how our Zamość grandparents persevered through a decade of wandering so that one day we could live and love and build this family of our own.

Afterword

For years, I traveled across countries and continents following the footsteps of our grandparents. Months into my search for our families' pasts, the far-flung geographies I was traversing became chillingly relevant to our violent present. I witnessed up close Russia's ruthless attack on Ukraine; the Kremlin's crackdown on transparency; its targeting of Americans, journalists, and LGBTQ people like us.

Meanwhile, peace had never felt so far away in the all-too-beloved sliver of land on the Mediterranean. Early in the morning of October 7, 2023, Hamas militants from Gaza breached the border wall and attacked a nearby target: kibbutzim. These were the agricultural communities that came out of the socialist vision shared by Zamość's Avigdoria. Our friend's cousin Maya was visiting her in-laws in Kfar Aza, a kibbutz founded by Jewish refugees from North African countries. She planned to attend a kite festival that day with her family. Instead, she was shot in front of her two young children; one among more than twelve hundred Israelis and foreign nationals murdered that day, along with hundreds more who were taken hostage.

Under the leadership of Prime Minister Benjamin Netanyahu—the inheritor and amplifier of Jabotinsky's militant ideology of an "Iron Wall"—bullets and bombs soon decimated tens of thousands of Palestinians; entire extended families were wiped out. The hollowed eyes of displaced residents of Gaza, starving and maimed children, stared back. Netanyahu maintained that the highly lethal assault was needed to free the hostages and destroy Hamas. As I completed writing this book, few reporters remained in Gaza to investigate his claims. International journalists had been banned from entering; Israel had killed nearly two hundred journalists. Around the globe, charges of genocide have been leveled against this country forged from the ashes of the Holocaust.

Back home, the United States was enacting its own forms of repression against the displaced. This country that served as a refuge and land of opportunity for my family slashed that promise for others. President Trump halted refugee resettlement in January 2025 for the first time since the aftermath of World War II. Thousands of attorneys like Talia have fought the shutting of our doors at a time of record global displacement and myriad assaults on immigrants living in the United States. But the justice system has proved much less effective in stopping this Trump administration from unleashing the most draconian enforcement actions in the nation's history.

I often return to the fickle nature of citizenship and survival in the face of state-sponsored violence that I uncovered in our grandparents' journey. Brutality often struck unexpectedly, even if in hindsight the build-up appeared obvious. Facing impossible choices, luck as much as foresight and courage guided who survived and who perished. But at a critical moment, our grandparents did follow their instincts and act, and leave, when they could. And along the torturous way, tight links to their heritage, community, and family proved transformative.

As Talia and I pass on the Jewish tradition to our children, with its legacy of displacement and survival, we are now the ones charged with sharing our ancestors' stories and the lessons we draw from them. One of the teachings of the Exodus is that it should become the wellspring of moral action: "You shall not wrong a stranger or oppress him, for you were strangers in the land of Egypt." My hope is that in reading these pages our children will not only learn their family's saga as victims but also feel a connection with today's migrants fleeing persecution. That they learn not to accept any one narrative as an ultimate truth, but to wrestle and probe to uncover what goes missing in the stories we tell. And I hope they will find in their great-grandparents' journeys, and the wanderers that preceded them, a personal legacy of resilience, community, and love that fortifies them and their descendants.

Acknowledgments

This book has been a consuming journey over the past four years, though in many ways my research started the first time my grandparents told me their story. For decades, I interviewed relatives, producing recordings that gathered dust in closets and on hard drives. Then Sarah Wildman masterfully edited an essay I wrote for *The New York Times* on my father's fake identity and refugee restrictions. When I told her about Talia's and my intersecting histories, she responded, "Now that's a book."

Savannah Ashour and Pete Nowalk took that spark of an idea and kindled it over drinks with me and Talia. In the years since that fateful night, Savannah has offered invaluable expertise, editing, and wit, and Pete provided writing insights and a place to retreat. Robert Asahina guided my proposal, fielded countless questions, and connected me with my inspired agent, Andrea Blatt, of WME. When an agent tells you she read your proposal on the way back from her wedding, you know she's your person. Andrea immediately got my story, brilliantly advocating for the project and calming my nerves across continents, even as she brought her own child into the world.

Mollie Weisenfeld took on editing *The Wanderers* with passion, vision and precision, shaping it from an idea into a book. Bernadette Murphy, as a writing coach, was in the trenches with me, and with wisdom and rapid edits, brought this book forth from the rabbit holes of my mind. Jacqueline Young received my book with open arms and as an editor brought new insights, as well as remarkably fast and clear communication. Ena Alvarado was a clear-eyed, multilingual, and fastidious fact-checker.

This project began in the years after our fathers died, and their spirits often carried me through the process. My father, Allan, with his unique intellect and passion for the past, and Nachum's joy and determination, urged me on as I worked.

Without them, I needed to rely even more heavily on other living relatives. My uncle Sam traveled with me in 2008 to the Föhenwald DP camp, his birthplace, and has patiently and lovingly contributed memories and editing since then. His wife, my aunt Shelley, and my cousins Mara and Nina have been eager readers and supporters. My father's cousin Sol Cooperman meticulously documented the family history; his wife, Eva, assisted with Yiddish and recorded family interviews with Sol for the Fortunoff Video Archive for Holocaust Testimonies. My father's other cousins—Calman, Charlie, Eda, Esther, Harry, Miriam, and Tamar—all graciously engaged with interviews. My cousin Ruthie was a particularly eager reader and shared recordings she made with her grandfather Moishe. The Argentine descendants of my grandmother's brothers, the Szajt family, helped dig up family stories and photos.

My extraordinary siblings have each played pivotal roles in this book. Merissa provided rabbinical knowledge, writing expertise, and enthusiasm that buoyed my spirits. David has been a research partner in our family story for more than twenty years, accompanying me from Bavaria to Brighton Beach, and digitizing and organizing family records. His wife, Liv, has been a steady source of wisdom and support.

I feel so fortunate to have landed in the Inlender family, for myriad reasons beyond our Zamość connection. Talia's brother Daniel interviewed Uncle Zyg and has tolerated too many questions from me. Her brother Aaron and his wife, Rachel, welcomed us on trips to Israel and have helped me talk through sections of the book and parenting. Talia's cousin Gosia Szymanska Weiss opened our minds to exploring Warsaw, translated Pepa's memory book, reviewed the entire manuscript, and was infinitely patient with my inquiries regarding the Holocaust and the Polish perspective. Zyg's children, Phyllis and Stephen Fleshler, connected me with family documents and stories. Bernie Enlander shared his genealogical research from London. Nachum's cousins Hedva Kadmoni and Zeevik Nosatzki and his wife, Holly, hosted our family, shared photos and memories, and introduced me to relatives. Nachom Inlender and Itzik Nosatzki tried to answer additional questions.

While this book is about our fathers' families, we would not be who we are without our mothers, and their families have their own fascinating immigration journeys that also shaped who we are. My mother, Joan Nathan, has taught me by example to ask everyone questions, taste local foods as part of the reporting process, and write my notes immediately! She is an inspiration on how to live as a writer and a mother. My mother-in-law, Tobi Inlender, has been a patient supporter, not pushing me about what I was going to write even as I asked her endless questions and dove through the boxes she has thankfully preserved. Her thoughtful eye, babysitting, and strong questions have improved this manuscript, and we are lucky to have her in our lives.

I connected with two writers, Adam Frankel and Mikhal Dekel, immediately after my father died, who inspired me to pursue my own book. Adam's *The Survivors* served as a reflection of postwar trauma and lies—and even had a surprise cameo of my mother. Mikhal's *Tehran's Children (In the East)* told my family's story in a way I'd never seen it represented, and she was generous with sources and insights. We also shared the bizarre and tragic coincidence that Mikhal's father died from the same rare disease as mine, Creutzfeldt-Jakob.

This book could not exist without the historians and immigration scholars who do the hard work of probing beyond the fickle nature of individual memory to preserve our collective past. Among the many whose research I relied on, who answered questions and in various instances read the book: Eliyana Adler, Vadim Altskan, Tarik Cyril Amar, Laura Auketayeva, Sarah Bridger, César Cuauhtémoc García Hernández, Roger Daniels, Sofia Dyak, Katharina Friedla,

Libby Garland, Atina Grossmann, Josef Hasitchka, Muhayo Isakova, Albert Kaganovitch, Kamil Kijek, Marek Kołcon, Paul Lerner, Zeev Levin, Heribert Macher-Kroisenbrunner, Adi Mahalel, Rebecca Manley, Tony Michels, Hiroshi Motomura, David Myers, David Nasaw, Markus Nesselrodt, Katarzyna Person, Naama Seri-Levi, Marci Shore, Alina Skibinska, Joanna Sliwa, Dariusz Stola, Julie Weise, Rona Yona, and Lidia Zessin-Jurek.

The troves of Holocaust research that captured survivors' testimonies and documents that have been made accessible to the public are invaluable. Vadim Altskan, Alina Skibinska, and Steven Vitto helped me navigate the US Holocaust Memorial Museum archives. Crispin Brooks guided me through the intricacies of the USC Shoah Foundation Visual History Archives, and Genie Glucksman spoke with me about the process of interviewing my grandmother. Joanna Sliwa helped me understand the complexity of reparations and Claims Conference documents, as well as Polish suffering in Zamość. Greta Barak assisted me at the Ghetto Fighters House Archive. JewishGen preserved the Yizkor Books and translated the Zamość one into English.

I am especially grateful to the survivor writers who captured their experiences in their own words. A great privilege of working on this book was reading their memoirs.

In Warsaw, Katarzyna Person welcomed us with warm clothes and toys, and was a steady source of brilliant knowledge and dark, delightful humor throughout my research. The Jewish Historical Institute provided archival assistance along with Anna Przybyszewska-Drozd's team at its Family Heritage Center. Rabbi Yehoshua Ellis introduced us to the Warsaw Jewish community and connected us to Bytom. Natalia Romik guided us on a memorable Pravda tour, and journalists Roman Fillinger, Sarah Nowotny, and Justyna Pawlak to reporting on the region. Blossom Preschool and the JCC Warszawa cared for our children. The Centre of Migration Research at the University of Warsaw provided Talia—and by extension me—with an intellectual home.

The contributions to this book of Marek Kołcon, a high school teacher in Zamość, cannot be overstated. For years, he has maintained the Facebook site Żydowski Zamość—Jewish Zamość. His trips to the archives for family records, his encyclopedic knowledge, and his unwavering patience with my questions built the sections of this book specific to Zamość. Daniel Sabaciński, director of the Zamość Synagogue, inspired me with his dedication and provided immeasurable generosity in sharing his work over many years with me.

Shelley Pollero and Sonny Putter, town leaders for Zamość, and Tomaszów Lubelksi respectively at Jewish Records Indexing-Poland, located family records. Ewa Koper guided us at the haunting Bełżec Museum and Memorial, and ensured our small children were appropriately occupied during the interview.

Rena Borow and Kamila Radecka-Mikulicz provided Yiddish translation. Yuliia Zhytelna, a student at California State University, Northridge, served as an able research assistant and interpreter, offering insights into the refugee experience, as did Elena.

In Lviv, Sofia Dyak, director of the Lviv Center for Urban History, welcomed me with a dinner with colleagues and introduced me to Marci Shore. The brilliant historians provided an unforgettable orientation, even as they mourned their friend, the poet Victoria Amelina, who died from wounds sustained when a Russian missile struck another Ukrainian restaurant. Olha Zarachnyuk, an architect and coordinator of the center's Lviv Interactive project, found records of Wigdor Inlender's building. Olha Honchar and the staff at the Territory of Terror introduced me to their challenging and creative work, and Liana Blikharska read sections from Ukraine. Johanna Mendelson Forman provided a bridge to connections in Lviv, among them historian Ihor Lylo. Inna was a highly knowledgeable and energetic guide.

In lieu of traveling to Russia, I relied on experts to help me bridge the gap with documents. Jan Szumski, a historian at the Instytut Pamięci Narodowej (Polish Institute for National Remembrance, or IPN), introduced me to the Index of the Repressed and assisted extensively with family archival requests. He also pointed me to the new Sybir Memorial Museum, and connected me with historian Marcin Zwolski, who was a patient and insightful guide throughout. KARTA's cofounder, Alicja Wancerz-Gluza, met with me on little notice to discuss how they researched victims of Soviet political crimes. The courageous Tatiana Kosinova, Alexander Guryanov, and Alexey Mosin led me to identify our family documents. They reinforced the very present need to push back against totalitarian regimes and preserve histories of oppression. My friend Larisa supported my research and even ventured out in minus forty degrees (incidentally where Celsius meets Fahrenheit) to the post office.

In Uzbekistan, Anait Garaeva was an extraordinary guide to Samarkand and Juma, and Ambassador Zehavit Ben-Hillel graciously met with me in Tashkent. It was also a great pleasure to reunite with Sherzod, whom I had not seen since we graduated from college twenty-five years earlier. And Oleg and Lilia, I'll always be grateful to you for enriching this transformational trip and my life. We stayed in two converted homes of Bukharan Jewish merchants, Amelia Hotel (Bukhara) and Rabat Hotel (Samarkand), which provided unforgettable sites to work and retreat.

Kamil Kijek provided a detailed overview of the so-called "reclaimed territories" over a Georgian dinner with our rambunctious children in Wrocław, Poland. Izabella Kuhnel guided us in Bytom and graciously shared her years of research.

In Austria, my friend Ruthi Orli Moshkovitz helped track down local sources. She identified historian Josef Hasitchka in Admont, who opened his home and archives to us, and connected me with historian Heribert Macher-Kroisenbrunner.

Hagar Cygler, a gifted artist, archivist, and genealogist, who took on her own father's past via a different medium, made key connections throughout Israel and was a thought partner and friend, as was her husband, Hemy Ramiel. I'll never be able to thank Adi Shalit enough for connecting us to photos of Kolonimus and Manya and then welcoming us with full enthusiasm to probe overlapping family stories.

When I first visited Föhrenwald in 2006, multimedia artist and musician Michaela Melián and her husband, Thomas Meinecke, invited me into their home and introduced the displaced persons camp based on her extensive research. Wibke Bergemann was a collaborator on our project "Too Many Geister" and has been a great friend and thought partner. Rhiannon Moutafis at the BADEHAUS Place of Remembrance, a museum about Föhrenwald, located historical records.

Amelia Klein introduced me to Reboot and later connected me to Max Wald, vice president of the Australian Jewish Genealogical Society. His curiosity helped me unravel the mystery of Abe Blumstein. And the real Albert Blumsztein graciously met with Max and later my mother. His great-niece, Natalie Shva, shared with me her extensive research and careful eye. Genealogist Jennifer Mendelsohn guided me through the slow process of accessing my family's US immigration records.

This type of deep reporting over many years demands outside financial support beyond a book contract. The fellowships I received to Germany, the Arthur F. Burns Fellowship and the Alexander von Humboldt German Chancellor Scholarship, broadened my historical and contemporary perspective, and provided language training. The Humboldt also connected me to my Russian peers, planting seeds decades ago. Unfortunately, the program was canceled in 2024 due to severe funding cuts. Reboot Studios was the first to come forward and give me financial support specific to this book to fund my research trip to Uzbekistan.

I am very fortunate that California State University, Northridge (CSUN), has been my professional home for nearly a decade. My students, most of whom have immigrant backgrounds, have shaped this project and encouraged me that, even in this digital age, reading remains important. I am grateful to have colleagues and an administration that supported and provided a sabbatical, research grants, and a fellowship for me to do this work. Public universities like CSUN, which support opportunities for first-generation college students and faculty research, are treasures of the best part of our democracy that we need to fight for now more than ever.

As Journalism department chair, Linda Bowen brought me to CSUN, with flexibility and patience, and was the first to say I was writing a book publicly. Melissa Wall has taught me how to carve out time for research, brought me into writing groups, and helped me stay sane in this process. Stephanie Bluestein and Marcella DeVeaux, as department chairs, and Dan Hosken as dean, have supported my untraditional academic path. Adriana Elegado, Jennifer Lu, Natali Papazyan, and Liman Wang have deftly handled my reimbursements and administrative questions. Gretchen Macchiarella has readily provided answers. The Jewish Studies department, where I'm an affiliated faculty member, has supported this project at a challenging time and connected me to the former Israeli consul in Tashkent.

Zócalo Public Square at Arizona State University, where I am an editor at large, provided a place to pursue my writing with enlightened colleagues. Moira Shourie, Eryn Brown, and team, I cannot thank you enough. Talib Jabbar, Jackie Mansky, Sarah Rothbard, and Sara Suárez read my manuscript and coached me through countless moments. Café Zinque Thursday mornings, and Paradocs Coffee and Tea on the other days. The West Tisbury Library was a summer residency of sorts, and the best community-serving library I know of in this country.

Elements of this book have been previously developed and published in or broadcast on Deustchlandradio Kultur, *The New York Times*, the *Los Angeles Times*, and *Afar* magazine. Susan Brenneman edited the *Los Angeles Times* essay on our family's refugee history in Ukraine. An earlier version of the chapter on finding my father's home in Uzbekistan ran in *Afar* magazine. My gratitude to editor in chief Julia Cosgrove, who was there when my father was first diagnosed, for seeing the promise in that story, and to executive editor Katherine LaGrave for her careful and insightful editing of that piece.

I was fortunate to also have a trove of unofficial editors on this project. Serena Jones was my not-so-secret weapon in the negotiating process and beyond. *New Voices* was my first journalism job, and it's fitting that Daniel Treiman returned to help edit here. The *New York Sun* was my next reporting job. Ira Stoll assigned me to the immigration beat back in 2002 and provided a generous read in 2025. Karen Frillmann, my editor at WNYC, advised me on an audio version and helped me launch the original reporting in Germany. Gal Beckerman,

ACKNOWLEDGMENTS

Debra-Ellen Glickstein, Ian Halperin, Jason Mandell, Michael Scott Moore, Mitchell Landsberg, Rebecca Lesser, Michael Lukas, Agnieszka Pikulicka-Wilczewska, Liz Robbins, and Audrey Singer provided insights, read, and listened to sections or the entirety of the book.

Rose Jacobs, a wise editor and friend, made a memorable dinner trip across borders to meet Talia and me in Austria. Deborah Kolben pushed me forward when I needed it most. And Xiao Mina's tarot cards readings steadied me and propelled the project. Gabriella Herman edited and sharpened photos. Jennifer Cheng made my first Wanderers map. Megan Woo created my website.

As a professor now, I especially appreciate the professors that shifted the course of my life. James McIlwain taught me how to pursue independent research into genealogy. Roberto Suro provided an opportunity for me to move to California, and I am forever grateful for that and the talks over so many years, wrestling through the intricacies of journalistic approaches, migration policies, and life. I wish that Michael Parks could have joined us for more conversations with some classical music in the background, adding insights on Cold War legacy, decision making, and the failures of global diplomacy.

Elizabeth Aguilera, my collaborator in Migratory Notes and other schemes, was a sounding board on immigration coverage and more. Yana Kunichoff provided Russian insights, found me the Old Mermaid Sanctuary in Tucson for a phenomenal self-directed writing retreat, and literally saved my life while there. Ama Anane, Walter Barrientos, Ali Berzon, Natalia Bogolasky, Lee Buchannon, Laurel Firestone, Jesse Hardman, Steffi Hoffrichter, Yvonne Hung, Suzy Jack, Cristina Jimenez, Ali Manzano, Eva Sanchis, Fernanda Santos, and Andrea Wenzel are among many friends and colleagues who enrich my life and championed this project.

The fellow parents who bring joy to our lives and our kids—and were always at the ready to help out on days I needed to work. María y David Ramírez: Somos tan afortunados de que sean parte de nuestras vidas. For a year of writing this book, we had the good luck to live among the books of historians Nathan Perl-Rosenthal and Jessica

Marglin. Our Nefesh and Shtibl communities nurture our Jewish lives and nourish our spirits.

Without Talia, there would be no story. The two strands of family history existed, but you brought the magic that created our lives together. Your unwavering faith in this project, support for me, and brilliance have steadied and inspired me throughout the writing and beyond. I am in wonder of a universe that brought us together.

And to our children, Alma and Aviv, who don't remember a time when I was not working on this book, I marvel daily at how lucky I am to be one of your mothers.

Note on Language and Reporting

The Wanderers is a work of nonfiction, as close as I could get to a true story. Oral histories, by their nature, contain gaps and uncertainties, which I have worked to address as faithfully as possible while acknowledging the limitations inherent in reconstructing the past. Historical recollections stated by other people are in italics. If a scene is re-created based upon outside testimonies, those are cited. If I was working from a personal memory, and did not have a recording, I confirmed with at least one other person. Dialogue is reconstructed from memory and research, and I made every effort to remain true to the spirit and content of those original conversations, as the precise words were not always available.

In a few instances, I only include the first name for people concerned about personal safety, or who I worried could be threatened if I revealed their identities. In Zamość, which I visited twice, elements of the time frame of my reporting were reconstructed to fit the narrative.

To avoid confusion when names change many times, I used Mottel and Peshke primarily when referring to my grandparents, even though my grandfather's names also included Mordechai and Mordko, as well as his Blumstein alias; and after they moved to the United States, they were known as Morton and Paula Gerson. In Marek's initial email about Leon's first wife, Marja Miriam (Manya), he wrote "Miriam" not "Manya." Because she had three names and was known to the family as Manya, I changed it for clarity. Leon often went by Leybl in archival documents from Poland, but since he also went by Leon and adopted that name upon moving to Israel, I use Leon. Pepa always went by Pepa.

Jews lived in Poland for hundreds of years as a minority prior to World War II but were considered a distinct nationality. When I refer to Poles, I'm referring to ethnically Polish citizens who generally are Roman Catholic.

Palestine was the name of the territory with shifting boundaries under Ottoman control from 1516 until World War I. Subsequently, under the British Mandate Jewish and Arab residents alike held Palestinian citizenship certificates and passports. I use Jewish residents of Palestine and Palestinian Arabs in the period prior to the establishment of Israel in 1948.

Lviv was one of many place-names that changed repeatedly. I use the Ukrainian name for the city since it officially shifted during the period I'm writing about from Lwow (Polish) to Lvov (Soviet) to Lemberg (German, Yiddish). With many names to keep track of, and since it is currently Lviv, I selected that.

Notes

"There is a literature both on the Holocaust and on the fate of Poles in the Soviet Union during World War II, but the history of this 'Siberian odyssey of Polish Jewry' seemed until recently to have largely disappeared from pubic memory," Antony Polonsky writes in the introduction to the book Katharina Friedla and Markus Nesselrodt edited, *Polish Jews in the Soviet Union (1939–1959): History and Memory of Deportation, Exile and Survival. Jews of Poland* (Academic Studies Press, 2021). Historian Eliyana Adler similarly observes, "Their choice to flee east—and subsequent choices—placed them outside the reach of the Nazi genocide. Yet it also placed them in a sort of netherworld of history and memory; on the *other side* of the stories we tell about the Holocaust and the Second World War," in *Survival on the Margins: Polish Jewish Refugees in the Wartime Soviet Union* (Harvard University Press, 2020).

I was very fortunate in writing that invaluable sources, such as these two, following closely on Mark Edele, Sheila Fitzpatrick, and Atina Grossmann's *Shelter from the Holocaust: Rethinking Jewish Survival in the Soviet Union* (Wayne State University Press, 2018), were published on the topic of Polish Jewish survival in the Soviet Union in recent years. Another book completed while I worked on this book, Albert Kaganovitch's *Exodus and Its Aftermath: Jewish Refugees in the Wartime Soviet Interior* (University of Wisconsin Press, 2022), provided additional detailed research. Kaganovitch concludes that "a comprehensive study of the migration of Jewish refugees to the eastern regions of the USSR and the conditions of their life during the war still has not been done, largely due to the full or partial unavailability of archival sources."

In addition to the history books published in the past five years, Mikhal Dekel's *Tehran Children: A Holocaust Refugee Odyssey*, republished as *In the East: How My Father and a Quarter Million Polish Jews Survived the Holocaust* (W. W. Norton, 2019), provided key details and a model for this type of book. Stefani Hoffman's translation of Julius Margolin's *Journey into the Land of the Zeks and Back: A Memoir of the Gulag* (Oxford University Press, 2020); and Meier Landau's richly detailed *A Lost World: The Galician Shtetl and Siberia* (Brill, 2023), edited by historian Lidia Zessin-Jurek, brought to life the experience.

While earlier scholarship was more limited, foundational sources include John Goldlust's "A Different Silence: The Survival of More than 200,000 Polish Jews in the Soviet Union During World War II as a Case Study in Cultural Amnesia" (*Australian Jewish Historical Society Journal*, 2012, pp. 13–60); and Antony Polonsky and Norman Davies' *Jews in Eastern Poland and the USSR, 1939–46* (St. Martin's Press, 1991).

PREFACE

Markus Nesselrodt, in the introduction to *Polish Jews in the Soviet Union (1939–1959)* writes, "Most historians agree that between 160,000 and 230,000 Polish Jews survived the Holocaust because they made it beyond Germany's grasp deep into the Soviet Union in a wide variety of ways." An estimated 300,000 to 350,000 fled east.

CHAPTER 1

The historical narrative of my grandparents, Mottel (Morton) and Peshke (Paula) Gerson, draws from testimonials they each provided to Gail Schwartz as part of the Oral History Project of the Jewish Community Relations Council of Greater Washington (1989); one my grandmother recorded with Genie Glucksman for what is now the USC Shoah Foundation (1998); and four additional interviews my siblings, Merissa and David, recorded with her between 1989 and 1998; and a brief autobiography my grandfather wrote.

The 1931 census recorded 24,241 people in Zamość, 54 percent Roman Catholic and 42 percent Jewish.

Bełżec descriptions come from the Museum and Memorial Site in Bełżec and an interview with Ewa Koper on-site and follow-up information on survivor testimony.

CHAPTER 2

The number of Jews in Zamość is not consistently recorded, with some sources stating there were 12,531 Jewish residents of the city before the war. I based the number 10,490 on Marek Kołcon's research. He found that the editorial board of the Krakow newspaper *Ilustrowany Kurier Codzienny* asked the Zamość authorities in June 1939 about the number of inhabitants. The town board answered that on June 1, 1939, three months before the German invasion, 28,502 people lived in Zamośc; among them, 17,732 Poles, 10,490 Jews, and 180 Ukrainians.

According to the Central Committee of Jews in Poland, there were 245 Jews in Zamość following World War II, in May 1945.

In the process of working on the book, I connected with a Moshe Inlender in Israel whose grandfather was Talia's grandfather Leon's cousin. Moshe's father left Zamość for Palestine before the war. I did not uncover any other Inlenders from Zamość who survived World War II.

CHAPTER 3

The narrative on family history, in addition to the testimonials from my grandparents, is based on interviews and oral histories provided by three of the five other siblings that survived the war with them. Eva and Sol Cooperman, with training from the Yale Fortunoff Video Archive for Holocaust Testimonies, interviewed Norma (Chuma) and Simon Cooperman. My brother, David, and I interviewed Moishe Gerson various times, as did his granddaughter

Ruthie Gerson. Simon was also interviewed by David and Sol and my father. My aunt Raya, who survived separately, also provided testimony to me and my brother. These testimonials all are used to reconstruct historical narrative.

CHAPTER 4

Various terms other than "Holocaust survivors" have been used to describe Polish Jews who survived in the Soviet Union, such as "flight survivors," "refugees," and "deportees," since they were not in Nazi territory when extermination was implemented as a policy. For more on terminology, see Adler's *Survival on the Margins*; and Katharina Friedla and Markus Nesselrodt, editors, *Polish Jews in the Soviet Union (1939–1959): History and Memory of Deportation, Exile and Survival. Jews of Poland* (Academic Studies Press, 2021).

The definition of who is a Holocaust survivor according to German restitution law is highly complicated. "The eligibility criteria for the West German Federal Compensation Law kept changing," Joanna Sliwa, historian at the Conference on Jewish Material Claims Against Germany, explained to me. "Jewish survivors who met strict persecution and geographical criteria established by the West German government were eligible for compensation through the *Bundesentschädigungsgesetze* (BEG or West German Federal Indemnification Law), introduced in 1953. Eligibility depended on the type and duration of persecution and imposed limits, such as a survivor's citizenship, legal status, and residency before and after the Holocaust. Relatively few survivors were eligible for this compensation."

CHAPTER 5

Adi Shalit's family archives provided the photos of Leon Inlender and his first family. She, and her mother, provided testimony passed down from her grandfather Khaim upon which this family history is based. The Israeli Organization of Zamość Jewry and their Descendants served as a repository for many of their photos.

Helen Epstein's *Children of the Holocaust: Conversations with Sons and Daughters of Survivors* (G. P. Putnam's Sons, 1979) was the book that my mother said most helped her understand the burdens my father lived with. My father and grandfather also both read it, and our copy had their respective notes in English and Yiddish. Epstein also provided an interview. Various other works have since then looked at the legacy from an academic and journalistic lens, such as Dan Bar-On's *Fear and Hope: Three Generations of the Holocaust* (Harvard University Press, 1995).

Ninety-one people were killed in the King David Hotel attack, which blew up the British military headquarters. Irgun leader Menachem Begin later maintained he had tried to limit casualties, and three calls were made to urge evacuation. He said they were ignored. See https://www.jewishvirtuallibrary.org/bombing-of-the-king-david-hotel.

CHAPTER 6

The Warsaw Uprising occurred fifteen months after the Nazis had liquidated the ghetto in their quest to systematically exterminate all Jews. While by then the vast majority of the city's prewar Jewish population of more than 350,000 had been murdered, hundreds of Jews who survived in hiding or escaped captivity fought alongside Poles in the Warsaw Uprising. For more see Marci Shore's "The Jewish Hero History Forgot," (*New York Times*, 2013).

Talia wrote about her experiences during the travel ban in Zócalo Public Square, providing more details to the case: "The courts deemed the first travel ban unconstitutional. Those wrongfully denied entry were permitted to return, including Mr. Vayeghan. Indeed, the court ordered the government to facilitate his return, and he entered the United States as a lawful permanent resident later that week" (/www.zocalopublicsquare.org/airports-became-battleground-deciding-belongs-america/). Garcetti's speech, "2017 State of the City," April 21, 2017, can be found at https://empowerla.org/mayors-message-121/. The *LA Times* profiled Talia's role in " 'Coordinated Chaos': Scores of Volunteer Attorneys Mobilized to Try to Stop Detentions and Deportations at LAX" (*LA Times*, January 31, 2017).

"A grenade was thrown into a room in the Peretz House, where Jews were being quartered. Fortunately, it did not explode, so no one was injured."

Julian Kwiek, Nie chcemy Żydów u siebie. Przejawy wrogości wobec Żydów w latach 1944–47, Warszawa 2021, s. 150 (Julian Kwiek, We Don't Want Jews at Home. Manifestations of Hostility Toward Jews in 1944–47, Warsaw 2021, p. 150).

CHAPTER 7

The *Zamość Memorial Book*, edited by Mordechai V. Bernstein, was published by the Central Committee for Pinkas Zamość in Buenos Aires in 1957. Originally written in Yiddish so all its diaspora community could understand, unlike a version in Hebrew published in Israel before that, it was translated to English in 2004 by Jacob Solomon Berger with support from JewishGen, a nonprofit organization created as an intergenerational resource for Jewish genealogy. For more on memorial books, see Eliyana R. Adler's "Narratives of Return: Preserving Lost Knowledge in Postwar Polish Jewish Memorial Books," *Journal of Migration History* 11, no. 1 (2025): 42–61.

The last name of the Inlenders I found in the memorial book had been transliterated to "Inlander." But the spelling in the Hebrew letters was consistent with how Talia's family spelled it.

The *Rough Guide to Poland* featuring Zamość on the cover is the eighth edition (Rough Guides, 2018).

CHAPTER 8

This chapter and others on the history of Jewish Zamość benefited immensely from Marek Kolcon's independent archival work, as well as from Adam Kopciowski's *Zagłada Żydów w Zamościu* (Wydawnictwo Uniwersytetu Marii Curie-Skłodowskiej, 2005); Moshe Frank's *To Survive and Testify: Holocaust Traumas of a Jewish Child from Zamosc* (Beit Lohamei Hagetaot, 1993); oral histories from Maria Krych and Henryk Lewandowski in the Centropa Archive; and articles authored in the *Zamosc Memorial Book*.

While Zamość was not immune to anti-Semitism, its local leadership was known to promote acceptance. On November 29, 1931, the by-then Polish-majority town council adopted a resolution condemning "anti-Semitic excesses by students in Warsaw, Vilnius, and Krakow."

The UNESCO World Heritage Convention documents for the Old City of Zamość (1992) and the World Monuments Fund publication on the "Revitalization of the Renaissance Synagogue in Zamość" (Foundation for the Preservation of Jewish Heritage in Poland, 2009) provided key historic and contemporary details. My sister, Merissa, affixed a mezuzah on the Zamość synagogue when she was coincidentally present for a dedication ceremony.

Broader histories such as Paul Kriwaczek's *Yiddish Civilization: The Rise and Fall of a Forgotten Nation* (Alfred A. Knopf, 2005); Miriam Weinstein's *Yiddish: A Nation of Words* (Random House, 2002); Norman Davies' *God's Playground: A History of Poland* (Columbia University Press, 2005); Adam Zamoyski's *Poland: A History* (Hippocrene Books, 2012); and Polin Museum's exhibit Paradisus Iudaeorum (1569–1648) each illustrated the pivotal and unique role of Zamość in Polish history. Although fiction, James A. Michener's *Poland: A Novel* (Fawcett, 1984) was also highly informative, with Zamość playing a central role and descriptions like this: "You are not about to enter a fort. This is a real town, and a most beautiful one. It was built by an Italian architect who gave it a chain of lovely arcades cool in summer, protecting in winter. I love Zamosc and would like to end my days sitting in the grand square."

Specifics about the history of Polish victims come from Elizabeth B. White and Joanna Sliwa's *The Counterfeit Countess: The Jewish Woman Who Rescued Thousands of Poles During the Holocaust* (Simon & Schuster, 2024), which relates in horrifying detail the devastation Poles from the Zamość region endured. They detail the debates of Hans Frank, governor-general of German-occupied Poland, with other members of the Nazi leadership about how to ethnically cleanse and exterminate Poles. This section also benefited from Tadeusz Piotrowski's *Poland's Holocaust* (McFarland, 1998); the United States Holocaust Memorial Museum's digital encyclopedia, "Polish Victims"; and Auschwitz-Birkenau State Museum, "Online Lesson About the Deportation of Poles Expelled from the Zamosc Region to Auschwitz."

Erica Lehrer's edited collection "Lucky Jews" (*Korporacja Ha!art*: 2014) presents an in-depth history of the figurines. Lehrer writes that historically a Christian Polish peasant would often believe Jews had magical powers and might even go to a rabbi for an amulet.

CHAPTER 9

Historian Kamil Kijek describes the generation of Polish Jews that came of age when our grandparents did as united by a "radical modernism." See Kamil Kijek, *Modern and Radical: Politics, Culture, and Socialization of Jewish Youth in Interwar Poland* (Indiana University Press, 2026), a translation of *Dzieci modernizmu: Świadomość, kultura i socjalizacja polityczna młodzieży żydowskiej w II Rzeczypospolitej* (Wydawnictwo Uniwersytetu Wrocławskiego, Wrocław, 2017). *Awakening Lives: Autobiographies of Jewish Youth in Poland Before the Holocaust,* edited by Jeffrey Shandler (Yale University Press, 2002) and based on a YIVO Institute for Jewish Research writing contest, provides extraordinary perspectives from young people of the time.

Descriptions of Peretz's social environment and attitudes toward Palestine relied on Adi Mahalel's *The Radical Isaac: I. L. Peretz and the Rise of Jewish Socialism* (SUNY Press, 2023); and Ruth R. Wisse's *I. L. Peretz and the Making of Modern Jewish Culture* (University of Washington Press, 1991). The section on Luxemburg drew from J. P. Nettl's *Rosa Luxemburg* (Oxford University Press, 1966); and Hannah Arendt's review in the *New York Review of Books* "A Heroine of Revolution," 1966; Robert S. Wistrich's "Rosa Luxemburg: The Polish-German-Jewish Identities of a Revolutionary Internationalist" (Leo Baeck Institute Year Book, July 2012); and Stephen Eric Bronner's *The Letters of Rosa Luxemburg* (Westview Press, 1978).

The *Zamosc Memorial Book* contains extensive biographies of I. L. Peretz and Rosa Luxemburg. Y. Zudiker, author of the Luxemburg chapter, titles the first section, "The She-Eagle That Flew Out of Zamosc." The name draws on the words of Vladimir Lenin, who often disagreed with Luxemburg, but ultimately admired her. "In spite of her mistakes she was—and remains for us—an eagle. And not only will Communists all over the world cherish her memory, but her biography and her complete works... will serve as useful manuals for training many generations of Communists all over the world," Lenin wrote in "Notes of a Publicist" (*Pravda*, April 16, 1924).

For discourse between Rosa Luxemburg and I. L. Peretz, see Adam Kirsch's essay "Non-Jewish Jews: Rosa Luxemburg and Isaac Deutscher," in *Who Wants to Be a Jewish Writer?* (Yale University Press, 2019); and for an interpretation on Luxemburg's connection to Jewish community, see Naomi Klein's *Doppelganger* (Farrar, Straus and Giroux, 2023).

The writing on the rise of Zionism benefited from the works of, among others, Sami Adwan, Dan Bar-On, and Eyal Naveh, eds., *Side by Side: Parallel Histories of Israel-Palestine* (New Press, 2012); *Memoirs: David Ben-Gurion* (World Publishing, 1970); Rashid Khalidi's *The Hundred Years' War for Palestine* (Macmillan, 2020); and Ari Shavit's *My Promised Land: The Triumph and Tragedy of Israel* (Random House, 2013).

"The Question of Palestine: Origins and Evolution of the Palestine Problem: 1917–1947 (Part I)," from the United Nations, includes the correspondence of Sir Edwin Montagu questioning the Balfour Proclamation. See https://www.un.org/unispal/history2/origins-and-evolution-of-the-palestine-problem/part-i-1917-1947.

Sources on the rise of Revisionist Zionism included Menachem Begin's *White Nights* (Harper & Row, 1979, originally published in Hebrew in 1957); Daniel Kupfert Heller's *Jabotinsky's Children* (Princeton University Press, 2017); and Zeev Tzahor's "The Struggle Between the Revisionist Party and the Labor Movement: 1929–1933" (*Modern Judaism* 8, no. 1, 1988). Jabotinsky's 1923 "The Iron Wall" essay, originally written in Russian, can be found at https://en.jabotinsky.org/media/9747/the-iron-wall.pdf.

On the growth of HeHalutz, and left-leaning Zionist social movements, I relied on Rona Yona's "A Kibbutz in the Diaspora: The Pioneer Movement in Poland and the Klosova Kibbutz" (*Journal of Israeli History*, 2012); and "From Russia to Palestine via Poland: The Shifting Centre of Interwar Labour Zionism" (*Cambridge European History*, 2021); Zachary Lockman's

Comrades and Enemies: Arab and Jewish Workers in Palestine, 1906–1948 (University of California Press, 1996); and Judy Batalion's *The Light of Days: The Untold Story of Women Resistance Fighters in Hitler's Ghettos* (William Morrow, 2021).

For specifics on Zamość, Kopciowski's *Zagłada Żydów w Zamościu* (Lublin, 2005) provided the titles of Zionist talks and details of the confrontation between progressives and the Agudath Yisrael movement. Polin Museum's Virtual Shtetl entry on Zamość provided additional details. See https://sztetl.org.pl/en/towns/z/17-zamosc/99-history/138301-history-of-community. Henryk Lewandowski, in an interview for USC Shoah Foundation Visual History Archive, describes his father's affiliation with Jabotinsky and the Revisionists in Zamość, and his general popularity in Poland.

CHAPTER 10

The descriptions of Zionist life in Zamość as Germany closes in come from a letter from Arie Fialkow dated 14 December 1938 and kept in the Ghetto Fighters' House Archives.

CHAPTER 11

Human Rights Watch's report, "Poland: Rule of Law Erosion Harms Women, LGBT People," December 15, 2022, describes the threats facing gay people.

CHAPTER 12

Descriptions of the onset of the war in Zamość come from the town's memorial book and family testimonies. The Tomaszów Lubelski memorial book describes gathering around the radio after Sukkot. Moshe Frank's *To Survive and Testify: Holocaust Traumas of a Jewish Child from Zamosc* (Beit Lohamei Haghetaot, 1993), provided details of Leon's brother-in-law's departure from Zamość.

The broader political situation relied on Jan Tomasz Gross's *Revolution from Abroad: The Soviet Conquest of Poland's Western Ukraine and Western Belorussia* (Princeton University Press, 2002); and Daniel Finkelstein's *Two Roads Home: Hitler, Stalin and the Miraculous Survival of My Family* (Doubleday, 2023).

For more about the Jewish Historic Institute, the history of the building, and its Family Research Center, see https://www.jhi.pl/en/about-the-institute/. More on the destruction of the Warsaw ghetto can be found at https://www.yadvashem.org/yv/en/exhibitions/warsaw_ghetto_testimonies/liquidation.asp.

CHAPTER 13

Adler's definition and conceptualization of the Other Side in *Survival on the Margins* informed this chapter.

Just how many Polish Jews fled across the border from German-occupied territory to Soviet-occupied is a matter of debate among historians, ranging from estimates of 100,000 to 400,000 people. Adler sums up the numbers analyses of different scholars in *Survival on the Margins* (2020), p. 27.

Ukrainians' views of LGBTQ people have grown increasingly positive since 2010. In May 2022, a survey by Kyiv International Institute of Sociology found that 38.2 percent claimed to hold negative views about LGBT people.

CHAPTER 14

Rebecca Manley's *To the Tashkent Station: Evacuation and Survival in the Soviet Union at War* (Cornell University Press, 2009), probes the origins and meaning of the concepts of "refugee" and "evacuee" in Soviet history, and shaped the development of this chapter.

On borderland history, Timothy Snyder's *Bloodlands: Europe Between Hitler and Stalin* (Basic Books, 2012) provided details on Stalin's deportations, the Gulag system, and the movement of information to Poland.

CHAPTER 15

The Lviv Center for Urban History helped identify the background and current locations of the Jewish hospital and Wigdor Inlender's building, and details about the corner tenement house at 3 Maja and Kościuszko Streets. Adam Kopciowski's book on Jewish Zamość detailed the fate of Wigdor Inlender's family.

Tarik Cyril Amar's *The Paradox of Ukrainian Lviv: A Borderland City Between Stalinists, Nazis, and Nationalists* (Cornell University Press, 2015); Marci Shore's chapter "Autumn in Soviet Galicia," from *Caviar and Ashes: A Warsaw Generations' Life and Death in Marxism, 1918–1968* (Yale University Press, 2009); Alexander Wat's memoir via interviews with Czesław Miłosz, *My Century* (NYRB Classics, 2003); and Landau's memoir all provided key details and context to the period when our grandparents arrived in Lviv.

Among the most illuminating and poignant reporting from Lviv during World War II came from the Ringelblum Archive. Created at the initiative of historian Dr. Emanuel Ringelblum, a group known as Oneg Shabbat undertook the task of gathering and documenting the fates of Jews following the Nazi invasion of Poland. One section is on accounts from the borderlands and includes Soviet annexation. In 1946, a survivor from the historical group dug up the metal boxes protecting tens of thousands of pages of handwritten documents from Jews detailing their systematic extermination. "What we were unable to cry and shriek out to the world we buried in the ground," read an attached note, written by a nineteen-year-old assistant in the archives. "We may now die in peace. We fulfilled our mission. May history attest for us." Andrzej Żbikowski, ed., *The Ringelblum Archive. Underground Archive of the Warsaw Ghetto, Accounts from Borderlands, 1939–1941* (Jewish Historical Institute, 2018).

Philippe Sands's *East West Street: On the Origins of "Genocide" and "Crimes Against Humanity,"* provided a detailed and highly insightful exploration of Lviv and its imprints psychological and physical, on the present (Vintage, 2017). Daniel Mendelsohn's *The Lost: A Search for Six of Six Million*, also describes arriving in Lviv on a journey to uncover the area's Jewish past (Harper Perennial, 2017).

Did my grandmother Peske's hair really go white instantaneously? It seems hard to believe, but this is one of the places where the testimonies line up from both my grandfather and my great-uncle Moishe. Witold Wrzosiński, director of the Warsaw Jewish Cemetery, informed me about the fate of children in Jewish cemeteries.

NOTES

CHAPTER 16

Descriptions of Zamość under the Nazis used here come from the town's memorial book.

Landau in his memoir provided more details of the human smuggling trade that emerged between German- and Soviet-occupied territories. "Peasants from the border villages became guides who smuggled people at night through the demarcation line, for a certain agreed-upon fee. It was a two-way traffic. Some guaranteed the crossing and others didn't. Some insisted on being paid in advance, some agreed for half to be paid upfront and for the rest to be paid after the crossing." For more, see Meier Landau's *A Lost World: The Galician Shtetl and Siberia* (Brill, 2023).

Holding a passport was a fundamental part of Soviet society, not to leave for other countries but to function within it. As Rebecca Manley writes in *To the Tashkent Station*: "Since the early 1930s and the introduction of the passport regime, residence and work had been the twin requirements for full inclusion in the Soviet polity. People who lacked a 'fixed residence' and were not engaged in 'socially useful labor' were routinely targeted in 'cleansing' operations designed to clear major cities of 'socially undesirable elements.'" Gross, in *Revolution from Abroad: The Soviet Conquest of Poland's Western Ukraine and Western Belorussia*, explains the rationale for the process and documents some of the testimonials cited. Nikita Khrushchev describes in *Khrushchev Remembers* (Little Brown, 1970) the report that Poles were signing up to return.

Wat and Amar provide descriptions of the respective January and February deportations in Lviv. The June deportation from Lviv is based on family testimonials, USC Shoah Foundation testimonials, and Landau's descriptions of the trucks arriving. Fiszel K, in testimony in Yale's Fortunoff Video Archive, states upon his deportation, he learned that in the Soviet Union, "No such thing as a refugee, either you are a citizen or a spy."

CHAPTER 17

The Soviet enforcement arms tended to target people asleep in their beds, when they were their most vulnerable, as described by Aleksandr Solzhenitsyn in *The Gulag Archipelago* (Basic Books, 1973): "The sharp nighttime ring or the rude knock at the door, the insolent entrance of the unwiped jackboots of the unsleeping State Security operatives... The arrested person is torn from the warmth of his bed. He is in a daze, half-asleep, helpless, and his judgment is befogged."

A digital guide to exhibitions at the Museum of Terror can be found at https://museumterror.com/exposition/.

Jan Gross writes in *Revolution from Abroad* that at the time of the deportation to the Gulag, those being deported by the Nazis received slightly better conditions. "In fact, the Germans provided somewhat better facilities at the time; for example, deportees might travel in regular passenger wagons."

Descriptions of Polish Jewish deportation to the Gulag come from family records, Landau, and various testimonies compiled in the USC Shoah Foundation Visual History Archive of those that were also deported to Sverdlovsk Oblast. One of them was Tina Jaffe, who provided the testimony about being deported as a child to Sos'va.

The anonymous witness and Stanisław Różycki's detailed accounts of Soviet-occupied Lviv are part of the Ringelblum Archive: Andrzej Żbikowski, ed., *The Ringelblum Archive. Underground Archive of the Warsaw Ghetto, Accounts from Borderlands, 1939–1941* (Jewish Historical Institute, 2018).

Pepa's older sister Sura had different ages recorded on a birth certificate from the Tomaszów Lubelski archives and the testimony left at the Yad Vashem World Holocaust Remembrance Center. I used the age from the official Polish document, since the conflicting age was submitted based on someone's memory after the war. I was unable to identify the man who left the testimony, who went by Sydney, lived in Canada, and claimed he was the brother of Sura's husband. He also could have been wrong about their means of death, and even that they had two children. But his is the only testimony I have, and I wanted it recorded.

For a background on the Golden Rose Synagogue and the Space of Synagogues, see https://www.lvivcenter.org/en/discussions/synagogue-space/. Victoria Amelina's essay on Lviv and memory, "Nothing Bad Has Ever

Happened," was published in *Arrowsmith Journal*, vol. 7. One among many features on her life and work can be found at "She Saved the Diary of a Ukrainian Writer Killed by Russia: Then She Was Killed, Too," by Joanna Kakissis, Claire Harbage, and Hanna Palamarenko (National Public Radio, July 15, 2023).

CHAPTER 18

Lidia Zessin-Jurek's "Whose Victims and Whose Survivors? Polish Jewish Refugees Between Holocaust and Gulag Memory Cultures" (*Holocaust and Genocide Studies*, 2022), provides a rich analysis of the difference of memory culture. As an example I found of the divide, the Kresy Siberia Generations Remembrance Conference took place September 15–17, 2023. Rosh Hashanah, the Jewish New Year, began the evening of September 15, 2023.

Numbers provided of Polish deportees in the Soviet Union during World War II have varied greatly. I went with sources drawing on Soviet archival data, which find that 70,000 Jews of the 315,000–325,000 citizens of the Second Polish Republic were deported, or about 22 percent of the total. *Polish Jews in the Soviet Union (1939–1959): History and Memory of Deportation, Exile and Survival. Jews of Poland.* (See Antony Polonsky's foreword, p. ix.) These are not the entirety of Polish Jews who survived in the interior of the Soviet Union, which also includes people arrested, evacuated, and who served in the Red Army. Kaganovitch, in *Exodus and Its Aftermath*, puts the number at 100,000 Polish Jews who were deported to the east—to labor camps, special settlements, and places of exile—between the autumn of 1939 and the summer of 1941.

Numbers on overall deportees to the Gulag come from Snyder's *Bloodlands*.

The descriptions of life in the Gulag draw from family recordings, historian Eliyana Adler's *Survival on the Margins*; Laura Auketayeva's dissertation, "Experiences of the European Jewish Refugees in the Soviet Interior, 1939–1946" (American University, 2022); Meier Landau's *A Lost World: The Galician Shtetl and Siberia*; Julius Margolin's *Journey into the Land of the Zeks and Back*; testimonies in the USC Shoah Foundation Visual History Archive; and the Sybir Memorial Museum Exhibition Catalogue (Muzeum Pamięci Sybiru, 2021). Certain Soviet statements about not being able to return and the necessity of work were frequently repeated across different sources with minor shifts in language. It was Landau who noted a Soviet guard described his group as "strange people" for praying and fasting on Yom Kippur.

Adela Burstyn, in a testimonial to the USC Shoah Foundation Visual History Archives, describes how her family wrote to her in code to defy censors to let her know they were going hungry in the ghetto. "The only thing they mentioned was a name from the baker that this man was not in the house for six weeks. So I understood they meant that bread wasn't in the house for six weeks. Otherwise, they could not write a bad thing."

Alexey Valeryevich Chevardin's "Поляки в Свердловской области в 1939—конце 1940-х гг/ Poles in the Sverdlovsk Region in 1939—Late 1940s" (PhD diss, Ural State University, 2009), included confidential government reports and other communications on the special settlements and Polish prisoners on work attitudes, hunger, and tools. Adler provided specific details from a memorandum of the chief of the Department of Labor Settlements of the Gulag of the June 1940 deportation. They were sent to thirteen oblasts, with 8,186 people and 2,728 families deported to Sverdlovsk Oblast.

CHAPTER 19

Anne Applebaum's *Gulag: A History* (Doubleday, 2003), provides a detailed history of a diabolic system. Timothy Snyder in *Bloodlands: Europe Between Hitler and Stalin* (Basic Books, 2012), describes how the Gulag, which the Soviets called a "system of concentration camps," began alongside the collectivization of agriculture. It eventually included 478 camp complexes, to which some 18 million people were sentenced, of which the special settlements' inmates counted less than 10 percent at roughly 1.5 million people.

For other accounts of tracking down deportation records, see Mikhal Dekel's *In the East* (W. W. Norton, 2019); and Ruth Franklin's "The Lucky Ones" (*New York Review of Books*, October 21, 2021).

Alexander Guryanov, former Polish Program coordinator at Memorial, compiled and coauthored "Repressions Against Poles and Polish Citizens" (Memorial, 1997); and coauthored and coedited the eighteen books in the "Index of the Repressed" series, jointly published by Memorial and KARTA (2007–13). The collection is now part of an online database managed by Poland's Institute of National Remembrance. He explained to me in an interview that financial constraints were why our family's records were not included in the printed or digital lists of Gulag victims.

Aleena Rieger, in her book *I Didn't Tell Them Anything: The Wartime Secrets of an American Girl* (Sunpetal Press, 2015), provided descriptions I drew from of growing potatoes: "It's always winter except maybe three to four months, June, July, August. Nothing can grow in that climate, even potatoes are difficult. If you want potatoes, the planting must be done before winter ends; the frozen ground must be chopped, then you plant, then you wait a few months for the thaw, for the potatoes to come up, before the next year's freeze."

M. Gessen's *New Yorker* article, "The Russian Memory Project That Became an Enemy of the State" (2022), helped conceptualize the challenges facing memorial and commemoration of political crimes in Russia.

CHAPTER 20

Menachem Begin writes about his experience in Beitar, relationship with Jabotinsky, and imprisonment and survival in the Soviet Union in *White Nights: The Story of a Prisoner in Russia* (Harper & Row: 1979, originally published in Hebrew in 1957).

Descriptions of the Zamość ghetto come from the memorial book.

Landau provided the description of "When the Russians let you go...," as well as the journey, noting "Stalin's picture hanging on the wall, they raced to the local bazaar for a quick purchase or a barter," and the fresh posters extolling all who saw them to join the effort to save "Holy Mother Russia."

Xavier Pruszynski, in *Russian Year: The Notebook of an Amateur Diplomat* (Roy, 1944), provides the description of the mass movement approaching biblical terms. David Nankin, in testimony to the USC Shoah Foundation archive, notes that "you couldn't go far because without documentation in Russia you were like a headless person."

Nahum M. Sarna's *Exploring Exodus: The Heritage of Biblical Israel* (Schocken Books, 1986), informed an analysis of the biblical story.

CHAPTER 21

The four monuments I identify in Timur Square—to Marx, Lenin, Stalin, and Timur—were just a few of many that had stood there. See https://globalconnect.uz/uzbekistan/sights/tashkent/amir-timur-square.

Many Polish Jews were influenced by Alexander Neweroff's novel *City of Bread* (Wildside Press, 1927), and its descriptions of a bountiful Tashkent.

The section on Tashkent was informed by Manley's *To the Tashkent Station*; Kaganovitch's *Exodus and Its Aftermath;* Wat's *My Century;* and Yitzchok Perlov's *The Adventures of One Yitzchok* (Award Books, 1967); as well as family testimonies. The exact number of refugees in the city at the time is impossible to know, Manley writes, since many lived illegally and "simply evaded the police and lived in the city without papers, under the constant threat of eviction... Given their success in evading the police, however, we will never know just how many there were."

The creation of the memorial to Polish Jews who survived in the Soviet Union was initially suggested by Zeev Levin, a scholar of Central Asian Jewish history, who composed the first variant of the inscription. See "Thanksgiving Monument in Tashkent, Uzbekistan, 2022: The Bezalel Narkiss Index of Jewish Art," https://cja.huji.ac.il/browser.php?mode=set&id=44829.

Uzbek and Russian relations warmed after the death of Islam Karimov in 2016. During a visit to the Victory Park shortly after it opened in May 2020, Vladimir Putin called Uzbek contributions "confirmation of our special allied relations." The Uzbek president responded: "This is our common history, our common victory" (Iteca exhibitions, 2020). In 2021, Russia edged out China as Uzbekistan's top trading partner, for the first time since

2014. See "Uzbekistan: Russia Reclaims Top Trading Partner Position from China" (Eurasianet, 2022).

Campana Aurélie's "The Soviet Massive Deportations—A Chronology" (SciencePo, 2007), provides a timeline that includes the Korean deportation. See https://www.sciencespo.fr/mass-violence-war-massacre-resistance/fr/document/soviet-massive-deportations-chronology.html.

Historian Katherine R. Jolluck, in an introduction to Jacob Margolin's *Journey into the Land of the Zeks and Back: A Memoir of the Gulag*, describes how he crusaded for years for recognition of the terrors he faced and prisoners continued to encounter in the Soviet Union.

Descriptions of hunger and coexistence in Uzbekistan come from Landau, Adler, and Manley's work as well as various testimonials and memoirs, among them Tobi Klodawski Flam's *Toby: Her Journey from Lodz to Samarkand (and Beyond)* (Childe Thursday, 1988).

CHAPTER 22

Rieger describes her mother's admonition to never return to Central Asia in *I Didn't Tell Them Anything: The Wartime Secrets of an American Girl*.

Oleg's shirt, "The Odious Smell of Truth" was from the RAGE Collective, which wanted to know what it would mean to tell the truth in a world of false news and social media. See https://rageartcollective.com/THE-ODIOUS-SMELL-OF-TRUTH.

We stayed in Samarkand at the Rabat Boutique, located in the old Jewish mahalla or quarter. It was the building of a rich Bukharan Jewish merchant of the late nineteenth century. Bukharan Jews are believed to have arrived in what is now Uzbekistan following the destruction of the First Temple via Persia. In Samarkand, a large Jewish community is first documented in the twelfth century. After Russians colonized the area, Ashkenazi Jews began to arrive as well. The population peaked at nearly one hundred thousand Jews in the 1980s, but more than 80 percent left between 1989 and 2021. At the synagogue in Samarkand's Jewish quarter, the manager said he could rarely make a minyan, the ten men needed to pray in an Orthodox community. For more, see "Community in Uzbekistan: World Jewish Congress," accessed April, 26, 2025, https://www.worldjewishcongress.org/en/about/communities/UZ.

When the American Jewish Joint Distribution Committee realized many of its aid packages sent via Tehran were not reaching Jews in Central Asia via Soviet or Polish distribution organizations, it attempted to send them directly. "By the end of the war and immediately thereafter, the AJJDC and some other Jewish organizations had stopped transferring money to the USSR, preferring to send parcels to available addresses, mostly Polish and Baltic Jews," Kaganovitch writes in *Exodus and Its Aftermath*. Mikhail Mitsel writes on the aid operation in *The JDC at 100: A Century of Humanitarianism* (Wayne State University Press, 2019). Mitsel, the senior archivist at the JDC, further clarified via email that to secure the addresses, "they likely relied on existing informal Jewish networks and communication channels, such as letters sent to Palestine, synagogues in Tashkent, Samarkand etc., Polish representation, the International Red Cross and other organizations, to obtain the necessary information."

To have your street named for Kaganovich was to live on one named for a murderer. "He bears as much guilt for crimes against humanity as many of the Nazis tried at Nuremberg," David Remnick wrote in a profile of him as an elderly man living free in Moscow. "But for Kaganovich there will be no trials. Kaganovich's onyx stare and dark brush mustache were once a fearful specter. As one of Stalin's key henchmen he conspired in the murder of millions and helped send many more to slave labor camps," in "An Old Stalinist Reflects on Jews: Henchman Calls Jewish People 'Confused,' 'Prone to Anarchy'" (*Washington Post*, 1990).

Family testimony recalled the loudspeaker in Juma announcing that the Red Army had liberated Zamość, which is likely what they would have heard in the Soviet Union. The Germans left the city and on the same day soldiers of the Home Army and the Red Army entered.

CHAPTER 23

About two hundred thousand Tatar and Slavs arrived during the famine in the Volga area to Central Asia in 1921–1922. More than 180,000 Crimean Tatars were forcibly relocated in May 1944 after Stalin accused them of being Nazis. Americans provided Studebakers used in some cases for the first leg of their deportation. From 1989 to 1994, more than 220,000 Crimean Tatars returned to Crimea from exile in Uzbekistan. For more, see Aigul Raimova's "History of the Formation of the Tatar Diaspora in Uzbekistan," *Oriental Journal of History, Politics, and Law*, June 2022; and "Deportation of Crimean Tatars and Their National Struggle under Soviet Rule," https://www.iccrimea.org/surgun/timeline.html.

Examples of black-market trade come from Adler, Kaganovitch, Rieger, and Landau. Roma Talasiewicz-Eibuszyc describes the fear that accompanied trade in *Memory Is Our Home: Loss and Remembering; Three Generations in Poland and Russia 1917–1960s* (ibidem-Verlag, 2015).

For more on the exclusion of Jews in Anders' Army, see Lidia Zessin-Jurek's "On a Melting Ice Floe: Polish Jewish Wartime Refugees in Central Asia," *Journal of Genocide Research* 26, no. 3 (2023): 286–306; and Israel Gutman's "Jews in General Anders' Army in the Soviet Union," *Yad Vashem Studies* 12 (1977): 231–296.

CHAPTER 24

While Manya and Kolonimus Inlender were most likely murdered by the time of the liquidation of the Zamość ghetto in October 1942, it is unlikely that Leon and Pepa Inlender knew their fate at the time or even in 1943. "Polish Jews who spent the war in the USSR do not report having learned about the Holocaust from Soviet media," Adler writes in *Survival on the Margins*. Our family reported that later, likely in 1944, they uncovered the truth via word of mouth, the Union of Polish Patriots, and letters sent back to Poland.

In Palestine, the efforts to reconnect were focused on a weekly broadcast and publication from the Search Bureau for Missing Relatives. It created its own paper in Hebrew, *To the Near and Far*, eventually counting more than 180,000 names. For more, see Search Bureau for Missing Relatives, Central Zionist Archives, http://www.zionistarchives.org.il/en/AttheCZA/AdditionalArticles/Pages/ChipushKrovim.aspx.

For more on Dzhambul as a key destination site for Polish Jews, see Albert Kaganovitch's "Stalin's Great Power Politics, the Return of Jewish Refugees to Poland, and Continued Migration to Palestine, 1944–1946," *Holocaust and Genocide Studies* 26, no. 1 (April 1, 2012): 59–94. I also draw from Rieger's memories of her family's time there as refugees. Hanche Waintraub, in an interview in her home in La Paz, Bolivia, with the USC Shoah Foundation Visual History Archive, described the situation in Dzhambul, where six couples would get married off at a time to protect the men.

"Stalin's Great Power Politics" explores Stalin and Kaganovich's motives in returning Polish Jews to Poland. The section on return also relies on details about the decision to repatriate Polish Jews from Adler's *Survival on the Margins*; Davies' *God's Playground*; and Grossmann et al.'s *Shelter from the Holocaust*.

My aunt Shelley recalled my grandmother telling her, as she changed one of her daughter's disposable diapers, that she only had one diaper during the return journey.

CHAPTER 25

Judt in *Postwar* writes that 150 Jews were killed in liberated Poland in the first four months of 1945. By April 1946 the figure was nearly 1,200. The accounts of anti-Semitism upon crossing the border back into Poland draw from testimonials recounted by Adler in *Survival on the Margins*.

Descriptions of a return to Zamość come from the *Zamość Memorial Book* and are written by M. Tzanin and Akiva Eierweiss.

Lidia Zessin-Jurek, in "Holocaust Survivors, Siberians, Refugees, Veterans—Memory and Choice of Jewish Returnees from the USSR to Poland (1945–2024)," in *Intergenerational Trauma in Refugee Communities* (Routledge, 2024), refers to this post-repatriation period as yet another stage of displacement and refugeedom. For Polish Jews, the fear of persecution made true return impossible; they had to seek safety in unfamiliar and only newly Polish territories.

Jewish postwar life in Poland's so-called "reclaimed territories" draws from research and descriptions in Kamil Kijek's "Aliens in the Lands of the Piasts:

The Polonization of Lower Silesia and Its Jewish Community in the Years 1945–1950," in *Jews and Germans in Eastern Europe: Shared and Comparative Histories* (De Gruyter Oldenbourg, 2018), edited by Tobias Grill, 234–56; and "Beyond Post-Holocaust Trauma: Polish Jewish Childhood in Dzierżoniów, Lower Silesia, 1945–1950," *Polin Studies in Polish Jewry* 36 (2024): 418–47 (coauthor Anna Podolska.)

Jacob Egit's role in creating a Jewish Communist settlement in Lower Silesia draws on his memoir *Grand Illusion* (Lugus, 1991). Although he uses the Hebrew word "Yishuv" to describe it, writing retrospectively Kamil Kijek explained via email that at the time Egit very consciously used the Yiddish word "Yishev," stemming from the Hebrew original "Yishuv," but having a different ideological connotation, underlining the non-Zionist or even anti-Zionist character of this project.

How many Polish Jews survived in the Soviet Union remains unknown. "Even with documentation now available, we are still unable to say exactly how many Jews returned to Poland from the Soviet Union," historian John Goldlust writes in *Shelter from the Holocaust.* "Some estimates suggest that as many as 200,000 had been repatriated by late 1946." Adler, in *Survival on the Margins,* notes that while overall numbers of Polish Jewish survivors is usually given at just over 10 percent, that includes those who had left for the Soviet Union and elsewhere in Europe. For those who remained in Poland, it was only 4 percent.

The section on Legnica is based on family testimonies; Rivka Agron Wolf, in Na'ama Seri-Levi's " 'Gypsy-Nomads': The Refugeeism of Polish Jewish Repatriates After World War II" (Jahrbuch Des Dubnow-Instituts /Dubnow Institute Yearbook 18, 2019); and Tamara Włodarczyk's *From the History of Jews in the Legnica Region* (Fundacja Rojt, 2016).

Bytom's history comes from the exhibition gallery book by Aleksandra Namysło, *Lost Hopes: Jews in the Silesian/ Katowice Voivodeship in Years 1945, 1970* (Oddział Instytutu Pamięci Narodowej—Komisji Ścigania Zbrodni przeciwko Narodowi Polskiemu w Katowicach, 2012), https://www.jewishvirtuallibrary.org/bytom; and Frank's *To Survive and Testify*. Most towns that the Nazis occupied renamed their central squares or boulevards after Adolf Hitler, as did Bytom.

On the Judenrat, Katarzyna Person, in "Jewish Councils and Jewish Ghetto Police in Eastern Europe," ed. Marion Kaplan and Natalie Aleksiun, in *The Cambridge History of the Holocaust* (University Press, 2025), writes it quickly became clear that hopes for a degree of "Jewish autonomy" were, as one employee of Warsaw Judenrat wrote, "based on nothing more than the shifting sands of German legislation that denied Jewish authorities any real powers." Adam Kopciowski writes that in the Zamość ghetto, "the moral decline of those at the head of the Zamość Judenrat during the war appears to be an indisputable fact." *Zagłada Żydów w Zamościu* (Wydawnictwo Uniwersytetu Marii Curie-Skłodowskiej, 2005).

Specifics on the Zamość Judenrat and the role of Wigdor Inlender come from the memorial book, which published Mieczyslaw Garfinkel's postwar testimony and Zwillich's accounts. Garfinkel, the head of the Zamość Judenrat, had sent a forty-six-page testimony to YIVO, which includes his encounters with the boy who survived Bełżec and was later killed. The account of Adolf Bohlman killing Wigdor Inlender is based on the memorial book and Kopciowski's *Zagłada Żydów w Zamościu*.

The fate of Roma Inlender and her mother is described in Henryk Lewandowski's testimony for the USC Shoah Foundation Visual History Archive. Yoram Golan provided specifics of the rest of the family to Kopciowski, to be found in *Zagłada Żydów w Zamościu*.

The Polish Institute of National Remembrance records cited Teodor Kalika as a witness of Wigdor's murder in Leon Inlender's lawsuit. His conflicting testimony was made January 29, 1947, and is in the Jewish Historical Institute archives.

Descriptions of the Kielce Pogrom draw from Jan Gross's *Fear: Anti-Semitism in Poland After Auschwitz* (Princeton University Press, 2006). Julian Kwiek's *Nie chcemy Żydów u siebie: Przejawy wrogości wobec Żydów w latach 1944–1947* (Wydawnictwo Nieoczywiste, 2021), describes the calls for a pogrom in Legnica.

CHAPTER 26

Descriptions of the formation of the Brichah come from Yehuda Bauer's *Flight and Rescue: BRICHAH* (Random House, 1970); and Yitzhak Zuckerman's memoir, *A Surplus of Memory: Chronicle of the Warsaw Ghetto Uprising* (University of California Press, 1993).

Albert Kaganovitch substantiates that Stalin permitted Polish Jews to move toward Palestine in "Stalin's Great Power Politics, the Return of Jewish Refugees to Poland, and Continued Migration to Palestine, 1944–1946," *Holocaust and Genocide Studies* 26, no. 1 (2012): 59–94.

Descriptions of the broad sweep of the Greek Bluff came from the USC Shoah Foundation Visual History Archive, Bauer, Adler, and the American journalist I. F. Stone's *Underground to Palestine* (Boni & Gaer, 1946). Bauer traces the origins of the "Greek Bluff," noting that "the documents, in a number of languages, showed the refugees to be Greek Jews liberated from German camps and destined for Athens, Salonika, or Larissa." I. F. Stone describes witnessing in 1946 what must have been the Greek Bluff, calling it "Z" so as not to expose the ruse: "A Haganah worker we had not seen before came up and warned us to be quiet. He told us that we were supposed to be natives of the country of Z. He said we were to speak only Hebrew, not Yiddish. The Yiddish recognizable because of its high German content, but the Hebrew would sound strange enough to pass for the language of that far country, Z."

Rothschild Hospital's role as a shelter is detailed in many Shoah testimonies and I. F. Stone's *Underground to Palestine*. United Nations Special Committee on Palestine's Jorge García-Granados, in *The Birth of Israel* (Knopf, 1949), describes a visit that would have been about a year later than our grandparents to the shelter in the summer of 1947, by then overrun with refugees from Romania.

CHAPTER 27

The section on the creation of displaced persons camps and the role of the Harrison Report benefited greatly from David Nasaw's *The Last Million: Europe's Displaced Persons from World War to Cold War* (Penguin Random

House, 2020); Mark Wyman's *DPs: Europe's Displaced Persons, 1945–1951* (Cornell University Press, 1989); and Judt's *Postwar*. Jan Jarboe Russell's *The Train to Crystal City: FDR's Secret Prisoner Exchange Program and America's Only Family Internment Camp During World War II* (Scribner, 2016), offers additional insights into Harrison's fascinating personal background, including administering immigration policies and incarceration camps in the United States.

Naama Seri-Levi writes on the post-1946 arrival to the DP camps of Jews who survived in the Soviet Union in "'These People Are Unique': The Repatriates in the Displaced Persons Camps 1946–1947," *Moreshet* 14 (2017): 49–100. Nasaw notes that of the DPs who lasted more than a year, the biggest group were Polish Catholics. Others included Christian Estonians, Latvians, Lithuanians, and western Ukrainians. Many were anti-Communists who faced potential charges of treason or war crimes if they returned to countries under Red Army control.

The context and history of Austrian displaced persons camps under the British relied extensively upon the scholarship of Heribert Macher-Kroisenbrunner and his dissertation "Re-establishment of Jewish Life in South-East Austria: Jewish Displaced Persons (DPs) in the British Occupation Zone of Austria" (Karl-Franzens University Graz, 2024). For Admont, his book, *We Hope to Go to Palestine: Das jüdische DP-Lager Admont 1946–1949* (CLIO Verein f. Geschichts & Bildungsarbeit, 2018); and Josef Hasitschka's "Auf Durchfahrt Nach Palästina / En Route to Palestine: The Jewish DP Camp in Admont 1946–1949"; and "Das jüdische DP-Lager Admont—ein emotionaler Ort," printed in the "Mitteilungen der Korrespondent:innen der Historischen Landeskommission Steiermark," were illuminating. Hasitschka also shared his collection of the camp newspaper *Admonter Hajnt*. The poem cited was called *Lager... Lager* by Blic Majer.

For more on the "soap myth," see https://www.jewishvirtuallibrary.org/the-soap-myth.

While the IRO charter was the foundation for international human rights protections, a fifth group was added when the 1951 UN Convention Relating to the Status of Refugees was ratified. A Swedish delegate pushed for the inclusion of a fifth principle, "membership in a particular social group," which would become the one that offered protection for gender-based persecutory and LGBTQ+ individuals and families.

The New York Times' coverage of Irgun strikes in Austria included "175 Britons Escape in Rail Blast Near Tunnel in the Austrian Alps," on August 13, 1947; and "Irgun Boasts of Alps Blast," August 20, 1947. Macher-Kroisenbrunner, in *We hope to go to Palestine*, provides additional context and specifics of the action in Admont.

The portrayal of the work of the United Nations Special Committee on Palestine and the *Exodus* ship drew on Jorge Garcia Granados's *The Birth of Israel: The Drama As I Saw It* (Alfred A. Knopf, 1948); Ruth Gruber's *Inside of Time: My Journey from Alaska to Israel* (Carroll & Graf, 2002); Rashid Khalidi's *The Hundred Years' War on Palestine* (Metropolitan Books, 2020); Benny Morris's *1948: A History of the First Arab-Israeli War* (Yale University Press, 2008); Kal Raustiala's *The Absolutely Indispensable Man: Ralph Bunche, the United Nations, and the Fight to End Empires* (Oxford University Press, 2023); Eugene Rogan's *The Arabs: A History—Third Edition* (Penguin, 2012); and Nasaw's *The Last Million*. Lucy S. Dawidowicz is quoted from a review she wrote in *Commentary* magazine in November 1953 on *The Redeemers: A Saga of the Years 1945–1952*.

CHAPTER 28

My initial reporting in Föhrenwald took place in 2006, and Heike Ander and Michaela Melián's book *Föhrenwald* (Revolver 2005) and accompanying radio program provided invaluable context. Melián also helped locate my father's home and guided my uncle and me on a visit to it with reporter Wibke Bergemann, with whom I reported on this trip in our radio documentary, "Too Many Geister" for Deutschlandradio Kultur (2008).

Further background on DP camps came from Kurt R. Grossmann's *The Jewish DP Problem: Its Origin, Scope, and Liquidation* (Institute of Jewish Affairs, 1951); and Philip S. Bernstein's entry, "Displaced Persons," in *The American*

Jewish Year Book 1947–1947, vol. 49 (American Jewish Committee, 1948). On congressional legislation, Nasaw's *The Last Million* was highly insightful. "No nation was invited or encouraged to take in displaced persons because they had suffered during the past war; no moral imperative was placed on the victors to care for or assist the most innocent and tortured survivors," Nasaw writes in *The Last Million*. This created a legacy that formed the backbone of international refugee policies that followed, stressing "utilitarian and political over humanitarian rationales for resettlement."

The congressmen cited as speaking against the admittance of Polish Jews who survived in the Soviet Union were Senator John Rankin of Mississippi and Eugene Cox of Georgia, quoted in Nasaw's *The Last Million*. Robert Rich of Pennsylvania spoke similarly: "I am not going to throw the doors wide open and permit America to be the dumping place for all humanity. That would mean a haven for Communists and every other person who would be unacceptable to our citizenship."

While the majority of Jews who survived in the Soviet Union never spied for the NKVD, Kaganovitch recounts in "Stalin's Great Power Politics, the Return of Jewish Refugees to Poland, and Continued Migration to Palestine, 1944–1946," that a small number likely did. "Joseph Schechtman describes a report to the US State Department from an American military official in Bremen on the presence of Soviet agents among refugees from the USSR who were in the displaced persons camps."

Rieger provides another example of crafting an alternative story to enter the United States. "Don't say you were in Russia. They'll never let you in," she recalled her family, which had survived in the Gulag and Kazakhstan, resolving in a DP camp as they made a plan to immigrate. "Once again, in nightly sessions, they planned and plotted. They didn't think about long-term effects. They had become accustomed to doing whatever was necessary to survive."

More about the role of Bernard Vogel, the Blumsztein's cousin, in running ammunition for the Irgun can be found at https://www.haaretz.co.il/misc/2008-08-31/ty-article/0000017f-dbfc-db22-a17f-fffdb54c0000.

CHAPTER 29

The reflections from diplomat and scholar Ralph Bunche on the UNSCOP decision making came from a speech at Southern Methodist University, Dallas, Texas, on April 8, 1958, as cited in Raustiala's biography, *The Absolutely Indispensable Man: Ralph Bunche, the United Nations, and the Fight to End Empires*. Diplomatic cables from the consul general at Jerusalem, Robert B. Macatee, about Garcia-Granados are cited in Peter L. Hahn's *Caught in the Middle East: US Policy toward the Arab-Israeli Conflict, 1945–1961* (University of North Carolina Press, 2004); and cables from the British embassy are cited in Benny Morris's *1948*. Arab reaction to the testimony is captured in Wahid Khalidi's *Before Their Diaspora: A Photographic History of the Palestinians: 1876–1948* (Institute for Palestine Studies, 1984).

The description of the flag being raised in Admont was published in the DP camp newspaper *Admonter Hajnt* in March 1948 and described by Josef Hasitchka in "Das jüdische DP-Lager in Admont 1946–1949—ein emotionaler Ort" (2025).

The description of the Inlenders' trip to Israel benefited from various testimonials in the USC Shoah Foundation's Visual History Archives. When they arrived on the Eilat ship, the Red Sea city with that name had not yet been created. USS *General C. C. Ballou* descriptions are based on my father Allan Gerson's memoir, *Lies That Matter* (New Academia Publishing, 2001); the USC Shoah Foundation's Visual History Archives; and the family's ship registry.

The location of where Polish Jews survived in more than twenty countries around the world is based upon the recording sites of USC Shoah Foundation Visual History Archives.

Portrayal of arrival of the Inlenders in Israel and the refugee experience benefited greatly from Tom Segev's *1949: The First Israelis* (Owl Books, 1998). For land acquisition and the establishment of Israel, I relied upon Adwan and others' *Side by Side: Parallel Histories of Israel-Palestine*; and Benny Morris's *The Birth of the Palestinian Refugee Problem Revisited* (Cambridge University Press, 2003).

The development of Gan Rashal and Herzliya benefited from Irit Amit-Cohen's *Zionism and Free Enterprise: The Story of Private Entrepreneurs in Citrus Plantations in Palestine in the 1920s and 1930s* (De Gruyter, 2012); and Arieh Avneri's *The Claim of Dispossession: Jewish Land-Settlement and the Arabs 1878–1948* (Routledge, 1982). The breakdown of Arabs and Jews in 1945 Herzliya and Al Haram comes from Jaffa Sub-District Village Statistics, gathered via a joint survey of the British Mandate Government Office of Statistics and the Department of Lands. The data were calculated as of April 1, 1945, and later served the UNSCOP committee in determining its partition map, https://users.cecs.anu.edu.au/~bdm/yabber/census/VillageStatistics1945orig.pdf.

Descriptions of Al Haram and its destruction rely on work from Eitan Bronstein, with Normah Musih's "Al-Haram (Sidna Ali) in the Memory of Herzliya" (Zocrot, 2007); Aida Essaid's *Zionism and Land Tenure in Mandate Palestine* (Taylor & Francis, 2013); Walid Khalidi's *All That Remains: The Palestinian Villages Occupied and Depopulated by Israel in 1948* (Institute for Palestine Studies, 1992); and Benny Morris's *The Birth of the Palestinian Refugee Problem Revisited* (Cambridge University Press, 2003). While Essaid documented an incident of Jewish support for an Arab neighbor in Al Haram in 1948, she writes, "Unfortunately village land archives do not reflect such events, especially when it comes to the interactions and individual relationships between Arab and Jewish inhabitants. In fact, they suggest the opposite, i.e., that Arabs and Jews in the village were as separated as possible."

Portrayal of the Gersons' arrival in the United States came from extensive HIAS social worker intake notes on their case, HIAS photo files held at the Center for Jewish History's archives, *Forverts* coverage, and family testimonials.

Judt in *Postwar* describes the lack of interest in returning Jews to the Soviet Union. The immigration law that applied to the Gersons was Public Law 85-316—Sept. 11, 1957 Sec. 7, https://uscode.house.gov/statutes/pl/85/316.pdf. Eisenhower addressed Congress on its merits on January 31, 1957: ol.103, Part 1—House pages 1354–1374, https://www.congress

.gov/bound-congressional-record/1957/01/31/103/house-section/article/1354–1374.

CHAPTER 30

Rashid Khalidi, in *The Hundred Years' War on Palestine*, writes that while Israel by 1967 had "overwhelming military superiority," its leaders "sincerely believed that the Jewish state was in danger of extinction, as did many Israelis, alarmed by the empty threats of certain Arab leaders."

The protest at the Western Wall had been to support a group of Jews from Leningrad that had unsuccessfully hijacked a plane to go to Israel. By 1970, Stalin, once crucially supporting Jews going to Palestine, now was doing everything in his power to keep them from leaving the USSR. In the wake of the 1967 war, Moscow had broken off diplomatic relations with Jerusalem. That June a group of Leningrad Jews had attempted to hijack a small, civilian aircraft to escape to Israel. Their plot was foiled, and the protest was to raise awareness to their plight. My mother, Joan Nathan, writes about it in her memoir, *My Life in Recipes: Food, Family, and Memories* (Knopf, 2024).

My father, Allan Gerson, also writes about their meeting in *Lies That Matter*. That memoir, published posthumously, recounts one of his first jobs as a Nazi hunter for the Justice Department's Office of Special Investigations, and its intersections with his family's own immigration story. My father's dissertation was published as *Israel, the West Bank and International Law* (Cass, 1978). He also writes more on the topic and his work at the United Nations in *The Kirkpatrick Mission: Diplomacy Without Apology America at the United Nations 1981–1985* (Free Press, 1991). While he supported Palestinian autonomy in the West Bank, he did not back negotiating with the Palestine Liberation Organization (PLO), which did not recognize Israel's right to exist and whose charter stated that "armed struggle is the only way to liberate Palestine." My father sued Libya for state-sponsored terrorism over the 1988 bombing of Pan Am Flight 103 over Lockerbie, Scotland, paving the way for the PLO and Iran to be also successfully taken on in US courts.

Khalidi, in *The Hundred Years' War on Palestine*, writes a perspective different from that of my parents on the Israel-Egypt peace accords, that Israel intentionally designed the agreement to remove Egypt from the conflict, freeze out the PLO, and negate Palestinian rights.

AFTERWORD

The tally of journalists killed in Gaza comes from the Committee to Protect Journalists, accessed September 10, 2025, https://cpj.org/full-coverage-israel-gaza-war/. The US-based watchdog wrote, "Israel is engaging in the deadliest and most deliberate effort to kill and silence journalists that CPJ has ever documented."

Index

Achitskiy Sector, 136–37
Adam and Eve, 146
Adler, Eliyana, 63, 225
Admont, 210–19
   author's visit, 207, 210–14, 217–18
   displaced persons camp, 207–8, 210–18
Admonter Hajnt, 213–14
Admont Town Hall, 210–11
Adolf Hitler Platz (Bytom), 189, 190
"Adon Olam," 41
Adventures of One Yitzchok, The (Perlov), 151, 182
agriculture, 60, 61, 150, 212, 238, 253
Aktion Zamosc, 50
Alexander the Great, 156
Allied Expeditionary Force, 242
Amelina, Victoria, 121–22
American Jewish Labor Committee, 187
Anders, Władysław, 173–74
anti-Semitism, 20, 28, 46, 58, 59, 62, 67, 69, 174, 185, 197, 198, 200, 209, 223
   stereotype of "Lucky Jews," 53–54, 63
Aparthotel Centrum (Bytom), 189

Arab Higher Committee for Palestine, 68, 216–17
Arab-Israeli War of 1948, 236
Argentina, 1, 42, 58, 79, 204, 234
Army 82nd Airborne Division, U.S., 19
Ashkenazi Jews, 46, 152
Auschwitz concentration camp, xvii, 6, 50, 168, 189, 204, 229
Australia, 42, 79, 217, 227–28
Australian Jewish Genealogical Society, 227–28
Austria
   annexation of, 69
   displaced persons (DPs) camps, 15, 203, 206, 207–19, 221–23
Avigdoria, 60–61, 253

Baikal, Lake, 131
Balfour, Arthur, 57
Balfour Declaration, 57, 58
Begin, Menachem, 143, 146, 173, 215–16, 250–51
Beirut, 238
Beitar, 143

Bełżec extermination camp, 6, 13, 30, 43, 92, 120, 122–23, 193–94
Ben-Gurion, David, 232, 236
Ben-Hillel, Zehavit, 151–53
Bergen-Belsen concentration camp, 217
Berlin, xvi–xvi, 54, 55, 131, 158, 159
Berlin Wall, 131–32
Beuthen, 189
Bezhenets, 96–98
Białystok, 124–25
black markets, 105, 109, 145, 168–70, 221
Black Sea, 123
Blumstein, Abe. *See* Gerson, Allan
Boeing CH-47 Chinooks, 19
Bohlmann, Adolf, 194
Bolivia, 42, 180
Bolshevik Revolution, 58, 60
Brazil, xvi, 10, 42
bread, 83, 100, 105, 128, 150–51, 152–53, 160, 180
Bremen, 233, 234
Brichah, 201–6, 218
Britain and Palestine, 67–68, 202–4, 231–32
  Arab Higher Committee and, 68, 216–17
  Balfour Mandate, 57–58
  displaced persons and, 209–10, 215–17
  "Greek bluff," 203–4, 224–25
b'shert, 9, 41, 205
Buenos Aires, 1, 40, 42, 170, 234
Bunche, Ralph, 216, 230–31
Bundism, 56, 63
Bytom, 188–91

Cain, 146
Camp David Accords, 251
Carpathian Mountains, 199
Caspian Sea, 166
Central Asian Soviet Republics, 146
Central Committee of Polish Jews, 186–89, 200
Central Database of Shoah Victims' Names, 28, 120
Central Zionist Archives (Jerusalem), 179
"Chalomot paz," xv
Chanukah, 245, 249, 251–52
Children of the Holocaust (Epstein), 26–27
Chilmark, Martha's Vineyard, 10–11
China and Silk Road, 147
CIA (Central Intelligence Agency), 231
Citizenship and Immigration Services, U.S., 241, 242
City College of New York, 243
Coast Guard, U.S., 232
Cold War, 20, 131–32, 216, 241–42
Communism, 56, 65–66, 100, 202–3, 241–42
Cooperman, Chuma
  exile and displaced person, 206, 222
  in Juma, 165, 168, 169–71
  in Lviv, 110
  move to America, 233, 234, 240
  Zamość pogrom, 197
Cooperman, Simon
  exile and displaced person, 203, 204, 205–6, 218, 223–24
  Gulag liberation, 145–46
  in Juma, 173
  in Lviv, 110, 113, 118
  move to America, 233, 234, 240
  repatriation, 182, 188
  Zamość pogrom, 197
Cooperman, Sol, 110, 171, 197, 222

Covid-19 pandemic, 11
Customs and Border Protection, 34
Cygler, Hagar, 25, 27
Cyrillic, 139, 140, 155, 176
Czech Republic, 37, 198, 199

Dawidowicz, Lucy S., 217
DDT, 206, 237
Deir Yassin, 235
Dekel, Mikhal, 133
deportations
   from Lviv, 111–15, 117–20
   Sybir Memorial Museum (Bialystok), 124–25, 129–30
   from Zamość, 6, 30, 43, 49–51, 193–96
diphtheria, 105, 170
diseases, 128, 153, 164, 170
displaced persons (DPs), 206, 207–19, 221–26, 235
Displaced Persons Act of 1948, 225, 234
Dodger Stadium, 181
Dominican Republic, xiv
Dror, 200–201
Drozd, Anna Przybyszewska, 77–79, 84
Dzhambul, 179–81

Echo Park, xvi–xvii
Egit, Jacob, 186–87, 197–98
Egypt
   Arab-Israeli War of 1948, 236
   Camp David Accords, 251
   Exodus, 146, 182, 232, 254–55
   Sadat's visit to Jerusalem, 250–51
   Six-Day War, 246–47
Eierweiss, Akiva, 185
Eilat, INS, 232–33
Eisenhower, Dwight, 241–42
El Haram, 238–39

Eliecer, 37
Elysian Park, 74
Elysian Valley, 74–75
English Channel, 234–35
Epstein, Helen, 26–27
Eretz-Israel, 232
Eskin, Raya, xv–xvi, 8, 40–43, 205
Estonia, 151
Exodus and Its Aftermath (Kaganovitch), 154
Exodus, Book of, 146, 182, 232, 254–55
exodus from Poland, 199–206
Exodus, SS, 215–16

Feiga, 43, 193, 233
Fialkow, Arie, 67
Fiddler on the Roof (musical), 54
Final Solution, 84, 144, 186
Fix Café, 74
Fleschler, Zyg, 14–15, 17, 230
   in America, 248–49, 250
   deportation, 136
   in Tashkent, 148–49, 153–54, 169
   in Zamość, 26, 47–48, 68, 84–85
Föhrenwald, 221–22, 233, 235
forced labor camps. *See* Gulag
forgery, 225–26

Gan Rashal, 238
Garaeva, Anait, 161–63, 164–65
Garcetti, Eric, 35
García Granados, Jorge, 217
Garfinkel, Miesczyslaw, 194
gay marriage, 72, 74
Gaza Strip, 236, 247
Gaza war, 253–54
General C. C. Ballou, USS, 234–35
Genghis Khan, 156

INDEX

German Chancellor Scholarship, xv, 54, 72, 131
Gershkovich, Evan, 132
Gerson, Allan
  Australia voyage, 227–28
  author's initial research, 16, 20–26, 30–31, 42
  Bezhenets, 96–98
  birth of, 69, 176
  David's interview of, 109–10
  death of, 31–32, 157
  exile and displaced person, 205–6, 220–23, 233
  identity of, 220–24, 226–29, 241, 243
  in Israel, 247–48
  in Juma, 167–68, 172–73, 174, 176
  law career of, 31, 249–50, 251
  in Lviv, 101, 103, 105–6
  Passover, 142–43
  repatriation journey, 181–83, 184–86
  in Samarkand, 157–58, 162–63
  Talia and, 9–10, 91–92
  United States, 229, 233–35
  in Zamość, 3, 60–62, 83
Gerson, Chaim, 43, 108–9, 193, 222
Gerson, David, 21, 35, 109–10
Gerson, Esther, 43, 83, 193, 222
Gerson, Merissa, 117, 196
Gerson, Moishe, 222
  determination to fight, 173–74
  Gulag and liberation, 134–35, 146
  in Israel, 220, 233
  in Legnica, 197
  in Lviv, 109, 113, 174
  repatriation, 188, 196, 197
  in Warsaw, 39
  in Zamość, 83
Gerson, Mordechai, 225–26
Gerson, Morris, 240–41
Gerson, Mottel "Morton," xi–xii, xv–xvi
  in America, 229, 233–35, 240–44
  Bezhenets, 96–98
  deportation, 114–15, 117–18, 125–26
  as displaced person, 218–19, 221–23, 233
  exodus, 198, 199–200, 203, 204–6
  Gulag and liberation, 125–28, 140, 144–47
  in Juma, 164–65, 167–75
  in Lviv, 98, 101, 105–6, 109, 111–13
  repatriation journey, 181–83, 184–86
  revealing hidden identity of, 220–21
  in Uzbekistan, 147, 149, 160–61, 164–65, 167–75, 181–83
  in Zamość, 1–3, 5–6, 44–45, 47–48, 55–56, 58–60, 62, 68–69, 80
  Zamość escape, xi–xii, 2–6, 82–84, 94
Gerson, Peshke "Paula," xi–xii, 245–46
  in America, 229, 233–35, 240–44
  Bezhenets, 96–98
  deportation, 114–15, 117–18, 125–26
  as displaced person, 218–19, 221–23, 233
  exodus, 198, 199–200, 203, 204–6
  Grynberg and, 12–13
  Gulag and liberation, 125–28, 142–47, 149, 175–76
  in Juma, 164–65, 166, 169–76
  in Lviv, 98, 101, 105–6, 111–13
  pogroms, 196–97
  pregnancy and birth of Allan, 69, 175–76
  repatriation journey, 181–83, 184–86
  revealing hidden identity of, 220–21
  in Zamość, 1–3, 44–48, 66–67, 68–69, 80, 81–85

INDEX

Zamość escape, xi–xii, 2–6, 82–84, 94
Gerson, Sam, 142–43, 220, 222, 234, 242–43
Golan Heights, 247
Golden Rose Synagogue (Lviv), 121–22
Gold Room, xvi–xvii
Granados, García, 104, 217
Great Britain. *See* Britain and Palestine
Great Purge, 97–98
"Greek bluff," 203–4, 224–25
Green Shelter, 218–19, 221–22
Griffith Park, xiii–xiv
Griner, Brittney, 132
Gross-Rosen, 186
Gruber, Ruth, 215
Grynberg, Eryk, 12–13
Gulag, 128–30, 187, 226
    diseases, 128
    Gerson family and, 126–28, 134–35, 142–47, 175–76
    hunger and starvation, 135, 143–44
    Inlender family and, 4, 20–21, 136–38, 141, 145–46, 147, 149
    liberation, 144–46, 150
    Sybir Memorial Museum (Bialystok), 124–25, 129–30
Gulom, Gafur, 156
Guryanov, Alexander, 133–34

Haganah, 197, 203, 235
Hamas, 253–54
Harris, Kamala, 34
Harrison, Earl, 208–9
"Hashkiveinu," 51–52
Hashomer Hatzair, 61–62, 200–201
Hasitschka, Josef, 210–14
"Hatikvah," 231
Hebrew, xiv–xv, 204

Hebrew Immigrant Aid Society (HIAS), 240–41
Hebrew University Law School, 247
HeHalutz, Hebrew for the Pioneer, 60–62, 200–201
Herzliya, 238–39, 244
Herzl, Theodor, 238
Himmler, Heinrich, 50
Himmlerstadt, 172–73
Hitler, Adolf, 6, 211
    annexation of Austria, 69
    Final Solution, 84, 144, 186, 226
    Gulag and, 144–45
    lebensraum, 118–19
    rise to power, 64, 67, 68
Hitler Youth, xvi
Hollywood Hills, 72
Holocaust, xvi
    memorials and museums, 114–15, 121–22, 124–25, 129–30, 149–55
Holocaust Memorial Museum, U.S., 13–14, 20, 222–23, 228
Holocaust Remembrance Day, 27
homophobia, 70–71, 93, 163
Honchar, Olha, 115, 116
Hood, John, 217
hunger and starvation, 14, 50, 98, 101, 113, 118, 119, 126, 128, 135, 144, 146, 153, 156, 164, 165, 169, 192, 212, 215

"infiltrees," 210
Inlender, Chaya, 6–7, 43, 192, 193, 250
Inlender, Daniel, 14, 104
Inlender, Kolonimus, 252
    author's initial research, 22, 23, 24, 27, 29–30
    in Zamość, 29–30, 48, 49, 80, 85, 87, 183, 193

Inlender, Leah, 6–7, 192, 193
Inlender, Lejba, 64–65
Inlender, Leon
    author's initial research, 14–15, 20–26
    as displaced person, 211–12, 215–16, 230, 231–32
    Gulag and liberation, 4, 20–21, 136–38, 141, 145–46, 147, 149
    in Israel, 229–33, 237–39
    in Lviv, 102–3, 105, 111–13
    marriage to Manya, 15, 29–30, 64–66, 84, 85, 136, 183
    marriage to Pepa, 136–37, 178–79
    reparations, 13, 20, 21, 195–96
    repatriation journey, 178–79, 181–83, 184, 188–91
    in Uzbekistan, 148–49, 149
    in Zamość, 29–30, 48, 62, 64–65, 66, 84
    Zamość escape, 84–85, 87, 94
Inlender, Marja "Manya"
    author's initial research, 22–27, 29–30, 64–66
    marriage to Leon, 15, 29–30, 64–66, 84, 85, 136, 183
    in Zamość, 29–30, 43, 44–45, 48, 61, 64–66, 68, 71, 78–79, 80–81, 84, 85, 136–37, 183, 193
Inlender, Nachum
    birth certificate, 180, 208
    death of, 16–17, 32, 34, 162–63
    as displaced person, 35, 207–8, 230–31
    in Israel, 26, 230–31, 232–33, 237–39, 246–48
    move to United States, 248–50
    name of, 244
    Shabbat dinner, 72–73
    Talia's interest in story of, 7–8
    Talia's interview and research of, 15–17, 22, 24, 26
    Talia's wedding and, 9–10
Inlender, Pepa
    author's initial research, 14–15, 20–26
    autograph book of, 104, 136–37
    as displaced person, 211–12, 215–16, 229, 230–31
    Gulag and liberation, 4, 136–37, 141, 145–46, 147, 149
    in Israel, 229–33, 237–39
    in Lviv, 103–5, 111–13, 120
    marriage to Leon, 136–37, 178–79
    marriage of Leon to Pepa, 15, 136–37, 178–79
    repatriation journey, 181–84, 188–91
Inlender, Roma, 7–8, 194–95
Inlender, Rywka, 195
Inlender, Talia
    in Admont, 207, 210–14, 217–18
    author's initial meeting of, xiii–xv
    author's initial relationship with, xvi–xviii, 4–5, 9–11, 72–74, 89–92
    author's wedding to, 9–10, 74–75
    in Białystok, 124–25
    in Bytom, 189–91
    Chanukah party, 245, 251–52
    family research of, 5–8, 11–15, 20–30, 32, 40–43, 65, 84–85, 103–4, 136, 139–40, 148–49, 178–80, 241
    immigrants' rights work of, xiv, 19, 33–35, 159, 254
    interview with father, 15–17
    video meeting with Adi, 27–30
    in Warsaw, 19–20, 33, 35–38, 39, 77–78, 123, 184

in Zamość, 18–19, 39–40, 44–45, 47–52, 53–54, 64–66, 70–72, 75–76
Inlender, Tobi, 9–10, 23–24, 72–73, 103, 249–50
Inlender, Tuvia, 6–7, 192–93
Inlender, Wigdor, 47–48, 60–61, 65, 102–3, 191–95
intergenerational transmission of survival trauma, 26–27
International Refugee Organization (IRO), 214–15, 225, 235
International Tracing Service, 20–21
Iran, 34, 146, 147
Iraq, 236
Irgun, 215–16, 229, 235, 250
Iron Curtain, 241–42
Islamic Jihad, 251
Israel
   Allan Gerson in, 247–48
   Arab-Israeli War of 1948, 236
   Camp David Accords, 251
   establishment of, 231–33
   Inlenders in, 26, 229–33, 237–39, 246–48
   Sadat's visit to Jerusalem, 250–51
   Six-Day War, 246–47
   UN Partition Plan, 230–31, 235–36, 251
   Zionism, 56–58, 61–63, 67–68, 200–201
Israel-Hamas War, 253–54
Israeli Declaration of Independence, 236
Israeli Navy and *Eilat*, 232–33
Israeli Organization of Zamość Jewry, 7
Israel the West Bank and International Law (Gerson), 251

Israel War of Independence, 236
Izbica, 194

Jabotinsky, Ze'ev, 28, 31, 61–62, 143, 200–201
Jaffe, Tina, 118
Jerusalem, xiv, 31, 51, 236, 246–50
Jewish Agency, 67–68, 203, 235–36, 238
Jewish Bolshevism, 118–19
Jewish Century, The (Slezkine), 46
Jewish Community Relations Council of Greater Washington, 12
Jewish Cooking in America (Nathan), 72
Jewish Historical Institute, 77–78
Jewish Records Indexing-Poland, 11–12
JFK Airport, 86
Joint Distribution Committee, 160–61, 222
Jordan, 247
Jordan River, 61
judenrein, 50, 172, 173, 186
Judt, Tony, 242
Jugendstil, 102
Juma, 160, 164–77
   author's visit, 164–77
   Kaganovich Street, 165–68, 172–73, 174–75
Justice Department, U.S., 31, 249–50

Kaddish, 173
Kaganovich, Lazar, 161–62
Kaganovich Street, Juma, 165–68, 172–73, 174–75
Kaganovitch, Albert, 154
Kalibr, 123
Karimov, Islam, 148, 155
KARTA Center, 133
Kathmandu, xv

308 INDEX

Katowice, 189
Katyn massacre, 174
Kazakh Soviet Socialist Republic, 179–81
Kazakhstan, 125, 180–81
Khrushchev, Nikita, 111, 161
kibbutzim, 212, 237, 253–54
kiddush, 10
Kielce Pogrom, 196–97, 199–200, 202
Kijek, Kamil, 56, 187–88
Kindertransport, 152
King David Hotel (Jerusalem), 31, 229
Kobee Factory, 34
Kołcon, Marek, 21–24, 25, 44–45, 47–51, 64–66, 76, 88, 192
Kollek, Teddy, 248
Komi Republic, 133
Koreans, 155
Kornmass, Wolf, 42
Kosinova, Tatiana, 132–34
Kresy, 58
Kristallnacht, 67
Kuehnel, Izabella, 189–90
kulaks, 98, 126

Latvia, 151
League of Nations, 58
Lebanon, 236
lebensraum, 118–19
Legnica, 188, 197–200
Lenin, Vladimir, 54, 59, 100, 169
Leopolis Hotel (Lviv), 99
LGBTQ, 70–72
lice, 117, 127, 128, 206, 237
Lithuania, 43, 133, 151
Los Angeles Dodgers, xvi–xvii, 181
Los Angeles International Airport (LAX), 33–34, 35–36
Los Angeles Times, 34
LOT Polish Airlines, 35

Lovers of Zion, 57
Lower Silesia, 186
Lubetkin, Zivia, 200–201
Lublin, 20, 68, 88, 193, 200
"Lucky Jews," 53–54, 63
Luxemburg, Rosa, 54–55
Lviv, 86–123
  author's visit, 86–89, 92–108, 114–17, 121–23
  deportations, 111–15, 117–20
  Golden Rose Synagogue, 121–22
  history of, 96–103
  name of, 268
  Nazi occupation of, 111–13, 118–20
  Russian invasion, 37, 86–87, 95, 101–2, 107–8, 116, 121–22
  Territory of Terror Memorial Museum, 114–17, 124
Lviv Jewish Hospital, 105, 106

Maccabiah Games, 59–60
Madagascar, 111
Majdanek, 43, 50, 78
Majer, Blic, 213–14
Mandatory Palestine. *See* Palestine
Manley, Rebecca, 154–55
March of the Living, xvii
Margolin, Jacob, 152
Martha's Vineyard, 10–11, 21, 86
Mauthausen Concentration Camp, 218
Mein Kampf (Hitler), 67
Meir, Golda, 235–36
Memorial International, 132–34, 138
Mexico City, xv
Ministry of Internal Affairs (Russia), 135, 139, 140
Montagu, Edwin, 57–58
Mosin, Alexey, 76, 134–36, 138–39, 140–41

INDEX

Mount Carmel, 232–33
Muhammad, 162
Muslim travel ban, 33–35

Nathan, Joan Gerson, 9–10, 31, 72, 89–92, 220–21, 248, 249–50
NATO (North Atlantic Treaty Organization), 18
Nazis
   annexation of Austria, 69
   battle of Stalingrad, 176
   Final Solution, 84, 144, 186, 210
   invasion and occupation of Zamość, xv, 2–7, 23, 30, 36, 50–51, 71, 80–81, 85, 144, 172–73, 191–92
   Kristallnacht, 67
   occupation of Lviv, 106, 108, 111–13, 118–20, 195–96
   record keeping, 6, 13
   reparations, 13, 20, 21, 195–96
   surrender of, 176, 208
   Warsaw Ghetto Uprising, 27, 186, 200–201
Nazi-Soviet Nonaggression Pact, 81
Netanyahu, Benjamin, 253–54
New York City, 240–41, 243
New York Harbor, 235
New York Public Library, 42
New York Sun, xv–xvi
New York Times, 110, 215
New Zion, 186–87
NKVD (People's Commissariat for Internal Affairs), 97, 171
   deportations and Gulag, 125–28, 135, 136, 138, 140, 143–44, 145
   in Lviv, 103, 110–11, 112, 114, 118
Nobel Peace Prize, 132–33
"Nothing Bad Has Ever Happened." (Amelina), 121–22

Obergefell v. Hodges, 74
Okunevskaya, Tatiana, 151
Operation Barbarossa, 97–98
Ostrava, 37

Palestine
   Arab Higher Committee, 68, 216–17
   Arab-Israeli War of 1948, 236
   Brichah and, 201–6, 218
   Britain's role. *See* Britain and Palestine
   displaced persons and, 209–10, 214–17
   early Jewish immigration, 28–29, 59–60, 67–68
   "Greek bluff," 203–4, 224–25
   Jewish exodus from Poland, 199–206
   Stalin and, 181–82, 202–3
   UN Partition Plan, 230–31, 235–36, 251
   Zionist mobilization, 31, 56–58, 61–63, 67–68, 200–201
Palestinians, 235–36, 238–39
Paris, 26, 224, 227, 229
Passover, 142–43, 146, 157, 193, 196
passports, 28, 93–94, 109, 122, 140, 157, 160
Pat, Jacob, 187
Patton, George S., 209
Peretz, I. L., 54–55
Perlov, Yitzchok, 151, 182
pogroms, 46, 59, 195–97, 210
   Kielce, 196–97, 199–200, 202
   Kristallnacht, 67
Poland. *See also* Zamość
   author's initial prejudice against, 35, 36
   election of 1991, 129
   exodus from, 199–206
   repatriation journeys, 181–98

Polish Catholics, 46, 79, 129–30, 185
Polish government-in-exile, 129, 145, 173–74, 201
Polish Institute of National Remembrance, 191
Polish-Lithuanian Commonwealth, 71
Polish-Soviet War, 46
Pollero, Shelley, 11–12
Portuguese, xv–xvi
Postwar (Judt), 242
Potocki, Alfred, 102
Potsdam Conference, 186
Pruszynski, Xavier, 146
Public Theater, 240
Purim, 1
Putin, Vladimir, 18–19, 132–33, 155–56, 158, 159

Quakers, 31, 208

"rainbow family," 70
Rainbow Square (Zamość), 70, 123, 183
Red Army, 186, 188, 200
    Gulag, 141, 143, 147, 187
    Lviv, 98, 104
    Tashkent, 150
    Zamość, 71, 82, 83, 172, 176, 179
Red Cross, 97, 161, 229
"refugee," 97
"refugium," 97
Registan Square (Samarkand), 162
Reich Industry Fat (RIF), 213
reparations, 13, 20, 21, 195–96
repatriation journeys, 181–98
Revisionist Party, 61, 201
Ringelbum Archive, 119
River Bug, 3, 82, 96, 174
Romania, 151, 216, 223
Roosevelt, Franklin D., 208

Roosevelt Square (Green Shelter), 221–22
Rosh Hashanah, 130
Rottenmann, 208
Rough Guide, 39–40, 47
Rózycki, Stanisław, 119
Russia. *See* Soviet Union
Russian invasion of Ukraine, 18–19, 20, 39, 45, 79, 132–33, 135, 253
    Lviv, 37, 86–87, 95, 101–2, 107–8, 116, 121–22
    Uzbekistan, 148, 155–56, 158–60
Rynek Wielki 3, Zamość, 22, 23, 48

Sabacinski, Daniel, 45, 47, 51, 64, 71–72, 88–89
Sadat, Anwar, 250–51
St. Petersburg, 158–60
Salt Square, Zamość, 66–67, 80, 183
Samarkand, 157–63, 170
San Fernando Valley, 14, 72, 250
Saudi Arabia, 236
Schaffner, Helena, 185
Scheid, Shmuel-Joseph, 43, 193, 222
Schimbu, 179–80
Schindler's List (film), 12
Search Bureau for Missing Relatives, 179–80
Sephardic Jews, 46, 71
Sfard, Dovid, 185
Shaar Ha'aliyah, 237
Shabbat, 196–97
Shalit, Adi, 23–30, 179
"Shalom Aleichem," 72–73
Shanghai ghetto, 152
Shehecheyanu, 77, 232
"Shema," 51–52
Sherf, Khaim, 23, 26, 28–30, 66, 179–80

INDEX

Shoah Foundation, 12, 14–15, 203
Siberia, 4, 114–15, 131–32, 134, 135–36, 138–41
Sikorsky UH-60 Black Hawks, 19
Silk Road, 147, 156, 181
Silver Lake, xvii
Sinai Peninsula, 251
Six-Day War, 246–47
Slate, 34
Slezkine, Yuri, 46
Slovakia, 199
Sound of Music, The (musical), 207, 219
Soviet Union
   army. *See* Red Army
   Bezhenets, 96–98
   Cold War, 131–32, 216, 241–42
   dissolution of, 121, 133, 167
   Great Purge, 97–98
   Gulag. *See* Gulag
   Katyn massacre, 174
   Nazi-Soviet Nonaggression Pact, 81
   Operation Barbarossa, 97–98
   Polish border, 94
Spielberg, Steven, 12, 228
Squadrilli, Alexander, 210
SS (Schutzstaffel), 43, 78, 194, 208–9
Stalingrad, 176
Stalin, Joseph, 6, 149
   death of, 166
   defeat of Nazis, 152
   ethnic cleansing, 155
   Great Purge, 97–98
   Gulag, 21, 126, 128–30, 133, 135, 144–45, 147, 161–62, 225, 226, 232
   Kaganovich and, 161–62, 167
   Katyn massacre, 174
   Lviv and, 105, 112, 116, 118–19
   Nazi-Soviet Nonaggression Pact, 81

   Operation Barbarossa, 97–98
   Palestine and, 181–82, 202–3
   post-war Poland and, 181–82, 189
   Potsdam Conference, 186
Star of David, 108, 187
Starry Night (Van Gogh), 88
stereotype of "Lucky Jews," 53–54, 63
Stern Gang, 235
Stola, Dariusz, 191
Stroop, Jürgen, 78
Sunset Boulevard, xvii
Survival on the Margins (Adler), 225
Sverdlovsk, 131–32, 133–34, 136, 138, 139
Sybiraks, 129–30
Sybir Memorial Museum (Bialystok), 124–25, 129–30
Syria, 236, 238, 247
Szarf, Szloma, 64

Talasiewicz-Eibuszyc, Roma, 169
Tamerlane, 149
Taraz, 180–81
Tarzana Notary, 139–40
Tashkent, 147, 148–56, 161
Tashkent, City of Bread (film), 150–51
Tashkent Station, 154–55, 156
Tatars, 155, 165–66, 167
Tehran's Children: In the East (Dekel), 133
telogreika, 141
Territory of Terror Memorial Museum (Lviv), 114–17, 124
Timur, Amir, 149
Tomaszów Lubelski, 20, 104, 122–23
Torah, 71, 76, 146, 242
To the Tashkent Station (Manley), 154–55
Trans-Caspian railway, 164–65
Transjordan, 236

Treblinka extermination camp, 78, 130
Truman, Harry, 208–10, 225, 231, 232, 234
Trump, Donald, 33–34, 254
Turkmenistan, 147
typhoid, 153, 164

Ukraine
   Holodomor, 98
   Lviv. *See* Lviv
   Russian invasion. *See* Russian invasion of Ukraine
Ukraine Air Alert, 87
UNESCO World Heritage Site, 40, 165
Union of Polish Patriots, 173
United Nations Displaced Persons. *See* displaced persons
United Nations General Assembly, 231, 235
United Nations Partition Plan for Palestine, 230–31, 235–36, 251
United Nations Relief and Rehabilitation Administration (UNRRA), 208, 213, 214
United Nations Special Committee on Palestine (UNSCOP), 216–17, 230–31
United Synagogue Youth, xvii
University of Pennsylvania Law School, 208
Ural Mountains, 125, 131, 144, 165
Uzbekistan, 4, 147–77
   author's visit, 148–77
   history of, 149–51
   Holocaust memorial, 149–55
   Juma. *See* Juma
   Samarkand, 157–63
   Tashkent, 148–56
Uzbek Soviet Socialist Republic, 150–51

"vanderers," 147
Van Gogh, Vincent, 88
Versailles Treaty, 58
Victory Park (Tashkent), 149–50, 151–52, 154–55
Vienna, 207–8
Vilna, 200
Vitto, Steven, 13–14, 20
Volga River, 118

Waintraub, Hanche, 180
Wajnstok, Devora, 120
Wajnstok, Rebecca, 120
Wajnstok, Szlomo, 120
Wald, Max, 227–28
Wall Street Journal, 87, 132
Warsaw
   author's visit, 19–20, 33, 35–38, 39, 77–78, 184
   Centre of Migration Research, 19–20
   Nazi invasion, 39, 202–3
   Russian invasion, 37, 39, 83, 123, 202–3
Warsaw Ghetto, 78, 119, 123
Warsaw Ghetto Uprising, 27, 186, 200–201
Warsaw Great Synagogue, 78
Warsaw Main Judaic Library, 78
Wat, Aleksander, 99–100, 110–11, 150–51
Wehrmacht, 81, 210
West Bank, 236, 247, 251
Western Ukrainian People's Republic, 100
Western Wall, 236, 247, 248
West Tisbury Library, 11
Wolsztejn, Lejb, 193, 194
World Holocaust Remembrance Center's Database of Shoah Victims' Names, 23

World War I, 58–59, 97, 100, 102
World Zionist Congress (1931), 61

Yad Vashem, Central Database of Shoah Victims' Names, 28, 120
Yekaterinburg, 132, 134, 135–36, 139
Yeltsin Presidential Center, 134
Yiddish, 5, 55, 243
Yizkor, 40–41, 42–43, 80
Yom Kippur, 137

Zamość
  author's planned visit, 18–19
  author's visit, 39–40, 44–45, 47–52, 53–54, 64–66, 70–72
  elections, 55–56, 62–63
  history of, 45–46
  LGBTQ in, 70–72, 75–76
  Nazi invasion and occupation of, 2–3, 80–81, 85, 108–9, 144, 172–73, 191–95
  repatriation journeys, 181–98
  Russian invasion and, 19, 45
  Soviet occupation of, 81–85, 108–9
Yizkor, 40–41, 42–43, 80
Zamoscer Progressive Branch, 19
Zamość Jews, xv–xvi, 1–3
  author's initial research, 11–12
  commemorative march, 49–50
  deportations, 6, 30, 43, 49–51, 193–96
  family commemoration, xi–xii, 4–7
  history of, 45–46, 54–63, 65–68, 71
  Judenrat, 23, 71, 191–95
  numbers killed, 5–6
Zamość Poles, 50–51
Zamość Synagogue, 70–72, 75–76
Zamoyski, Jan, 45–46
Zelenskyy, Volodymyr, 19, 116
Zhytelna, Yuliia, 108
Zionism, 56–58, 61–63, 67–68
Zionist Federation of Great Britain and Ireland, 57
Zuckerman, Yitzhak, 186, 200–201, 202–3
Zwillich, Jekuthiel, 191
Zwolski, Marcin, 124–25, 129–30
Zyklon B, 189

About the Author

Daniela Gerson is an award-winning reporter whose work has appeared in *The New York Times, Der Spiegel*, Public Radio International, and the *Financial Times*, among other outlets. An associate professor of journalism at California State University, Northridge and editor-at-large at *Zócalo Public Square*, she previously worked as a community engagement editor at the *LA Times* and as a staff immigration reporter for the *New York Sun*. She also has directed programs at the intersection of civic engagement and news representation for the University of Southern California's Annenberg School and City University of New York's Newmark School. She lives in Los Angeles with her two children and her wife, an attorney specializing in immigrants' rights.